The Methodist Church on the Prairies

McGILL-QUEEN'S STUDIES IN THE HISTORY OF RELIGION

Volumes in this series have been supported by the Jackman Foundation of Toronto.

SERIES TWO   In memory of George Rawlyk
Donald Harman Akenson, Editor

Marguerite Bourgeoys and Montreal, 1640–1665
Patricia Simpson

Aspects of the Canadian Evangelical Experience
Edited by *G.A. Rawlyk*

Infinity, Faith, and Time
Christian Humanism and Renaissance Literature
John Spencer Hill

The Contribution of Presbyterianism to the Maritime Provinces of Canada
Charles H.H. Scobie and G.A. Rawlyk, editors

Labour, Love, and Prayer
Female Piety in Ulster Religious Literature, 1850–1914
Andrea Ebel Brozyna

Religion and Nationality in Western Ukraine
The Greek Catholic Church and the Ruthenian National Movement in Galicia, 1867–1900
John-Paul Himka

The Waning of the Green
Catholics, the Irish, and Identity in Toronto, 1887–1922
Mark G. McGowan

Good Citizens
British Missionaries and Imperial States, 1870–1918
James G. Greenlee and Charles M. Johnston, editors

The Theology of the Oral Torah
Revealing the Justice of God
Jacob Neusner

Gentle Eminence
A Life of George Bernard Cardinal Flahiff
P. Wallace Platt

Culture, Religion, and Demographic Behaviour
Catholics and Lutherans in Alsace, 1750–1870
Kevin McQuillan

Between Damnation and Starvation
Priests and Merchants in Newfoundland Politics, 1745–1855
John P. Greene

Modernity and the Dilemma of North American Anglican Identities, 1880–1950
William Katerberg

The Methodist Church on the Prairies, 1896–1914
George Emery

The Methodist Church
on the Prairies, 1896–1914

GEORGE EMERY

McGill-Queen's University Press
Montreal & Kingston · London · Ithaca

© McGill-Queen's University Press 2001
ISBN 0-7735-2183-6

Legal deposit second quarter 2001
Bibliothèque nationale du Québec

Printed in Canada on acid-free paper

This book has been published with the help of a grant
from the Humanities and Social Sciences Federation of
Canada, using funds provided by the Social Sciences
and Humanities Research Council of Canada.

McGill-Queen's University Press acknowledges the
financial support of the Government of Canada
through the Book Publishing Industry Development
Program (BPIDP) for its activities. It also acknowledge
the support of the Canada Council for the Arts for its
publishing program.

**National Library of Canada Cataloguing
in Publication Data**

Emery, George Neil, 1941–
    The Methodist church on the Prairies, 1896–1914
    (McGill-Queen's studies on the history of religion)
    Includes bibliographical references and index.
    ISBN 0-7735-2183-6
    1. Methodist Church – Prairie Provinces – History.
    I. Title. II. Series.
    BX8252.P7E44 2001   287'.09712   C2001-900058-8

Typeset in New Baskerville 10/12
by Caractéra inc., Quebec City

Contents

Tables

Acknowledgments

This book revises a doctoral thesis of 1970 that Dr Margaret Prang supervised at the University of British Columbia. The United Church Archives in Toronto furnished the research materials. Glen Lucas, the archivist, assisted my work over an eight-month period and gave me a room in his apartment, at nominal rent. Glen's kindness, friendship, and support left me with a debt for life. I thank Peter Neary and Philip Cercone for encouraging me to revisit the thesis after a hiatus of twenty-six years.

The revision benefits from postdoctoral research in the three prairie archives of the United Church (1972, 1999) and from interviews with former missionaries (1972–74). I thank the university of Western Ontario for grants from internal SSHRC funds and the Agnes Cole Dark fund in 1999.

McGill-Queen's University Press and the Aid to Scholarly Publications program arranged for four expert readers for two versions of the manuscript. I have an immense scholarly debt to a reader who appraised both versions. His or her reports were models of constructive criticism for work in two research fields (church history and prairie regional history). They impelled me to revisit the three prairie church archives, engage more of the literature, and sharpen the argument and presentation.

To my wife, Anne Sawarna, and our children, Alexandra and Nicholas, thanks again for seeing me through a book. I have debts to Brock Silversides, archivist at the Public Archives of Saskatchewan, Saskatoon; Dianne Haglund, the archivist at the United Church Archives in Winnipeg;

several staff in the Public Archives of Alberta in Edmonton; Trish Caplan and David Mercer of the Cartographic Section of Western's Geography Department; many staff at Western's D.B. Weldon library; and Peter Neary for his interest, support, and scholarly example. I thank Judy Emery for her typing and editing of the original thesis manuscript. Finally, I thank Ron Curtis for his meticulous copyediting.

Introduction

I began the revision of my doctoral thesis of 1970 with trepidation but rapidly became immersed in the work. First, I had additional research materials, obtained during the 1970s from three prairie church archives and interviews with former missionaries. I acquired more information in April and May 1999 by returning to the archives (now located in the Public Archives of Alberta, Edmonton; the Public Archives of Saskatchewan, Saskatoon; and the United Church Archives, in Winnipeg). Whereas my thesis research drew primarily from records of the administrative centre of the church in Toronto, the regional archives held local and district records, minutes of conference stationing committees, and manuscript minutes of conference proceedings. Historical photographs from the three archives, and also from the Glenbow Museum and Archives in Calgary, breathed life into the written record.

Second, advances in the literature have enriched the context for the subject of the book. Neil Semple's *Lord's Dominion: The History of Canadian Methodism* (1996) is an erudite history of the long-term national tradition of the church and is an indispensable reference work. Lynne Marks's *Revivals and Roller Rinks* (1996) sets a high standard for the social history of religion, with an account of three Ontario communities. David Marshall, *Secularizing the Faith* (1992), Phyllis Airhart, *Serving the Present Age* (1992), and Nancy Christie and Michael Gauvreau, *A Full-Orbed Christianity* (1996), frame a major scholarly debate about whether the protestant evangelical tradition declined or was redeployed.

In prairie regional history, Paul Voisey's *Vulcan: The Making of a Prairie Community* (1988) is a carefully crafted case study that speaks to general issues, including religious behaviour and a modernized version of the frontier thesis. Voisey's, *Preacher's Frontier* (1996), an edited collection of letters from an Anglican pastor in Castor, Alberta, is a gem. Randi Warne's *Literature as Pulpit* (1993), Valerie Korinek's "No Women Need Apply" (1993), and Catharine Cavanaugh's "No Place for a Woman" (1997) brilliantly expose gender aspects of prairie church culture.[1] Orest Martynowych's *Ukrainians in Canada* (1991) and John Lehr's "Peopling the Prairies with Ukrainians" (1991) revise conventional wisdom about ethnic-Ukrainian history, mainstream Canadian history, and Methodist Ukrainian missions. Canada's Ukrainian peasant-settler families, it turns out, were active agents in their history, not passive recipients of initiatives from Anglo-Canadian and Ukrainian elite groups. Their traditions were dynamic and evolving, not static and medieval, as Methodists believed.

This book focuses on the Methodist response to the settlement boom in the prairie West during the years 1896–1914. The book is intended for readers with interests in Canadian history, prairie regional history, Canadian and prairie church history, and Canadian religious studies. It emphatically is *not* a regional case study for the scholarly debate about secularization in Canadian society (as one expert read it). As discussed below, however, it advances that debate as a byproduct of its central problem.

THE REGIONAL LITERATURE

There is no recent scholarly monograph on prairie church history during the years 1896–1914, the time of the Laurier settlement boom.[2] John Webster Grant's *Church in the Canadian Era* (1967) does give a nice overview. But Semple's *Lord's Dominion* treats Methodist history from a central Canadian viewpoint and provides only a cursory treatment of home missions in the prairie region. Rosemary Gagan's *Sensitive Independence* (1992), on the other hand, devotes part of a chapter to Methodist women missionaries in Alberta, and Paul Voisey's *Vulcan* and *A Preacher's Frontier* treat church life in two Alberta communities. In addition, three useful anthologies are *The Anglican Church and the World of Western Canada* (1991), *Prairie Spirit: Perspectives on the Heritage of the United Church of Canada in the West* (1985), and *Visions of the New Jerusalem, Religious Settlement on the Prairies* (1983).

THE LITERATURE ON CANADIAN CHURCH HISTORY

Recent scholarship favours a noninstitutional focus on religious history rather than church history. It is strong as intellectual history but weak in social history and in the use of quantitative evidence.[3] With its superficial treatment of the social profiles of confessional populations, it tends to inflate the role of elites and consensus and understate the socially variegated and contested nature of religious ideas. Its broad characterization of the Methodist Church as "middle class" has, until recently, blocked the serious investigation of social class tensions in Methodist religious culture.

This book treats the social history of the Methodist church, with particular attention to social class, gender, and life-course influences. It contests Semple's characterization of the church as a middle-class institution whose leaders imposed class values on a passive membership. It finds that the church was a cross-class institution whose membership and culture drew heavily from farmers, skilled labourers, and shopkeepers. As Mark's *Revivals and Roller Rinks* and Louise Mussio's "Holiness Movement" (1996) show, many church members contested Methodist religious trends and some of them defected to sectarian splinter groups such as the Salvation Army and holiness movement churches. As Marks, Randi Warne, and Catharine Cavanaugh demonstrate, gender and life-course, as well as social class, influenced Methodist culture, religiosity, and the popularity of church membership in Methodist families. Simply put, Methodists had a complex social profile and contested values, not a cohesive middle class tradition.

THE RELIGIOUS STUDIES LITERATURE

A major debate in the literature concerns the *declension* (or *secularization*) theorists, who argue that an evangelical tradition declines and religion gets secularized. Supporters of this position include S.D. Clark (1948), W.E. Mann (1955), Emery (1974), Ramsay Cook (1985), Paul Voisey (1988), William Westfall (1989), and David Marshall (1992). Opponents of this position, the evolutionist theorists, include Marguerite Van Die (1989), Phyllis Airhart (1992), and Nancy Christie and Michael Gauvreau (1996).

The declension theorists see evangelical decline as a byproduct of capitalist economic development, social change, consumerism, and new intellectual currents. Protestant belief in the supernatural and personal salvation for heaven weakened over time, and Protestants placed a growing emphasis on moral reform and social justice on earth. In the process, religion ceased to be an intellectual super-system that organized other systems of explanation. Instead, it became a subsystem for what science and materialism failed to explain. Hallmarks of the secularization process included a popular disinterest in theology, an emphasis on Christ as preeminently a social worker rather than the Son of God, elaborate places of worship and emphasis on respectability in urban congregations, a shift from traumatic conversion to personal salvation and then to a belief in personal salvation as a gradual, educative process, and a falling off of church attendance and financial support.

The evolutionist theorists (Van Die, Airhart, and Christie and Gauvreau) find that the evangelical tradition was redeployed to suit changing times: it was not declining. The evangelical concern for personal salvation persisted but became subordinate to the social gospel, which was an application of evangelicalism to mass society. The social gospel marked a return to emotion and experience in the Methodist tradition, not secular drift. A popular indifference to theology was not irreligion but rather a rejection of an elite, "overly intellectualized" religion that had developed during the late nineteenth century.

As a scholarly exchange between two of the combatants, Airhart and Marshall, shows, the debate turns on definition. The declension theorists, with an "all-encompassing definition of secularization" and "narrow and surprisingly static" definition of religion, "find little in the way of change that does not lead to decline." By contrast, the evolutionist theorists, with "all-encompassing definitions of religion," find that "only change, never decline, is possible."[4]

My doctoral thesis told a declension story. It described how an Ontario-centred church failed to transfer its strength to the prairie region, in part because its evangelical tradition was dying.[5] The argument suited its times. The declension thesis, cogently expressed in S.D. Clark's *Church and Sect in Canada* (1948), was then conventional wisdom. Declension also described mainstream protestant church life during the 1960s. After having flourished during the early postwar years, it was losing ground. Pierre Berton's best seller *The Comfortable Pew* (1965) captured popular fascination with the change.

In contrast to my thesis of 1970, this book sides with the evolutionist theorists and therefore uses a broad, dynamic definition of religion rather than a narrow, static one. First, biographers of Nellie McClung (1873–1951) presented a vivid historical example of a Methodist woman whose religion was deeply spiritual and yet downplayed personal salvation for an afterlife. Belief in the power of the spirit sustained McClung's optimism about banishing social evils and achieving the millennium. She was impatient with doctrine and theology and pressed for "spiritual exercise," by which she meant active service modelled on Christ's life.[6] For McClung, a dampening of emphasis on the supernatural did not express secularism, as in the declension theory.

Second, the evolutionist definition fits my understanding of how tradition works. Tradition, for a given domain such as religion, summarizes what its adherents have learned from experience. People use the lessons of old experience to order new experience. The core assumptions of their tradition identify problems to be solved and supply acceptable solutions. When a tradition struggles to provide solutions to important problems, its adherents modify it to make it effective. Thus, tradition evolves through feedback from new experience, while retaining the core assumptions that define it. A tradition is progressive as long as it supplies its followers with solutions for important problems. Otherwise it stagnates and loses support.[7]

Methodism was a progressive religious tradition that originated in eighteenth-century England and became global in outreach. It began as a movement within the Church of England and evolved into several Methodist religious denominations. The tradition arrived in British North America during the eighteenth century and entered the prairie region in 1840. Church unions in 1874 and 1884 united Canada's several Methodist denominations into the Methodist Church of Canada. In 1925 the Canadian Methodist Church entered into the United Church of Canada. This change ended the Canadian Methodist tradition as a religious denomination, but not as a religious movement: that movement was an evolving bundle of values that preceded and transcended institutional Methodism.

As evolutionist scholars find, Methodism was not a static tradition whose template was fixed by John Wesley and/or saddle-bag preachers on the early Canadian frontier and which declined as the conditions of its founding vanished. Rather, it evolved through feedback from experience in an ever-unfolding present age. In the process it became variegated, like the social and economic milieus in which Methodist lives were lived.

Although religion is not its focus, this book advances the scholarly debate about religion. First, it posits definition as the central issue. The literature offers a choice between the definitions of religion of the declension theory and the evolution theory, although neither definition is the correct one. In the circumstances, scholars must choose between definitions, justify their selection, and discuss its implications for their project.

Second, the text enriches the literature on the social locations of Methodist religious ideas and practices. Using primary data and recent literature, it reveals the complex social profile of Methodists and the socially grounded, contested nature of their religious behaviours.

Third, it challenges the declension theorist's conventional wisdom about prairie religious history. For example, Rosemary Gagan portrays women missionaries in Alberta as failed evangelists who succeeded as social workers. By contrast, this book presents them as effective missionaries whose social work was inseparable from religion. Similarly it finds that Paul Voisey's information about the social profile of the population in Vulcan, Alberta, works against his speculation that Vulcan society was highly secular. In the process, it calls for a fresh application of his theory, a modernized version of the frontier thesis.

The years 1896–1914 evidenced a spectacular spread of white settler society in the prairie region. Migration and immigration to the region moved from a trickle to a flood in 1896. Over the next eighteen years, agricultural settlement served up a golden age for prairie economic growth and Canada's National Policy. Immigration and settlement halted during the First World War (1914–18). They resumed during the 1920s, but on a smaller scale, and stopped definitively during the Great Depression of the 1930s.

The endpoint for this study, 1914, is not the breakpoint in Canadian history that scholars once believed it to be. In areas of activity such as immigration, settlement, and the protestant church union movement, the decade of the 1920s extended trends from the prewar years. Even so, 1914 marked the passing of an era for Methodists in the prairie region. The physical challenges that Methodists faced were lessening, and the church's missionary program was shifting definitively from expansion to consolidation. Some of the following chapters provide evidence after 1914 to underscore the transition.

Chapter 1 surveys the challenges that Methodists faced in the region. Chapters 2 and 3 provide background information: on the political organization of the church (its polity), the social profile of its members, and the Methodist religious tradition that came into the prairie region, primarily from central Canada. Chapters 4, 5, and 6 deal with the church's mobilization of resources for expansion: the raising of money, the supply of clergy, the recruiting of laity, and the rivalry with Presbyterians and Anglicans. Chapters 7, 8, and 9 treat the church's encounter with non-Anglo-Saxon immigrants.

The church faced extraordinary challenges in the prairie region during the settlement boom. By and large, it rose to the occasion. The spread of its regular missions and the growth of its membership were impressive, given the difficulties in place. Its influence on non-Anglo-Saxon immigrants surpassed what one would guess from membership statistics. Overall, the Methodists kept pace with the Presbyterians and surpassed the Anglicans. In the process, they forged a regional variation on the national tradition of their church. Much of prairie Methodism's regional uniqueness, however, expressed temporary frontier conditions. As a religious challenge, the prairie West called on Methodists to perform heroic roles as preachers, preachers' wives, missionaries, and lay leaders. As a secular challenge, the prairie West called Methodists to the very heart of Canada's nation-building process. Thus, with bright hopes Methodists locked horns with prairie realities.

Wesley Methodist Church, Edmonton, ca. 1911–12. Young People's group bound for Sandy Lake, south of Edmonton, for picnic, 24 May. Glenbow Archives, Calgary, Canada. Image NA-1848-1

Methodist Church, Crossfield, near Calgary, ca. 1906–7. Glenbow Archives, Calgary, Canada. Image NA-1961-2

Joe Bainbridge, Methodist student minister, Bon Accord, Alberta, 1913. Glenbow Archives, Calgary, Canada. Image NA-1646-13

Canada's First Ukrainian Methodist Church (John "Olexiuk's church"), three miles east of Pakan, Alberta, ca. 1912. Glenbow Archives, Calgary, Canada. Image NA-1649-1

Methodist Ukrainian mission staff, meeting at Kolokreeka (Smoky Lake),
Alberta, 1916. *Left to right, back row:* Michael Bellegay, Rev. J.K. Smith and
Mrs Smith, Nicolai Veranka, Rev. P.G. Sutton, E. Hickman, Rev. D.M.
Ponich, R. Robinson, M. Brown. *Left to right, middle row:* Rev. T. Hannochko
(standing), Mary Yarwood, unknown, Mrs T.C. Buchanan, Mrs W.H. Pike
and Vera, unknown, Mrs Lawford. *Left to right, front row:* Mrs C.W. Ross and
Rev. C.W. Ross, Rev. T.C. Buchanan (superintendent of missions for
northern Alberta), Dr C.H. Lawford and daughters Alice, Kate, and Ruth.
Glenbow Archives, Calgary, Canada. Image NA-1649-2

Rev Oliver Darwin, Methodist
superintendent of missions for
Saskatchewan, n.d. Glenbow Archives,
Calgary, Canada. Image NA-642-7

Methodist Ladies' Aid, Mossbank, Saskatchewan, 1914. Public Archives of Saskatchewan, Saskatoon, Image S-P 65

Methodist church, Earl Grey, Saskatchewan, n.d. Public Archives of Saskatchewan, Saskatoon, Image S-P 25

J.J. Hughes and his wife (Dolly Mcguire), All People's Mission, Winnipeg, 1914, on the twenty-fifth anniversary of Dolly Macguire's founding of the mission. United Church Archives at Winnipeg

Children and staff, All People's (Maple Street) Mission, ca. 1903. United Church Archives at Winnipeg

All People's Mission, Winnipeg, lean-to that held the first kindergarten, 1890. United Church Archives at Winnipeg

All People's (Maple Street Mission) 1903–13. United Church Archives at Winnipeg

Top: Jessie Munro, WMS co-founder
of the Wahstao mission. Provincial
Archives of Alberta, Edmonton

Right: Rita Edmunds, WMS co-founder
of the Wahstao mission. Provincial
Archives of Alberta, Edmonton

Ukrainian missionaries, Pakan. *Left to right* (adults
only): Mrs Sanford, unknown, Ethelwyn Chace
(kneeling with camera), Rev. Percy Sutton. Provincial
Archives of Alberta, Edmonton

Ukrainian mothers and children in ethnic dress
at Wahstao or Kolokreeka. Provincial Archives
of Alberta, Edmonton

"Bundles for Charity": All People's Mission, Christmas, 1910. United Church Archives

Members of the first Alberta conference, 1905, photographed in 1925. *Left to right, back row:* R.E. Finley, L.R. McDonald, A.S. Tuttle. *Left to right, third row:* S.H. Johnson, W.S. Haggith, W.H. Irwin, J.B . Francis, J.K. Smith, Joseph Coulter. *Left to right, second row:* A.A. Lytle, R.W. Dalgleish, C.H. Huestis, Thomas Powell, A.C. Farrell, J.H. Wilkinson. *Left to right, first row:* P.E. Butchart, Arthur Barner, T.C. Buchanan, George F. Driver, Joseph F. Woodsworth, R.T. Harden. United Church Archives

1 The Prairie West as a Methodist Challenge

Canada's supreme opportunity at home is not in the development of her resources, or in the regulation of her trade, or in the
improvement of her political relations, or even in the establishment of a navy, or in all these combined – her supreme opportunity at home is in making the religion of Christ a real and vital
thing to all her people ... The supreme question in Canada today
is, what will be the religious life of our new communities? The
Churches must act now. Our whole future depends on what the
Churches do now. Was there ever given to the Churches of any
land a greater opportunity and a graver responsibility?

Newton Wesley Rowell, 1909[1]

Economic development transformed Canada's prairie region during
the years 1896–1914. The white settler population grew explosively
through migration from central and eastern Canada and immigration
from Britain, the United States, and Europe. Native peoples paid the
price. During the decade 1901–11 they lost a third of their population
and dropped from 11 to 0.9 percent of the regional population. Nature,
too, fared poorly as indigenous plants and animals gave way to the wheat
farmer's monoculture and weeds and the rancher's livestock.[2]

Except for native converts, Methodists were part of the predatory
white settler population. Anglo-Methodists lamented neither the
native's price nor nature's plight. Rather, they celebrated the homesteader's plough as the harbinger of "civilization" in Canada's "wild
and savage" West. Even so, for them the Christian character of prairie
"civilization" was a question to be decided. The region gave them
opportunity, but it also tested them.

PRAIRIE METHODISM BEFORE 1896

Prairie Methodism began as a British Wesleyan native mission enterprise and evolved into a Canadian white settler denomination.[3] In
1840 four Wesleyan pastors and two native clergy from Ontario
opened Cree missions at four Hudson's Bay Company posts, including
two in the prairie region (Norway House, north of Lake Winnipeg,
and Edmonton House). Each missionary reported directly to the
Wesleyan missionary society in London. James Evans, a veteran of

native missions in Upper Canada, served the society as local superintendent of missions.

The Wesleyans were invited guests of the Hudson's Bay Company, whose Rupertsland Charter of 1837 obliged it to promote Christianity among the natives. The company gave them board and lodging, interpreters, medicines, means of travel – and its discipline. If a missionary displeased a company officer, then he found himself at the servants' table. In the hierarchical fur-trade society such signs of disfavour meant loss of face among the natives whom the missionary sought to impress.

In 1841 Evans became famous as the inventor of Cree syllabic, which used simple, easily learned symbols to represent syllables in Cree words. After fashioning a crude printing press, Evans issued syllabic versions of Wesleyan hymns and portions of scripture. In 1861 the British and Foreign Bible Society published a Cree syllabic Bible that gave the missionaries a written form of the Cree language with which to counter traditional beliefs in the Cree oral tradition.

Meanwhile, Evans in particular offended the company by opposing travel on Sunday, promoting a native agricultural settlement (Rossville) near Norway House that threatened to remove natives from nomadic fur trade work, encouraging natives to engage in private trade so that they could contribute money to missions (a violation of the company's trade monopoly), and setting himself up as a rival to the company's authority. As a result, the company made life difficult for the missionaries, so that the four Wesleyans and one native missionary quit during the years 1846–54, leaving Henry Steinhauer, the remaining native missionary, to carry on.

In 1854 the Wesleyan Methodist Church of Canada sent four white missionaries with Steinhauer to reestablish the native missions in Rupertsland, and in 1860 George McDougall moved from Ontario to Norway House to become chairman of the missions. In 1862 he located a mission at Victoria, near Edmonton, to reach the far western prairie tribes. With his death in a snow storm in 1876, he became, after James Evans, prairie Methodism's second missionary hero. His son John McDougall continued the work. Thirty years later Methodists opened the George McDougall Memorial Hospital at his Victoria mission site.

During the 1870s and 1880s Methodist missionaries acted as advance agents for the white settler society.[4] They favoured the slaughter of the buffalo herds and the government's native treaties and introduction of the reserve system. They sought to convert natives in order to save the region from "heathen paganism" and Roman Catholicism. By shifting Indians from a nomadic, hunting life to settled farming on reserves, they could more easily observe native religious behaviour and establish settled institutions. They built churches, orphanages, and day schools on the reserves, boarding schools near reserves, and industrial schools away from the reserves.[5]

The native missions gradually changed, however, and they declined in Methodist priorities. As long as the Methodist goal was to convert nomadic populations, the missionaries travelled with natives, learned their ways, studied their languages, and trained converts as missionaries. But their sensitivity to native culture weakened as their goal became the assimilation of settled populations. They came to treat natives as children in a controlled environment. Once large-scale white migration came into the West during the 1890s, they regarded natives as just another minority group to assimilate.

The nonnative side of the enterprise dated from 1868, when George Young arrived from Ontario to open mission work among settlers along the Assiniboine River. When Louis Riel led métis resistance to Canadian authority at Red River in 1869–70, Young became a vocal Canadian patriot and chaplain to Riel's prisoners, including the ill-fated Thomas Scott. In 1871 he superintended the construction of Grace Church, Winnipeg, which developed as the "mother" church for the prairie region.

In 1874 the Wesleyan and New Connexion Churches united to form the Methodist Church of Canada, and when the union church created a Manitoba and Northwest conference in 1882, it named Young as superintendent of prairie missions. Two years later, in 1884, the Methodist Episcopal, Bible Christian, and Primitive Methodist Churches came into the union church. In 1887 James Woodsworth replaced the ailing Young as superintendent. Manitoba Methodists founded Wesley College in 1888, to offer degrees in liberal arts and theology, and by 1896 prairie Methodism was predominantly a white settler denomination. In that year, native missions accounted for just 10 percent of the church's prairie stations, down from 25 percent in 1883 and 78 percent in 1872.

THE EXPLOSIVE SPREAD OF WHITE SETTLEMENT

During the years 1896 to 1914, the Canadian prairies underwent massive economic development and population growth. Agricultural settlement, the engine of growth, was organized around two types of farming. The one, commercial wheat farming, pushed back ranching in grassland areas. This sector benefited from a rise in the world price for wheat, a decline of transportation costs for shipping prairie wheat to European markets, the exhaustion of unoccupied humid lands in

Table 1.1
Transformation of the Prairie Region: Census Populations, 1891–1921

	Prairies	Winnipeg	Calgary	Edmonton	Regina	Saskatoon
1891	219,305	25,639	3,876	–	–	–
1901	414,151	42,340	4,392	4,176	2,249	113
1911	1,322,709	136,035	43,704	31,064[1]	30,213	12,004
1921	1,956,082	179,087	63,305	58,821	34,432	25,739

[1] Includes Strathcona, North Edmonton, and West Edmonton.

the American west, the development of dry-farming techniques, and a rising demand for dryland farms, which were abundant in Canada's prairie region. Land speculation, not profit from crops, argues Paul Voisey, was the chief attraction for settlers. They arrived expecting to practise their traditional mixed farming but planted mostly wheat.[6]

Subsistence agriculture, the second type of farming, developed in forested park-belt lands to the north of the grassland ecological zone. The settlers were peasant families from central Europe. They shunned treeless prairie lands that Anglo-Canadian, American, and British settlers chose, because their goal was subsistence farming, not wheat farming. The park belt held what they were looking for: timber for fuel and building materials, meadowlands for livestock grazing and roof-thatching materials, abundant cheap land to furnish farms for their children – and no landlords.[7]

Railways and resource industries were other components of prairie economic growth. From 1896 to 1914 Canada's second and third transcontinental trunk lines crossed the park belt, and branch lines fanned out from the trunks. The resource industries included coal mining in Crow's Nest Pass and Lethbridge and park-belt lumber camps that produced for urban and dryland-farm markets.

Rail lines gave farmers access to markets. At the same time, the construction of new lines and resource industries provided seasonal employment for men from cash-strapped peasant settler families in the park belt. Increasingly after 1907 this seasonal employment attracted Central European sojourners: young, single men who aimed to return to the Old Country with savings, not to set up park-belt farms.[8]

Successive censuses tracked the transformation of the prairie region (table 1.1). The 1891 census found less than a quarter of a million people, most of them in southeastern Manitoba. Winnipeg was the only city with a population over twenty-five thousand. The 1911 census reported 1.3 million people in a vast triangle whose points were Winnipeg, Edmonton in the northwest, and Lethbridge in the southwest. Calgary, Edmonton, and Regina now joined Winnipeg in the large-city group. The 1916 census of the prairie provinces reported 1.7 million people, and the 1921 census reported two million and a fifth large city, Saskatoon.

The Prairie West and the Methodists

The Methodists' expectations for the prairie inflated the challenge before them. In their experience, agricultural, forest, and mineral resources were the motors of economic and population growth, and Canada had vast reservoirs of each. Thus, in 1902 the prominent Methodist layman N.W. Rowell judged that "not more than one-eighth of the Province of Ontario is really settled." The province's northlands had "vast acreages of agricultural land that have never been touched by the plough, and belts of timber stretching to the shore of Hudson's Bay, not to mention vast mineral resources that are only just beginning to be developed and understood. Settlement is pouring into this new country."

Although the church's obligation to settlers in "New Ontario" was "in itself ... a great work," Rowell noted that "further west the task was even greater. Think of the broad sweep of these western prairies and how the towns and villages are springing up. I travelled along the line of the Calgary and Edmonton Railway, and the towns and villages are growing up almost in a night. One point which I touched is called Ponoka. It is a thriving town of 500 inhabitants, yet I was told that two years ago all that was there was a signboard on a telegraph pole with the single word, 'Ponoka,' on it."[9]

Such thinking was infectious. In 1905 the Reverend J.H. Riddell, principal of Alberta College, predicted a population of fifty million for the North Saskatchewan valley. In 1909 Rowell was certain that the territories open for settlement "must be the home of many millions of people ... in the four years preceding 1907 more Government land was taken up, more homestead entries made in provinces west of the Great Lakes than in the whole 28 years preceding. It seems as if in the no distant future the balance of the population may be west of the Great Lakes."[10]

Thus, Methodists viewed the prairie region as a huge long-term project. At a minimum, they wished to provide religious services for their own people, who numbered 206,000 in the census for 1911.[11] Beyond that, they sought to implant Anglo-Protestant values in prairie society. As an Ontario Methodist politician opined in 1906, "any nation goes up or down on the scale of civilization in proportion as that nation maintains the principles of the Christian religion and endeavours to have its citizens live as closely as possible to the principles set forth in the Christian religion as based upon the word of God.[12] If the prairie West, with its vast potential, were not won for Christ, then Canada's Christian values would be at risk. If, however, the region received a Christian foundation, then Canada would strengthen an Anglo-Saxon mission to bring about the Kingdom of Heaven on Earth. As the general board of missions exclaimed in 1908: "increase the missionary force adequately in the West, spend $500,000 annually in Canada, and the Methodist Church will soon have a force of 500 missionaries, and the annual income of $1,000,000 which are needed for the proper discharge of our duty in the foreign field. *The mission of the Methodist Church is to save Canada, that through Canada we may do our part toward saving the world.*"[13]

Partisan denominationalism influenced some Methodists.[14] In 1896 their church was Canada's largest Protestant denomination. To remain so, it had to win the West and, in the process, carry forward the achievement of Methodist saddle-bag preachers on the Upper Canadian frontier. "Hearing such names in the country as Staples, Grandy, Darling, Matchett, Wilson, Sutton, Fallis, Richardson, Magill, etc.," mused the Reverend Thomas Argue when presiding at the opening of a church building in Manitoba in 1898,

we are reminded of life in Cavan and Manvers ... when the parents and grandparents of these people assisted in establishing Methodism in Cavanville, Bethany, Lifford, Newry, etc. Nor can we forget pastors Watts, Rolson, Pirrette, Tindall, Johnson, O'Hara and others, who led the hosts of the Lord onward to glorious victory. Among the best Christian workers in this progressive and hopeful western country are the descendants of these early Methodists of Ontario. None succeed better than they, and we are always glad to welcome them to our churches, and to assist them in securing suitable locations.[15]

AREAS OF METHODIST DIFFICULTY IN THE PRAIRIE REGION

Methodists faced five areas of difficulty in the prairie region: rural problems, problems with a large population of bachelors, problems with non-Anglo-Saxon immigrants, urban problems, and problems with native missions.

Rural Problems

The prairie region presented two types of rural problems. The one, well-known in central Canada, was depopulation and the dwindling number of supporters for rural churches. By 1905 this problem was

Table 1.2
Percentage of Population Classified as Rural in Census Enumerations, 1901–21

	1901	1911	1921
Canada	62	54	50
Ontario	57	47	42
PRAIRIES	74	64	64
Alberta	72	62	62
Saskatchewan	81	73	71
Manitoba	72	56	57

evident in southern Manitoba, where a trend to larger farms and an exodus of Methodist families reduced four self-supporting circuits (Austin, Bagot, Macgregor, and Sidney) to the status of missions. The Lenora mission fell into difficulty when the entire membership at one of its preaching places moved to Saskatchewan.[16]

Population dispersal was the more serious problem. Rural populations, compared to urban ones, were more scattered and less accessible for churches. Prairie society was more rural than Ontario society (table 1.2).[17] Its farms were larger, moreover, so its population density was lower. Whereas the hundred-acre farm was the norm in Ontario, prairie settler families worked quarter sections and half sections. Thus, as the *Christian Guardian* noted in 1896, many prairie Methodist families were "located eight or ten miles from church," and "regular attendance at Sunday school [was] quite impossible."[18] A related problem was "the growing diversity of population in newer districts [which was] breaking up the old simple denominational unit, such as Presbyterians, Methodists, Anglicans, etc. so that in few districts there are sufficient numbers of any denomination to form a congregation."[19] The Methodist church at Morris, Manitoba, met with hard times in 1906 when Germans and Mennonites replaced many of the original families.[20]

The Bachelor Problem

The feminine character of Protestant religious culture clashed with popular notions of a bachelor's masculinity. Thus, young men were less likely than other adults to be church members, as Lynne Marks found for Methodists in the small Ontario towns of Thorold and Campbellford during the 1880s, where just 12 percent of bachelors were church members, compared to 36 percent of single women and 44 percent of both married men and married women.[21]

The prairie region presented Methodists with an extreme version of this problem. In 1911, for example, in Ontario's adult population (age 20 and over) there were 1.4 bachelors for each unmarried woman. In contrast, the statistic was 5.1 for the prairie region, 6.9 for each of Alberta and Saskatchewan, and 3.0 for Manitoba).[22] In 1910 one Vulcan district had "31 single men and only 1 single woman."[23]

The Non-Anglo-Saxon Immigrants

During the decade 1901–11 the non-Anglo-Saxon European population in the prairie region rose from 110,000 to 507,000 and from 26 to 38 percent of the total population (table 1.3). In 1911 non-British peoples (including Francophones and natives) comprised 47 percent of the prairie population, compared to 24 percent in Ontario. "The situation in the West," warned the Reverend Andrew Stewart, professor of Old Testament exegesis at Wesley College, in 1909, "is different to that in the East. There we have whole sections of the country settled by foreigners; that is not possible here in the East. There you go and get twenty-five thousand people of the same tongue, all with the same social customs."[24]

Methodists commonly judged the newcomers harshly. As the Reverend Samuel East of Winnipeg wrote in 1908, "the foreigners have brought with them very low standards of morality, propriety and decency. We see sights every day, especially in warm weather, which cause us to blush ... The Catholic churches (Roman and Greek), which have been the only religious institutions known to most of these people, have succeeded in keeping them in ignorance; consequently superstitions and superstitious practices abound."[25] In 1909 a Winnipeg "Old Timer" remarked that every European community had three classes, the last being "the lowest class ... the drinking class ... the rag-tag ... the criminals." "We in the west," he complained,

have come to believe that the last class is the one we are being loaded up with. They come here full-fledged graduates of the habits mentioned, and almost at once they sign up with some department of the criminal record. If they "wager" in any matter "they bet the beer." At marriage "Festivals" instead of laying in stuff to eat, they stock up in things to drink ... these people seem to carry an innate morbid passion to shed blood. Their bringing up, religion, education or lack of education, seems to generate an absolute disregard for human life ... They fight with anyone, fight without rules, and generally fight to a finish.[26]

Methodists perceived the non-Anglo-Saxon immigrants as posing a problem with many dimensions. First, the immigrants were a moral threat. In 1909 Principal J.W. Sparling of Wesley College saw "a danger, and it is national! Either we must educate and elevate the incoming

Tableau 1.3
Ethnic Composition of Prairie Census Populations, 1901 and 1911 (Percentages)

	Manitoba	Saskatchewan	Alberta	Prairies
1901				
British	64	44	48	57
French	6	3	6	6
German	11	13	11	11
Scandinavian	5	2	5	4
Slav[1]	5	18	10	9
Aboriginal	6	19	18	11
Other	2	1	2	2
Total population	255,211	91,279	73,022	419,512
Total Non-Charter[2]	58,674	30,817	20,183	109,674
Non-Anglo-Saxon (%)	23	34	28	26
1911				
British	58	51	51	54
French	7	5	5	6
German	8	14	10	11
Scandinavian	4	7	7	6
Slav[1]	13	13	10	12
Aboriginal	2	2	3	2
Other	9	8	13	10
Total population	455,614	492,432	374,663	1,322,709
Total Non-Charter[2]	150,379	206,453	150,510	507,342
Non-Anglo-Saxon (%)	33	42	40	38

[1] Austro-Hungarian, Polish, Russian.

[2] Total population, less British, French, and Native Peoples.

multitudes or they will drag us and our children down to a lower level."[27] Second, as J.S. Woodsworth warned, they undermined working-class living standards by accepting low wages and crowded, unsanitary housing. The steady arrival of newcomers, moreover, prevented earlier arrivals from improving their lot.[28]

Third, because "aliens" were eligible for Canadian citizenship after three years of residence, they were a political threat. In 1902 the Reverend A.E. Smith feared that the government planned to divide the Northwest Territories into two provinces along an east-west line. Such a division, he warned electors in the Colleston district, near Prince Albert, would "throw the whole foreign population into the northern province" and "give the foreigners a controlling influence."[29] "The party which gets the foreign vote," lamented a *Christian Guardian* editorial in 1908,

will be the party which will sweep the west at the next Dominion elections. Not great moral issues, not questions of vital moment to the country ... will decide whether the Liberals or Conservatives will carry the west, but simply which party is able to cajole into their ranks the vast army of foreign voters … Over-anxious political partisans have seen that they have been made citizens, and have thrust into their hand the ballot. They are ignorant of our institutions, ignorant even of our language. Controlled by corrupt politicians, they can outbalance the thinking and intelligent electorate, hold a balance of power, and be a menace to our country.[30]

In 1910, on the eve of his election as general superintendent, the Reverend S.D. Chown asked, "how shall the foreigners govern us?"[31]

Fourth, the non-Anglo-Saxons were a Roman Catholic threat. By 1910 the francophone hierarchy of the prairie Roman Catholic Church was proselytizing Slavic immigrants with Greek Catholic and Russian Orthodox religious traditions. The *Christian Guardian* doubted whether Protestant ideals could triumph west of the Great Lakes if the Roman Catholic mission succeeded.[32] Fifth, the "foreigners" might turn to "atheistic socialism" if they escaped Rome's embrace.[33]

Finally, the ethnically mixed immigrant population threatened to balkanize Canadian society. For healthy nationhood, argued the Reverend John Potts, secretary of the Methodist Educational Society, in 1903, Canada had to "become one in language, in institutions, in manners and customs, and in political and industrial interests, and if not one in religious belief, at least one in that common Christianity which is the only foundation of true morality."[34]

Methodists responded to the non-Anglo-Saxon immigrants in four basic ways. First, they urged the Canadian government to adopt a selective immigration policy that would reduce the influx of "non-preferred" peoples and weed out the physically and mentally unfit. Second, they pressed national, provincial, and municipal government for prohibition, observance of the Sabbath, and other moral legislation. Third, they campaigned for provincial laws that would provide for compulsory English-language instruction in public schools. Fourth, they established missions among the "foreigners" in a bid to give them Protestant, Anglo-Canadian values.

Methodist mission work among the non-Anglo-Saxon immigrants raised several questions. How were Anglo-Canadian missionaries to communicate with people who spoke no English? If they were to learn the ethnic language, then should they learn it locally or in Europe? What was the role of the ethnic convert missionary who could preach the gospel in the "foreigner's" tongue but whose commitment to Anglo-Canadian values and nationalism was doubtful?

Money was the other basic concern. In 1909 the general secretary of the home missions department, James Allen, shrank at the thought of the four thousand dollars required to *begin* work in *one* non-Anglo-Saxon colony to the north of Winnipeg.[35] Unlike regular English-speaking missions, the non-Anglo-Saxon missions were unlikely to become self-supporting. They opened with no church members, and "foreigners" who became Methodists had no experience with the voluntary system of church support. In the old country their priests lived on government salaries and land endowments and by dispensing ceremonies on a fee-for-service basis. For George Moody, a Winnipeg barrister and a member of the general board of missions, the solution was for Methodists to concentrate on their own people. As he argued in 1909,

We have a large task in establishing our own mission work. Every mission grows into a big church and contributes liberally. The foreigners do not ... I feel it would be foolish to go into the foreign, Chinese or any other work ... while we have our own people neglected as they are, English-speaking people who would rapidly develop into a great religious centre. I think it would be madness to sink money into such work and leave our own undone ... I say as a citizen and a resident I would not touch these foreign people.[36]

The Urban Problem

The prairie region had few large cities before the First World War. In 1911 Winnipeg had 136,000 souls, and three other cities, Calgary, Edmonton, and Regina, had populations ranging from 30,000 to 44,000 (table 1.1). Even so, Methodists expected the prairie region to develop large cities as its population surged into the millions. Urbanization was a trend in Canadian, American, and British populations, and the prairie region was no exception.[37] In 1911 the census classed 36 percent of its population as urban, compared to 26 percent in 1901.

A general problem with cities was that secular influences competed with religious ones: profane entertainments competed with Sunday services and midweek prayer meetings for the leisure time of Anglo-Protestants. Street railways, railways, and smelters continued operations on Sunday, desecrating the Lord's Day and depriving their employees of the chance to attend church services. Compared to farm families, urbanites worked less directly with nature and felt less connected to the Creator. Men of his day, observed Ernest Thomas, a Montreal conference pastor, in 1905, were "living in highly complicated social, industrial and political conditions, and it is not easy for them to recognize the prompting of God in the new complex process."[38]

Second, prairie cities presented Methodists with the early stages of urban social problems that had emerged elsewhere. The starting point

Tableau 1.4
Urban Populations, 1911 Census

	Population	Non-British (%)		Population	Non-British(%)
Winnipeg	136,035	38	Toronto	376,538	14
Calgary	43,704	29	Ottawa	87,062	39
Regina	30,213	31	Hamilton	81,969	19
Edmonton	24,900	33	London	46,300	9
			Brantford	23,132	16
Mean (%)		35			18

was a deterioration of the urban environment: a widening gap between rich and poor and the beginnings of slums in downtown-core areas. Poverty, crowded tenement housing, poor sanitation, and the absence of recreational facilities made the urban core a breeding ground for vice and crime. A weakening of Protestant church influence in the core areas aggravated matters. Large downtown churches lost members to new suburban congregations, suffered financial collapse, and left the ground to city missions.

Third, prairie cities became magnets for non-Anglo-Saxon immigrants who were ignorant of Protestant values and British democracy. Language barriers, high population turnover, and so-called decadent religious traditions obstructed the Anglo-Protestant mission workers who sought to reform the "foreigners." As table 1.4 shows, the non-British percentage of census populations was notably higher for prairie cities than for Ontario cities (other than Ottawa, with its large francophone population).

Native Missions

After 1896 native missions were a declining priority for Methodists. The demand for resources in the white population was soaring, and Methodists were frustrated with the native's slow progress from "heathen paganism" to "civilization." Although the financial cost of the native missions was substantial, the results were meagre, and the missions had no immediate prospect of becoming self-supporting. Furthermore, the converts had moral lapses and could not suppress their nomadic instincts (as witnessed by their aversion to eating vegetables, according to one missionary).[39]

In retrospect, Methodist schools helped to impose aspects of white culture on native children but not to integrate them into white society. Church schools prepared the children poorly for employment, either on or off the reserves. In the process, they turned the church's gloomy prognosis for native adjustment to "civilization" into a self-fulfilling prophecy.

That was not the perspective of Methodists at the time, however. Rather, misguided generosity by church and state had turned the natives into dependents.[40] They were a perishing race, genetically sinister, alien, prone to violence, shiftless, lazy, and inferior. As Clifford Sifton, Canada's Methodist minister of the interior judged in 1904, "The attempt to give a highly civilized education to the Indian child is practically a failure. I have no hesitation in saying – we may as well be frank – that the Indian cannot go out from school and compete with the white man. [He has not] the physical, mental or moral get-up to enable him to compete. He cannot do it."[41]

Administrative changes helped to isolate the native missions. In 1897 the Manitoba and Northwest conference "consolidated" its Manitoba and far-west native missions into a separate "Indian District." In 1898, to prevent the conference stationing committee from using native missions as a dumping ground for hard-to-place clergy, the general conference gave the missionary society control over stationing for native missions, thereby ending administrative contact between the conferences and native missions. Finally, in 1906 the general conference divided the Missionary Society into home and foreign departments and placed native missions in the foreign department.[42]

By 1910 the native mission field was stagnating. The old missionaries were dying off, and the Missionary Society had difficulty replacing them. The church had four fewer native missions than the twenty-four listed in 1902 (including orphanages, industrial schools, and residential schools). Over the next four years, the Missionary Society cut in half its constant-dollar expenditures on prairie native missions. This contrasted with the sharply rising trends for its expenditures on regular and non-Anglo-Saxon missions in the region. "While Indians and Half-breeds have held sway there in the past," wrote a Methodist in reference to Willow Bunch, Saskatchewan, in 1907, "now the day has arrived for the homesteaders and advanced civilization."[43]

SCARCE RESOURCES

Money

The church faced long-term costs for native and non–Anglo-Saxon missions and severe short-term costs for English-speaking stations in newly settled areas. As an Alberta missionary explained in 1907, "You cannot get blood out of a stone. The homesteaders have practically no income for the first three years & fearful outlay – houses and fences to be built – stock and machinery to buy and provisions expensive. Flour for instance [is] $4.00 and $4.25 per hundred pounds. Many of the people regard the preacher as a burden & will not come to Divine worship because they have nothing to put into the collection. I wish I had the means of giving them the gospel without burdening them with my support."[44] In addition, prairie communities with small, dispersed Protestant populations hesitated to support more than the first church to reach them.[45] The Methodist Church's failure to be first in such places meant the loss of Methodists in them.

Population movement made financial outlays hazardous. In 1882 Methodists installed a missionary and log church in Sheho, Northwest Territories, following news that the community was to receive a rail connection to Yorkton. When the railroad failed to arrive, the settlers left, one by one. The church was about to withdraw its missionary in 1904 when, abruptly, a revival of the railway project brought settlers back to the area.[46] About the same time, as discussed above, rural depopulation placed several southern Manitoba circuits on the mission list.

Ironically, "acts of God" caused financial setbacks. In 1907 fire destroyed a $2,500 church at Grenfell, Saskatchewan, but only half its value was insured.[47] In 1912 a cyclone gutted Metropolitan Methodist Church in Regina, an $80,000 building, though "not a hotel nor a theatre in the city suffered any damage." Allowing for insurance coverage, this natural disaster saddled the congregation with a debt of $30,000 when it was about to launch a church-expansion program in the city.[48]

The Supply of Clergy

In 1901 James Woodsworth, the superintendent of missions for the Manitoba and Northwest conference, sought twenty-five additional clergy for the coming year. After 1907 the prairie conferences needed over one hundred additional pastors annually. Population growth and high quit rates for pastors kept the demand for clergy high, but the church's bachelor-male and high-school matriculation requirements for clergy kept the supply low.

The prairie pastor's job description offered no enticement to the faint of heart. In 1907 the Reverend Frank Coop travelled fifty miles each Sunday to serve four preaching appointments in the vicinity of Wilcox, Saskatchewan. Also in 1907 the Reverend Charles H. Hopkins was the lone Methodist parson in thirty townships that opened to settlement in Alberta's Peace River country.[49] Chores left the frontier

missionary little time for preaching. As the wife of the Reverend
F.W.H. Armstrong, a missionary in the Peace River country, wrote in 1913,

Mr Armstrong has been compelled to work like any other homesteader from
Monday morning to Saturday night ... For weeks at a time [he] has not had
time to glance at a paper to say nothing of books. I wonder that he is not
discouraged with the situation ... but had he devoted his time to studying and
preaching and visiting etc., we would have died long ago from either cold or
hunger.

   You cannot be of service to any community until you have a house to live
in and food to eat. So far we have accomplished that much.

She also noted the missionary family's deprivations: "We are seventy-
five miles from a Doctor, and our letters are three weeks old before
they arrive, and they don't often appear for six or seven weeks after
they are mailed ... We never tasted butter, milk or eggs after October."[50] For the bachelor majority of the Alberta pastorate, the hard-
ships were greater. In 1908, after living in a series of tents and
granaries, William T. Young moved into a typical "preacher's shack"
that measured eight feet by fourteen. An inventory of its furnishings
revealed "some board bookshelves, a tin stove, with a pipe three inches
in diameter, a home-made chair composed of birch limbs and twigs,
an oil lamp and lantern, a few nails to hang clothes upon, a tin trunk,
a box of Sunday-school papers, a box for a washstand, and a home-
made bed. One window, along with many cracks, served to illuminate
and ventilate the rooms ... in this humble abode the pastor spent the
leisure hours of his life, and also did his studying."[51]
   Young probationers from England were especially at risk of failing.
In 1908 acute homesickness drove John W. Roberts, a Lancashireman,
from the ministry.[52] In April 1905, Fred Corry drowned while trying
to cross the swollen Oldman River in southern Alberta.[53] In March
1909 George Cook was

very badly frozen ... He was stationed on the Richardson field ... about 20 miles
outside Regina. He was living in a shack. During the cold weather which we
had in January he drove home from Regina; and on reaching the place where
he lived he began to unhitch his horse, his hands being very cold; he tried to
thaw them by rubbing them with snow, but seemed to make them worse. He
then got excited and left his horse, and dropping his mitts started off for a
house which was half a mile away. On reaching the place his hands were frozen
solid. He was brought to the hospital next day, and has been there ever since;
until last Saturday morning when he went back to his field. His right hand

will be alright again, although all the fingernails came off. The Doctor had to take off four fingers from the left hand.

Three weeks later, Cook got his feet wet, contracted congestion of the lungs and typhoid fever, and died.[54]

The Laity

The church sought lay members laity for its prairie congregations from three groups of prospective supporters: Methodist migrants and immigrants to the prairie region, the children of church members, and other Protestants who lacked access to services of their own denomination. Each group presented difficulties for the church. Methodist immigrants from Britain and the United States, for example, came from Methodist denominations that had vanished in Canada in the course of Methodist church unions of 1874 and 1884. Thus, immigrant coreligionists were slow to embrace the somewhat different religious practices of the Canadian church. Sunday schools were a key instrument for bringing the children of Methodists into membership. For various reasons, however, many rural congregations did not have one. Methodist families commonly resided some distance from the preaching place. Thus they came with their children to church service but declined to come earlier, or stay later, to accommodate Sunday school at a different time of day.

Methodists had general concerns as well as specific ones. In 1902 Newton Wesley Rowell, the Toronto layman mentioned earlier who had a strong interest in the West, noted that "men were not forced by the time-honoured custom to attend divine worship on Sunday in the west, and in many instances did not go."[55] In 1903 T.C. Buchanan, the mission superintendent for the Alberta conference, remarked that "people do things when they get into a new country that they would never dream of doing at home."[56] Several Methodist observers also believed that the "scarceness of old people" weakened Protestant traditions in the Canadian West.[57]

James E. Hughson, an Alberta pastor, despaired of the materialism in the prairie West. "People are coming," he noted in 1908, "not to get educational advantages, not to get religious privileges, not to secure the comforts and sanctities of home; these things were found much more easily in the communities from which they have come; but they are coming to make money ... and the material side of life is uppermost in their thought – wheat and lands, dollars and acres, the thirst to have, the rush to get, these are the things that are absorbing the lives of men to the exclusion of other and higher things."[58] To R.R. Morrison, the Methodist pastor in Outlook, Saskatchewan, in 1910, the slogan of the prairie-bound was "Good-bye God, we are going West."[59] The church had to respond quickly. Based on evidence from the American West, prairie communities would become "Gospel-hardened" if they lacked religious services during their formative years.[60]

CONCLUSION

The massive spread of the white settler society into the prairie region presented Methodists with opportunity but also challenge. By establishing a strong presence in the booming West, they hoped to forge a powerful Protestant-Christian Canada that would be a major force in the Protestant world mission. The prairie region, however, was a minefield of obstacles, with rural problems, urban problems, large numbers of unmarried men, immigrant coreligionists and non-Anglo-Saxon immigrants, a climate of materialism, continuing demands from native missions, and competition with other denominations that was overtly hostile with Roman Catholics and not so friendly with Presbyterians and Anglicans. In these circumstances Methodists raised, husbanded, and deployed that scarce resources they could: in the form of money and clergy.

2 The Methodist Polity and the Social Profile of the Church

The religious culture, church members, financial resources, and administrative direction for prairie church expansion came largely from central Canada. This chapter treats two inputs from the national church: its political organization, or polity, and the social profile of its members.

The polity of the church evolved during the settlement boom. As the western Canadian conferences acquired a rising proportion of the church's national membership, the church's political centre of gravity shifted westward and undermined the church's bureaucratic central management of Western affairs.

The church was a cross-class institution in which farmers, skilled workers, clerks, and shopkeepers helped to forge threads of the church's pluralistic religious culture. Gender and life course also played on Methodist fortunes. The church's heavily feminine religious culture, for example, kept male bachelors at bay. This was ominous for the prairie mission field, where bachelors composed a high proportion of the population and were the church's prime source of recruits for its all-male pastorate.

THE METHODIST POLITY

Ontario was home for most Canadian Methodists (table 2.1). In 1891 the province held 77 percent of the Methodist census population, compared to 44 percent of the national population and 60 percent of the Anglican and Presbyterian census populations. With the spread of settlement in western Canada after 1896, the geographical concentration

Table 2.1
Geographical Distribution of Census Populations, by Denomination, 1891–1921
(Percentages)

	Total Population	Methodists	Presbyterians	Anglicans	Baptists	Roman Catholics
1891						
Maritimes	18	12	24	18	56	14
Quebec	31	5	7	12	3	65
Ontario	44	77	60	60	35	18
Prairies	5	4	7	7	1	2
British Columbia	2	1	1	4	6	1
1901						
Maritimes	17	12	21	17	54	14
Quebec	31	5	7	12	3	64
Ontario	41	73	51	54	37	18
Prairies	8	8	11	10	5	3
British Columbia	3	3	4	6	2	2
1911						
Maritimes	13	10	16	12	45	12
Quebec	28	4	6	10	2	61
Ontario	35	62	47	47	35	17
Prairies	18	19	24	21	14	8
British Columbia	5	5	7	10	5	2
1921						
Maritimes	11	9	13	10	42	11
Quebec	27	4	5	9	2	60
Ontario	33	59	44	46	35	17
Prairies	22	23	30	24	15	10
British Columbia	6	6	9	11	5	2

of Methodists lessened. Even so, Ontario held 59 percent of the church's census population in 1921, compared to 33 percent of the national population and less than 50 percent of the Anglican and Presbyterian census populations.

Ontario, Canada's industrial heartland geographically contiguous to the prairies, was a major source of settlers and capital for prairie economic development. Similarly, the heavy concentration of Methodist resources in Ontario helped the church stock its prairie conferences with clergy, church members, and mission funds.

The Centralized Polity

Methodist governance diffused up and down a centralized, hierarchical polity. The quadrennial general conference was the national church's governing body, and the Missionary Society and Woman's Missionary Society (wms) were national bodies under its authority. Below the national level were regional bodies, the annual conferences; sub-regional bodies, the annual districts; and local bodies, the quarterly official boards of stations (or circuits). Each station held one or more preaching appointments.[1]

The general conference comprised equal numbers of clerical and lay delegates from the annual conferences. The general conference could change the church's rules and regulations, subject to a three-fourths majority of the delegates present. As provided by the basis of the Methodist church union of 1884, it could not alter the articles of religion, destroy the itinerant system for stationing clergy, or abolish the privileges of ministers and probationers.

The general superintendents, general conference special committee, and general conference boards and standing committees managed national affairs between the quadrennial meetings. The church's central bureaucracy developed steadily after the union of 1884, as a result of the adoption of business methods in Methodist governance.[2] The central bureaucracy also helped Ontario Methodists to influence church decisions for the prairie region.

The general conference could elect two general superintendents, one for an eight-year term and the other for a four-year term. The superintendents presided over the quadrennial meetings and were members and ex officio chairs for each of the standing committees. Between the quadrennial meetings, they represented the church and settled disputes, subject to right of appeal by those affected. Finally, they nominated forty-eight men for the special committee, from whom the general conference chose twenty-four.

The Reverend Albert Carman was a general superintendent during the years 1884–1914. In Carman's hands, the position took on many characteristics of a bishop's office. Although Carman's views gradually lost support, the general conference was unwilling to unseat him. Its remedy was to team him with a younger, energetic man whose views were fashionable.[3] In 1910 it elected a second general superintendent, the Reverend Samuel D. Chown, for a four-year term and required him to reside in Winnipeg. Meanwhile, the general conference had difficulty unseating the Reverend Alexander Sutherland from the position of general secretary of the Missionary Society. Its remedy in that case was to divide the society into home and foreign departments and put the Reverend James Allen in charge of home missions.

In 1896 the church had ten annual conferences (one of them in Newfoundland). It had twelve after 1904, when the general conference divided the Manitoba and Northwest conference into three. The

Toronto, London, Hamilton, and Bay of Quinte conferences and six of the eleven districts in the Montreal conference were in Ontario. The Manitoba conference included the Port Arthur and Rainy River districts in northwestern Ontario.

The annual conference, the workhorse of Methodist organization, comprised its ordained clergy and an equal number of elected lay delegates. Its president and presiding officer was the pastor elected at its previous annual meeting. The clergy met alone in a ministerial session to examine the character and qualifications of ministers and probationers. The ministerial session also staffed the all-important stationing committee, which assigned pastors to their circuits for the coming year, created missions, and reorganized preaching appointments, circuits, and districts. The itinerancy system barred the committee from stationing a pastor on the same circuit for more than three consecutive years until 1902, when it allowed four years. In 1906 a two-thirds majority vote on the committee could suspend the rule in special cases, such as for pastors of non–Anglo-Saxon and city-core missions.

A conference divided its territory into several districts, each holding from eight to twenty stations. A station had one to six preaching appointments. Its quarterly official board managed local affairs and prepared for the district meeting, which treated district affairs and preliminary work for the annual conference. Thus its clergy met in a ministerial session to examine the character and qualifications of the ministers and probationers and recommend changes to circuit boundaries. The district chairman presided over his district's annual meeting, had oversight of church affairs between meetings, and supervised (or delegated the supervision of) probationers and lay supplies on other stations. The chairman's heavy duties meant that he was unavailable to his own congregation(s) for several days of the year.

An Ontario-Centred Polity

Ontario men made up 64 percent of the delegates to the general conference in 1902 and 57 percent in 1910. In contrast, Ontario men were never a majority at the general synod, the Anglican national body. By 1910 they had ceased to be a majority of the general assembly, the Presbyterian national body.

Ontario men influenced prairie church affairs through their strong representation on general conference committees. In 1906, for example, they were chairs for nineteen of the thirty committees (63 percent). Ontario men also had strong representation on Presbyterian committees that dealt with the prairie region. The general assembly's three most important committees (including the committee on home

missions and the board of finance) had Eastern sections for the
maritime region and western sections for central and western Canada.
In 1911 Ontario men were the conveners for western sections of the
three committees and for seventeen of the thirty-two other committees
that had national jurisdiction. In contrast, Ontario men had no influence on Anglican general synod committees that dealt with the prairie
region. In this case, each national committee had Eastern and Western
sections, and its Eastern section combined central Canada with the
maritime provinces.

Methodist journals expressed an Ontario influence. Except for the
Wesleyan, a weekly for the Maritime conferences, the church published
its official journals in Toronto. Although prairie Methodists published
local journals during the years 1904–10, they lacked official status.
The *Christian Guardian* was the official church weekly for the central
and western Canadian conferences, where one in nine church members were subscribers. The other journals included the *Missionary
Outlook,* the monthly publication of the Woman's Missionary Society;
the *Missionary Bulletin,* the quarterly publication of the Missionary
Society; the *Epworth Era* and the *Banner,* the journals for the Epworth
Leagues and Sunday schools; the *Christian Steward,* which promoted
systematic giving; and the monthly *Methodist Magazine and Review.*

Ontario Methodists had strong representation on the church's Missionary Society and WMS, each of which had its headquarters in
Toronto. In 1910 the WMS drew 76 percent of its members and
66 percent of its revenues from the five central Canadian conferences.
In 1906 Ontario men accounted for twenty-three of forty-four members of the general board of missions, the Missionary Society's governing body. They were always a majority at the general board's annual
meetings, in part because its members from western Canada had
difficulty attending them.[4] What is more important, Ontario men
dominated the twenty-four-man executive committee, which exercised
the general board's authority through the year. In 1906 the Reverend
James Woodsworth, in Winnipeg, was the sole non-Ontario man on
the executive. "To save travelling expenses," half its members were
Toronto residents.[5]

Prairie Discontent

In 1906 the bureaucratic centralism of the church drew criticism from
Arthur R. Ford, a Winnipeg newspaper editor; George W. Brown, a
Regina corporation lawyer; and W.G. Hunt of Calgary, the Massey-
Harris company's manager for Alberta. The Missionary Society,
insisted these critics, practised "bad business" by withholding authority

"from those on the ground who understand local conditions" and keeping it for "those at a distance [who] get their information second hand."[6] "In the commercial world," Ford reasoned, "every important eastern manufactory and wholesale house has found it imperative to establish a western branch. The eastern officials and managers, no matter how far their foresight, how keen their business acumen, have found it impossible to keep closely enough in touch with western affairs to hold their own with their competitors without headquarters west of the lake [Superior]. It is just as true in the religious world."[7] Brown felt so strongly about the issue that he refused to subscribe funds to the Missionary Society.[8]

Prairie critics of centralized management developed three general complaints. First, the general board issued regulations that were unsuited to prairie conditions. In 1906, for example, it made a grant conditional upon the mission's use of the weekly envelope "or some systematic and continuous method" to raise money. In time, experience persuaded most prairie quarterly boards that the weekly-envelope system was effective for raising money, paying pastors their minimum salaries, and doing so at regular intervals.[9] In 1906, however, the general board's critics argued that wheat-growing areas were cash-poor through most of the year and that a single canvass in the harvest season was preferable.[10]

Second, the general board's church expansion program was too timid to suit the critics.[11] One difficult problem was that the prairie conferences created more missions than the Missionary Society could adequately fund. In 1912 the general board responded with a plan to put the conference mission programs on a budget. To the Reverend S.W.L. Harton, the *Christian Guardian*'s correspondent for the Saskatchewan conference, the new policy statement "read like a statement of a board of directors at a financial meeting" and ignored the moral obligation to reach new fields "where no Gospel is preached." His remedy was to "give the west larger control and greater powers in the administration, distribution and expenditure of its missionary income, for it sees its own need at closer range, and note how it will rise to that need. The west is restive under the limitations within which it has to work ... and certain occasions call forth this restiveness. The general board does not hear as much about it as do those living on the ground."[12]

Bureaucratic "red tape" in Toronto was the third complaint. In 1906 the Reverend Fred Langford, the *Christian Guardian*'s correspondent for Alberta, found that the "the delays resulting from the concentration of everything in Toronto" were a serious hindrance in the purchase of church and parsonage sites. As he explained, "all applications must be sent there, which means at best two weeks, and where further information is needed, a month. Often the replies to the application are not very prompt. In the meantime, the price of lots is being advanced, and when loans are received, more money has to be paid. It is discouraging to those working hard in this pioneer work to be delayed and hampered in what seems an unnecessary way. Let us have some board official in Winnipeg who can settle these things."[13]

In 1907 the Reverend J.S. Woodsworth found that the general board's management of "too many petty details" delayed routine matters such as salary payments at Winnipeg's All People's Mission.[14] Also in 1907, for reasons of "insufficient information," the general board executive rejected two recommendations for grants from Oliver Darwin, its superintendent of missions for Manitoba and Saskatchewan. Darwin learned from the episode that the general board was unwilling to trust the judgment of its own man on the ground.[15] Another incident in 1907 arose from a joint missionary and educational society program to staff missions with student summer supplies. Due to a misunderstanding, the Saskatchewan conference placed some of its students in self-supporting stations rather than missions. When the general board refused to pay them, an angry Darwin lambasted it for evading payment to save a paltry sum of money.[16]

Yet another incident, in 1909, became a cause célèbre. At the conclusion of the general board's annual meeting in Toronto, Oliver Darwin visited James Allen's office to communicate verbally the relevant information about parsonage loan applications for three Saskatchewan villages. To expedite matters, he took the applications directly to the general board's committee on appropriations, instead of forwarding them through Allen. He advised the applicants that the money was on the way and told them to start construction. But on returning to Saskatchewan, Darwin was shocked to learn that the Toronto office had refused two of the requests and deferred action on the third, pending additional information.[17] In acute embarrassment, Darwin got "two or three of the brethren here to endorse a note, with myself, and get the money out of the bank [to] relieve the trustees."

Darwin, a self-educated blacksmith from Yorkshire and plain-spoken man of action, pulled no punches in his letter to James Allen, MA, the head-office bureaucrat. "I should like to say at the very outset Bro. Allen," wrote Darwin,

I have always regarded you, and look upon you still as a dignified, scholarly, cultured Christian gentleman, possessing gifts and graces that I could covet … But as an administrator of Missionary affairs, and a man to deal with the emergencies and detail of work as it pertains to our Great West, you are weak, exceedingly weak ... I am trying to do the most work on the least money, with fairness to all and you can contrast this conference with any other. Our conference gives more than it receives, and the committee on appropriations, recognizing that we are not a charge on them, [has] more than once indicated a willingness to accept my statements. You ought to give us credit for knowing what we are doing and not holding us up over forms. Life is too short and the task too big ...

I have been humiliated by your action in the presence of men who cannot understand the situation; the young men have been given the impression that I have no more power concerning a grant than a young probationer for the ministry has. [With] great personal inconvenience, humiliation, and loss [I] had to go to businessmen, and explain why my word has not been kept, for in good faith I said those grants would be forthcoming.[18]

Uproar ensued in the Saskatchewan conference, whose special committee endorsed Darwin's position.[19] When the general board was slow to respond, D.L. Thom, a member of the special committee and a Regina corporation lawyer, alluded to "a policy of silence on the part of officials in Toronto."[20] In his letter to the general superintendent, George W. Brown, Thom's law partner, demanded an end to the church's "inelastic methods of doing business in Saskatchewan. If the Methodist church is to succeed ... then Mr Darwin's position must have greater latitude or Mr Allen must come out here and come in personal contact with the situation himself." The people in the three villages in question, he added, were nearly all American immigrants who knew nothing of Canadian Methodism. Thus Darwin had been severely embarrassed when the general board declined to support him.[21]

The church was slow to respond to the critics' grievances. To free themselves of "red tape" from Toronto, for example, Edmonton Methodists established an Edmonton church and parsonage aid fund. In 1906, however, the general conference denied them permission to establish an Alberta conference fund and ordered them to merge the Edmonton fund with the Missionary Society's regular funds for church and parsonage aid. The Edmontonians grudgingly complied when James Allen threatened to cut them off from the regular funds.[22] Alexander Sutherland, the foreign-mission secretary, was a strong defender of bureaucratic centralism. In 1910, when a joint committee of the three prairie conferences petitioned for a Western office of the general board of missions, with its own general secretary, Sutherland denounced any transfer of control "to some irresponsible committee in the west."[23]

In the end, the prairie men achieved some gains. In 1906 the general conference allowed conferences to create city mission boards that could raise and spend money for mission work within the city limits.[24] In 1907, after its misunderstanding with the Saskatchewan conference, the general board gave the conferences lump-sum grants for student summer supply programs, to spend as they saw fit.[25] Then in 1910 the general conference agreed to three major changes.[26] First, it elected a second general superintendent, Samuel Chown, and directed him to reside west of the Great Lakes. Second, it provided for a Western committee of the general board with advisory powers. Its members included the officers of the Missionary Society, Western members of the general board, and the western Canadian mission superintendents.

Third, it provided for conference missionary committees. Each such committee was to include conference members of the general board's Western committee; a minister and laymen from each city mission board; and a minister and laymen elected by the conference. The committee was to prepare estimates of the conference's needs for the coming year. Based on the estimates, the general board was to advise the committee of the total amount that the conference could expect. The general board was then to issue grants according to the committee's recommendations, up to the amount of the allotment. Thus, by forming a missionary committee, the conference could acquire a voice in the general board's plans. The price was to put its mission work on the general board's budget. The general conference's provision for conference missionary committees, in other words, prepared the ground for the "too-timid" church-expansion policy that the general board was to unveil in 1912.[27] Interestingly, the Manitoba and Northwest conference had used the missionary committee system until in 1904, when, as mentioned, the conference divided into three.[28]

Prairie autonomists and Toronto centralists battled over church journals, as well as missions. In 1892 the Manitoba and Northwest conference called for a prairie journal to replace the *Christian Guardian* as the conference's official journal.[29] In 1904 the Reverend T.E. Holling of Moose Jaw founded the monthly *Assiniboia Church Advocate* for Methodists of the "Soo line" and Moose Jaw districts. In the same year, the Reverend Robert Milliken founded the monthly *Western Methodist Bulletin* (later the *Times*) in Winnipeg. Holling's paper died through a merger with Milliken's paper in 1905, when the "iron rule of the itineracy" transferred him from Moose Jaw. In 1906 the Manitoba conference memorialized the general conference to make Milliken's paper the official journal for the prairie region.[30] By then Milliken's monthly had five thousand subscribers. In contrast, the weekly *Christian Guardian* had less than three thousand prairie subscribers, and the number was declining.[31]

The outcome disappointed all parties concerned. After a spirited debate, the general conference established a Western section of the general conference book committee and authorized it to found a Western journal.[32] The proposed journal never got off the ground, however, and in 1914 the general conference removed the provision for it.[33] In the meantime, the editor of the *Christian Guardian*, the Reverend W.B. Creighton, tried to improve his journal's coverage of prairie events. In 1907 he toured western Canada and hired four subeditors to gather Western news.[34] In 1912, however, his correspondent for northern Alberta was "in the position of people who once had to make bricks without straw. We have received one letter in eight weeks pertaining to correspondence for this column."[35]

Prairie Centralists

Some prairie Methodists opposed the decentralization of the governance of the church. In 1906 the Reverend G.W. Kerby of Calgary urged the general conference to deny authorization for a western Canadian journal. In 1907 the Alberta conference voted to appoint a conference subeditor to improve Western coverage in the *Christian Guardian* rather than to support a Western journal at Winnipeg.[36] In 1909 the Reverend Walter A. Cooke, then president of the Manitoba conference, praised the general board's efficiency and interest in the West.[37] Also in 1909, W.H. Cushing, a Calgary businessman on the general board, argued that the executive of the general board understood Western needs and did not need a western Canadian office.[38] In 1913 the Alberta conference probationers' association thanked James Allen and Alberta conference officers for their efforts [the missionary committee system] to secure for missionaries their official minimum salaries.[39] While some prairie Methodists wanted autonomy to expand the non-Anglo-Saxon missions, others, such as the Winnipeg barrister, George Moody, regarded them as a waste of money.[40]

METHODISTS AND SOCIETY

Social Class

The Methodist church was a cross-class institution, with large numbers of farmers, skilled workers, and shopkeepers, and relatively few members that one could style middle class. All social classes contributed to Methodist religious culture and notions of respectability. Thus the church developed a class-variegated religious culture rather than a monolithic middle-class culture.

The interpretation here differs sharply from conventional wisdom, which characterizes the church as a middle-class institution whose leaders imposed class values on a passive membership. In the tradition of S.D. Clark (1948) and W.E. Mann (1955), Neil Semple's *Lord's Dominion* (1996) describes the late nineteenth-century Methodist church as "pre-eminently a middle class institution" that was "dominated by middle-class values." The "middle class sustained the church's operations" and strove to "serve all segments of society by remaking the world in its own image." Conversely the church "reinforced" and gave "added sanction" to "middle-class attitudes and social understanding [that] were generally accepted by Victorian and Edwardian Canada. They were the common intellectual currency of secular, as well as sacred, forces and were widely shared by farmers and labourers as well as merchants and industrialists."[41]

Semple's model allows middle-class Methodists to debate respectability, but not other Methodists. Once the church's middle class sorted out its values, everyone got them. A "small group of wealthy commercial and industrial leaders" played an exceptional role within the "upwardly mobile middle class" that defined Methodist goals and social values. An "expanding class of skilled professionals who helped run the commercial and industrial operations" ("lawyers, accountants, and business administrators") worked closely with them. During the late nineteenth century, these elite groups made indispensable contributions to church finances and administration. To this end, the Methodists increased the lay representation on church courts with their church union of 1884 and developed a national bureaucracy with "sound business practices" after 1884. The construction of "impressive, even monumental, regional churches" in the major cities expressed the elite groups' influence and the church's rising "middle class respectability."[42]

Semple's interpretation presupposes an implicit two-class model of middle class and others. The composition of his middle class, however, is unclear. One learns, for example, that "farmers and labourers" widely shared "middle-class attitudes and social understanding," but not whether these groups were in the middle class. Other recent studies muddy the waters of definition. In Marguerite Van Die's examination of revivalism in Brantford, Ontario, for example, the middle class, which includes skilled workers, was a social juggernaut that held 77 percent of the city's labour force in 1881.[43] In contrast, the urban middle class in Louise Mussio's study of the holiness movement churches excludes skilled workers.[44]

With *Revivals and Roller Rinks*, Lynne Marks became the first scholar to give precise empirical definitions and quantitative evidence for the social profile of Methodists. Her middle class includes merchants and professionals, small employers and foremen, and clerks and agents. Her working class includes artisans, skilled workers, unskilled workers, factory workers, and servants. Her investigation of small urban places, however, leaves unresolved the social locations of rural Methodists.[45] Any two-class model, moreover, misses the range of social locations in the population. The fewer the categories, the greater the chance that differences within categories are more striking than differences between categories.

Although Marks argues brilliantly against the notion of a monolithic protestant religious culture in Ontario's small towns, she implicitly accepts Semple's model of middle-class hegemony for Methodists. Although noting working-class counter-discourses that challenged church-based respectability, she locates them outside the church, in the Salvation Army and Knights of Labour movements.[46] Within the church, poor working-class women were less likely than middle-class women to join ladies aids, which were fund-raising institutions. Even so, Marks attributes this to financial and social constraints and constraints of time, rather than to alternative values.[47] In contrast to Marks, Louise Mussio finds that "farmers and skilled labourers" opposed "middle-class urban values" *within* the church, as well as *outside* it.

Gordon Darroch's recent study of nineteenth-century central Ontario argues for the existence of a rural middle class of farmers "who had won some degree of prosperity from their work." He uses two sets of empirical indicators of middle-class status. One includes middling or large farms (seventy or more acres), family status and the number of children residing at home, servants, home ownership, and type of housing. The other includes "declines in marital fertility and heightened interest in schooling with increased family privacy, domesticity, and deepened gender divisions of labour in the household."[48] Darroch reports that middle-sized farms held 59 percent of the province's landed-farmer heads in 1871 and were above average for his social indicators. In his view, these findings show a large rural middle class in the process of formation.[49] If so, then many of them would have been Methodists.

Much of Darroch's evidence, however, belies his argument. For example, although "a servant was an essential part of any middle class household," just 4.3 percent of his medium-sized farm households had a servant in 1861, and the percentage followed a declining trend. Similarly, although his middle class led a drop in marital fertility, the mean number of children on medium-sized farms was above average and rising between 1861 and 1871. Finally, the influence on the data of the life-course of families needs investigation. Tenancy, for example, was a strategy for young couples "starting up" and old couples "winding down," rather than an indicator of low status.[50]

Table 2.2
Rural-Urban Population Distribution, by Denomination, 1911 Census (Percentages)

	Ontario	Manitoba	Saskatchewan	Alberta	Prairies
RURAL AREAS					
Population	47	56	73	62	64
Methodists	56	59	68	61	63
Presbyterians	50	54	65	50	57
Anglicans	35	49	62	49	54
CITIES[1]					
Population	24	30	7	15	18
Methodists	17	23	7	18	15
Presbyterians	22	29	7	16	20
Anglicans	35	36	9	18	25

[1] The figures are for cities with more than 25,000 inhabitants.

A Cross-Class Institution

The Methodist social profile was not middle class except by definitions that include almost everyone and make class analysis pointless. Rather, the church was a cross-class institution with large numbers of farmers, skilled workers, clerks, and shopkeepers. Farmers probably were the largest occupational group. The census enumeration of 1911 found 56 percent of Ontario Methodists and 63 percent of prairie Methodists in rural places (table 2.2). The comparable statistics for Presbyterians (50 and 57 percent) and Anglicans (35 and 54 percent) were notably lower. Second, workers probably made up a majority of Methodists in small towns. In the Ontario towns of Campbellford and Thorold, for example, Lynne Marks's working class included 72 percent of Methodist families and 63 percent of Methodist families with church members.

Third, the majority of Methodist men in Toronto probably were workers, shopkeepers, and clerks, in occupations that one might style as working class and lower middle class. As table 2.3 shows for a random sample of males in the Toronto *City Directory* for 1911, only 10 percent of Toronto men were in categories that held wealthy laymen (professionals and manufacturers).[51] Simply put, few Toronto Methodists were in an upwardly mobile middle class, because few Toronto men were. Conversely, the church's price of membership – pew rents, envelope subscriptions, and the cost of Sunday clothes – helped to keep unskilled workers from its congregations.[52]

Given the social profile of Methodists, the notion that middle-class values defined the church is implausible. That interpretation denies agency to the majority of Methodists. At best, it allows them to resist

Table 2.3
Occupational Profile for Toronto Men, 1911

Occupational Category	Number	Percentage
Skilled labourer	153	40
Shopkeeper	42	11
Clerk	70	18
Professional	26	7
Unskilled labourer	58	15
Manufacturer	11	3
Employee (undesignated)	25	6
Total	385	100
Unclassifiable	1	
Total	386	

Source: Toronto City Directory, 1911.

the middle-class hegemony but not to express their own values. In an age of rising real incomes, consumerism influenced all social classes. Thus, all classes, not just the small middle class, included consumer values in their social constructions of respectability. Similarly, Methodists sought to impress their social peers, not their putative middle-class social betters. Workers and farmers wore good Sunday clothes to impress other workers and farmers, not distant millionaires in Toronto's Sherbourne Street congregation. Similarly, by joining the Odd Fellows, a Methodist artisan or farmer signalled his breadwinner's respectability to other artisans or farmers; he could afford the lodge's joining fees and dues, and his family members were not headed for paupers' graves.[53] Finally, alternative notions of respectability, ranging from bachelor rowdyism to farmer holiness, had Methodist followings. As Louise Mussio notes, Methodist farmers and artisans in the holiness movement disputed "urban middle class *conceptions*" of respectability, not respectability itself.[54] Effectively, Methodists developed overlapping, competing social and religious respectabilities, not a monolithic middle-class respectability.

Gender and Life Course

In the Ontario communities of St Catherines and Huron County in 1913–14, 60 percent of persons at church services were women, as were two-thirds of persons at midweek prayer meetings. In London two-thirds of the persons at morning service were women, as were 57 percent of persons at evening service. Although the men's organizations outnumbered the women's and mixed-sex organizations combined, "the women far outnumber[ed] the men ... in enrolment."[55]

Bachelors were the problem. As Lynne Marks shows for Thorold and Campbellford during the years 1886–92, 65 percent of Methodist church members were women, because 90 percent of the church's bachelors declined to join.[56] As Marks explains, "protestant discourse was imbued with female imagery. The close fit between the notions of the ideal woman and the ideal Christian – in piety, gentleness, morality, and submission to the will of God – could not help but make the upright Christian man uneasy." Church and parsonage improvements tended to feminize and domesticate sacred space. In raising money for the purpose, ladies' aids extended women's responsibility for the beauty and comfort of their homes. The feminized religious culture fit poorly with bachelor masculinity, with its values of strength, independence, and self-assertion. In contrast, the domesticated church suited married men whose masculine ideals included the roles of family provider and breadwinner.[57]

The gender influence sharpened on the prairie frontier, where there were large numbers of bachelors. In expansionist discourse, notes Catharine Cavanagh, the West was manly space. Men were the settlers ("men of muscle who were willing to hustle"); women were the civilizers, the tamers. Thus the Dominion government refused women the right to take up a homestead, lest they keep the land from becoming productive. The effort of a man to get rich was a struggle for essential manhood. The frontier was "no place for a woman." Indeed, the young man's quest for manhood required women's absence. The churches tried to accommodate bachelor masculinity. They barred women from the pastorate to keep it "manly." The Presbyterian pastor Charles W. Gordon promoted muscular Christianity in his popular Ralph Connor novels. Paradoxically, however, the frontier needed women to civilize it.[58]

SUMMARY AND CONCLUSION

The Methodists managed church expansion in the prairie region with a centralized polity and heavy influence from the Ontario conferences. During the years 1906–14, the church conceded some autonomy to prairie conferences to appease and co-opt regional discontent. At the same time, important numbers of prairie Methodists withheld support from critics of the church's bureaucratic centralism.

Contrary to conventional wisdom, the church was not a middle-class institution whose leaders imposed class values on a passive membership. Rather, it was a cross-class institution with heavy representation from families of farmers, skilled workers, and lower-middle-class men. The various class groups developed multiple, overlapping, conflicting notions of respectability. Within each group, individuals sought primarily to impress their peers, as opposed to deferring to values of social "betters."

Gender and life course, as much as social class, shaped Methodist notions of respectability. Women formed a majority of the members, and the church's evangelical doctrine matched values of domestic feminine culture. Their contributions to church decoration developed naturally from work they did in their homes. The feminine content of Methodist respectability clashed with the masculine values of bachelors, but not with the masculine values of married men. Thus bachelors seldom became church members, while married men commonly did.

As in the larger society, men filled the church's leadership positions. Images of muscular Christianity and an all-male pastorate helped to shore up their masculine insecurities in an institution heavily influenced by women. This reinforcement of masculinity probably was essential for the recruitment of probationers from the ranks of bachelors, the church's most difficult constituency.

Methodists were less attached to church life than one might suppose. A minority of Ontario Methodists attended morning services on a given Sunday. In three small Ontario towns, less than half the Methodist families included a church member. Bachelors stayed aloof from the church, and they did so in droves.

3 Methodist Traditions

Long-term Methodist traditions from outside the region exerted the primary influence on prairie Methodist religious culture during the Laurier settlement boom from 1896 to 1914. The prairie environment and frontier conditions created distinctive short-term features in the regional culture. In contrast, the settlement boom largely severed the regional culture from its early years (1840–95), when it was organized around Native missions.

THE LONG-TERM TRADITIONS

The Wesley brothers, John and Charles, founded Methodism as a religious movement within the Church of England during the mid–eighteenth century. The movement spread to North America and spawned Methodist religious denominations on both sides of the Atlantic. Although the Wesleys originated the movement's doctrines and organization and the means of grace, Methodism developed distinctively on the North American frontier. Whereas Wesleyan doctrines identified four bases of authority – scripture, tradition, reason, and experience – North American Methodists emphasized experience, emotional fervour, and scripture – at the expense of tradition and reason.[1]

In Methodist doctrine, salvation for the afterlife required a life that was perfect according to Creator's law. After Adam's original sin (the Fall), humanity was depraved and deserved eternal damnation. Magnanimously, God gave his only Son, Jesus Christ, to atone for humanity's sins by dying on the cross. Under Christ's new covenant with humanity, personal salvation merely required that one accept God's undeserved offer of eternal life.

Methodists believed that humans had moral choices.[2] Thus, if a person was unsaved, that person had not willed to be saved. The first step to salvation was an experience of conversion. This second birth "made a new person who could only act to further God's work." Methodists commonly attained conversion with difficulty, after years of anguish and uncertainty.

After conversion the Methodist worked toward entire sanctification (complete holiness), whereby the heart was cleansed of sin and filled with perfect love. John Wesley doubted that many could attain entire sanctification, but what mattered was the struggle for it. In contrast to Wesley, certain North American revivalists presented sanctification as an essential "second blessing of the Holy Spirit," akin to conversion but more important. As such, this state of holiness marked the start of a Christian life, not its culmination.[3]

Methodists formed a centralized connexion whose polity grouped societies (at preaching appointments) into circuits; circuits into districts; and districts into annual conferences. The society's job was to promote spiritual growth and maintain discipline. Sunday public worship, weekday prayer meetings, and the weekly class meeting were its regular means of grace.

The class, a small group of adherents who sought salvation, was the germ cell of early Methodism. One had to belong to a class to be a Methodist. The class leader's power to drop backsliders was a key instrument of Methodist discipline. The class acted as a group confessional to promote spiritual growth. It was also a proxy family for "lonely individuals who joined the fellowship," a training ground for lay preachers, and a link between the members and preachers.[4]

Methodists used mass evangelism to invigorate their revival message and carry it to new groups, through outdoor camp meetings, lasting several days, and protracted indoor meetings that were held in the evenings, to avoid disrupting secular activities during the day. Local clergy or professional evangelists led the work.

Canadian Methodism after 1850

Social diversity marked Methodists after 1850. Methodism had begun as a movement of the rural frontier masses. With Canada's urban-industrial development, it came to include a wealthy elite, urban working-class families, and established farm families. Rising real incomes and consumerism crept into church life, as evidenced by the construction of permanent places of worship with elaborate interior decoration. The development of railway and road networks and telegraphic communications eroded the geographical insularity of local congregations. Rising levels of schooling diffused unevenly through the membership, and new intellectual currents pressed Methodists to recast their religious beliefs and practices. In Canadian Methodism, in contrast to British Methodism, a professional pastorate displaced lay preachers, and university courses became important in the pastoral apprenticeship. Congregations increasingly recruited church members from among the children of Methodists rather than unchurched adults. Thus, the Sunday school and youth organizations became major means of grace, while the class meeting and prayer meeting declined in popularity. Other influences on Canadian Methodism came from immigrant British and American coreligionists who joined the church, an aging population trend, and an intake of members from other protestant denominations through marriage to a Methodist or out of convenience.

Trends and countertrends made Methodist religious culture as diverse as its membership. The trends included a dampening of emotional display, a revival of reason and tradition as religious authorities, the experiencing conversion and sanctification as gradual processes, rather than as sudden, traumatic events, and the development of a liberal (modernist) theology and social gospel in reaction to new intellectual currents and emerging social problems. The countertrends included a resurgence of emotional revivalism, a holiness movement that treated sanctification as an emotional, traumatic event, the defection of members to Methodist splinter groups such as the Salvation Army and holiness churches, a popular rejection of theology and attraction to the social gospel as a return to emotional, experiential religion, and the proliferation of modest places of worship on Canada's settlement, forest, and mining frontier.

The literature locates Methodist trends among wealthy urban laymen, the faculty of theological colleges, and young, university-trained clergy. It positions the countertrends among rural and working-class Methodists and older clergy. In W.E. Mann's study of Alberta, the countertrends held a special attraction for socially marginal families with below-average levels of schooling, working-class families with average incomes, farm families with below-average incomes, and persons who were weakly integrated with their social classes, such as workers who ignored working-class communal activities.[5]

The trends and countertrends were complex phenomena. Each had a cross-class appeal and social-class, gender, and life-course meanings. Their complexity makes Methodist religious culture tricky to interpret.

The elaborate interior decoration of urban churches, for example, expressed consumerism, but also sacred space and women's home-decoration skills. Yes, raising money through pew rents did sharpen social class distinctions by relegating the poor to the back of the church. By the 1890s, however, Methodists were shifting from pew rents to subscriptions to raise money.[6]

The trends and countertrends in the church's pluralistic religious culture evolved from long-term continuities in different ways. The shift from traumatic conversion to a more rational approach of "gradual growth to a state of grace," notes Semple, harkened back to "Wesley's original understanding of salvation." In contrast, the social gospel and a growing popular rejection of theology, argue Christie and Gauvreau, returned Methodists to the emotional, experiential religion of the North American frontier.[7]

Christian Nurture

As their offspring became the chief source of church members, Methodists increasingly expected children to reach a state of grace without a traumatic conversion experience.[8] Yes, infants were depraved because of Adam's fall, but they were innocent of sin while too young to know right from wrong. By the 1870s many Methodists believed that infants were born in a state of grace through Christ's atonement. Thus, a conversion experience was unnecessary for children who became enlightened before they were old enough to actively sin.

Apart from spiritual concerns, peer pressure, parental expectations, and a quest for acceptance and respectability nudged children into church life. In many cases, speculates Lynne Marks, "the conversion experience may have [been] as much scripted as spontaneous." Similarly, church membership could signal worldly concerns as well as "some level of belief."[9]

The Earthly Kingdom

By the early twentieth century Methodists widely anticipated the Kingdom of Heaven on Earth. In 1901 Alexander Sutherland, the Missionary Society's general secretary, wrote that "we are entering, with the new century, the last decisive stages of the great world conflict."[10] "The message of today," argued a Methodist in 1905, "is wider than the narrow personal salvation of the past."[11] "In the moral history of the world today," opined S.D. Chown, the general superintendent, in 1913, "the world is marching forward, and ... the upward angle of its advance has recently become more acute."[12] All three men voiced the spirit of the popular missionary slogan, "The evangelization of the world in this generation!"[13]

Notions of Anglo-Saxon superiority underlay Methodism's optimistic post-millennialism.[14] Methodists expected Canada to play a major role in an Anglo-Saxon destiny to civilize "lesser" peoples. Compared to Britain and the United States, Canada was a "young" country with vast, untapped resources. The settlement of the West led toward a population in the millions. Thus, Canadian protestant churches joined with British and American churches in a massive global mission.[15] Canadian Methodists aimed to present the gospel message to 14 million heathens in Japan and China – a large task for their 300,000 members.[16]

During the years 1900–14, the church increased the number of its West China missionaries from 9 to 104, in addition to operating a large mission field in Japan.[17] Although this missionary outreach stimulated Canadian church life by giving it global significance, non-Anglo-Saxon immigrants, social problems, and materialism were eroding Canada's protestant character and capacity for outreach.[18] Methodists responded with the social gospel.

The Social Gospel

The social gospel aimed at the salvation of mass society, as opposed to personal salvation for an afterlife. It sought to model society on the golden rule ("Do unto others as ye would have them do unto you"), Christ's Sermon on the Mount, and Christ's life. Its environmentalist approach to sin assumed an immanent God who was active in transforming humanity. Its tools included education and Christian nurture; collectivist action through organizations such as "business associations, labour unions, farm cooperatives, women's groups, and reform societies"; and government legislation of moral standards. At first glance, the social gospel complemented the task of personal salvation. A thoroughly Christian environment, one that applied Christian teachings to social problems, clearly helped the Methodist quest to regenerate sinners.

Even so, the social gospel tended to make personal salvation a secondary priority. In the individual's spiritual progress, a commitment to social salvation was to "precede, not follow, individual salvation." On the one hand, a highly individualistic theology could "prevent personal salvation by encouraging selfishness and even pride." On the other hand, personal salvation developed incidentally from the subordination of self to the welfare of society.[19]

Nellie McClung, the prairie-Methodist social activist and feminist, exemplified the shift in Methodist priorities. She believed that she would one day meet God in heaven, but "until then she strove to know God's presence in her day to day living." As she argued in 1917, "The Church must renounce the idea that, when a man goes forth to preach the Gospel, he has to consider himself some sort of glorified immigration agent, whose message is, 'This way, ladies and gentlemen, to a better, brighter, happier world; earth is a poor place to stick around, heaven is your home.' His mission is to teach his people to make of this world a better place – to live their lives here in such a way that other men and women will find life sweeter for their having lived. Incidentally, we will win heaven, but it must be a result, not an objective." Similarly, "the Church has directed too much energy to the business of showing people how to die and teaching them to save their souls," because "the soul can be saved only by self-forgetfulness."[20]

For J.S. Woodsworth, the superintendent of All People's Mission in Winnipeg (1907–13), the social gospel replaced the gospel of personal salvation.[21] By 1906 he had lost faith in Christ's divinity and personal salvation for an afterlife. At the same time, his social gospel built on the Methodist tradition of personal holiness and Christ's life and teachings as a model for social reform. He spoke against the traditional evangelical goal because he saw it as competing with the social gospel.

Woodsworth's version of the social gospel was radical as a religious program in its outright rejection of otherworldly individualism,[22] but moderate as a program of social reform. Marxist socialism, for example, sought to abolish capitalism through working-class violence and revolutionary change. In contrast, Woodsworth's Christian socialism aimed to reform capitalism by basing social relations on brotherhood rather than class differences. It called employers and employees to treat each other according to the golden rule and envisaged social change that was evolutionary, not revolutionary.

This moderate version of Christian social reform attracted business promoters of welfare capitalism during the First World War and the 1920s. Large firms in the United States and Canada devised corporate benefits for their employees in a bid to weaken labour unions, reverse government's intervention in labour relations, and secure labour peace. The social gospel helped to legitimate their program. As Owen D. Young, the American chief executive and publicist for the General Electric Company, pronounced, "The Golden Rule supplies all that a man of business needs."[23]

Winnipeg's working men showed scant interest in Woodsworth's social gospel and rejection of personal salvation. Few of them attended the independent labour churches in which Woodsworth and William Ivens preached, whereas they flocked to old-time gospel meetings at the Methodist Bethel Mission and other churches in the city's working-class districts.[24]

In contrast to Woodsworth's religious mix, Nellie McClung's views were moderate as a religious program but radical as a social program.[25] McClung, a wife, popular author, and feminist and religious social activist, lived in Manitoba until 1913 and then in Edmonton. Her beliefs in personal salvation, personal purity, and temperance were in the Methodist mainstream, but her crusade for woman's rights within the church and in the larger society challenged convention. Having been denied ordination in her church by virtue of her gender, McClung used "literature as pulpit." In McClung's Pearlie Watson trilogy, as Randi Warne shows, God worked through women to grant absolution to men. Implicitly, the church's exclusively masculine pastorate was a social shame.[26]

New Intellectual Currents

Higher criticism of the Bible and Darwin's concept of evolution initially challenged Methodist belief. Nevertheless, Methodist educationalists managed to reconcile the new currents with Methodist tradition. In the process, they reinforced trends such as postmillennialism, the social gospel, and the dampening of emotion.

Higher criticism, the examination of the Bible in the light of historical and archaeological findings, suggested that much of the Bible was not literally true. Several authors had compiled the Old Testament over time. Biblical accounts of supernatural events, such as the collapse of the walls of Jericho at the blast of trumpets, were inspired legend, not fact.[27]

Evolutionary theory gave a naturalistic reading of history that ignored providential design and cast doubt upon the biblical account of the fall of man. Humanity had not slipped from a state of perfection but, rather, had evolved from lower forms of life. But if original sin was a myth, then what need had humanity of a redeemer? Could Christianity survive if biblical supernaturalism was myth?[28] Such questions became compelling as nineteenth-century technological developments increased the stature of empirical science. The more that Methodists sought rational explanations for things, the greater their difficulty in holding religious doctrine by faith alone.[29]

At Victoria College the professors Samuel Nelles and Nathanael Burwash used "reverent criticism" to incorporate the new currents into their church's evangelical tradition. On the critical side, they accepted certain insights from science and biblical scholarship. On the side of reverence, they held that original sin had dulled humanity's rational faculty. Hence they subordinated reason to faith and screened out claims that clashed with Methodist core beliefs, such as God's presence in history and Christ's divinity.[30]

Viewed in this light, empirical science and higher criticism provided a progressive revelation of God's will. Social gospellers, for example, came to view the Old Testament prophets as religious reformers who fought decadence in official Judaism. As such, they were models for Methodist reformers who battled Roman ecclesiasticism, the traffic in drink, and immigrant vice.[31] Liberal theologians discarded the notion of a transcendent God who stood apart from his creation and intervened through miracles and substituted an immanent God-in-the-world who "used the natural, ongoing processes of evolutionary creation to fulfil His purpose." A key attraction of a liberal theology was its reconciliation of Darwinism with Christianity. It did this in part by "changing survival of the fittest into survival of the best."[32]

Clergy in Winnipeg illustrated the range of Methodist reactions to the new intellectual currents. At one extreme, J.S. Woodsworth had lost his faith in biblical supernaturalism and salvation for an afterlife. At the other extreme, John Maclean, pastor of the Maclean mission, and Henry Kenner, a retired minister, supported Albert Carman, a general superintendent and a champion of biblical literalism.[33] Burwash's middle-ground modernism attracted the majority, including William Sparling and Samuel P. Rose – the pastors of the prestigious Grace and Broadway Street Churches – and the Wesley College theologians Salem Bland, Andrew Stewart, and J.H. Riddell.[34]

Elsewhere Stephen Byles, a twenty-one-year-old probationer in Lashburn, Saskatchewan, was proudly modernist in theology. Although Byles was a former farmhand who lacked junior matriculation, let alone college training, prized holdings in his personal library included Dr [Robertson] Smith's scholarly commentaries on the major and minor prophets. Byles never learned how his rural congregations viewed his preaching, but they made no trouble for him.[35]

Countercurrents

Evangelical revivalism and holiness revivalism countered the consumerism, respectability, formalism, and liberal theology that had crept into Methodist religious culture. Albert Carman, the general superintendent mentioned in the previous section, championed both movements.[36] The countermovements extended also into Methodist splinter organizations: the Salvation Army and holiness movement churches.[37]

The Salvation Army, an offshoot of British Methodism, came to Canada in 1882 and had 25,000 members by 1886. As Marks notes, the "shouting, crying, and jumping up and down in the name of salvation" at Army meetings was a throwback to old-time emotional revivalism.[38] The Army's turnover of members was high; while some converts left the churches to join the Army, others quit the Army to join the churches or lapsed in their commitment to the movement. In 1911 the Army had 10,308 members, including 2,690 in the prairie region. By this time its emphasis had shifted from evangelicalism to rescue work.

The holiness movement came to Canada from the United States and produced twenty-five holiness churches during the years 1893–1907.[39] It supporters valued plain dress and avoided fashionable clothes. Whereas Wesleyan tradition viewed entire sanctification as a gradual rational process, supporters of the holiness movement likened it to a traumatic conversion experience, only more important.

METHODISM AS A RELIGIOUS MOVEMENT

Denominational Methodism and religious-movement Methodism were complementary, yet mutually corrosive. Methodism began as a religious movement within the Church of England but eventually spawned several denominations, each with its own clergy, congregations, property, and polity. Paradoxically, denominationalism weakened even as it developed.

First, Methodist differences from other Protestants began to blur at midcentury.[40] With the separation of church and state in the 1840s, Anglicanism and Presbyterianism ceased to be establishment religions, and as denominations they were evangelical in outlook. Conversely, Methodist religion became less emotional and more rational, and protestant divisions over new issues, such as biblical criticism, crossed denominational lines.

Second, the Canadian Methodist church unions of 1874 and 1884 consolidated Methodist denominationalism, but they were also compromises that diluted denominational loyalty. For example, the union church discontinued features of polity (e.g., the position of bishop in the former Methodist Episcopal Church) that some of its members had known in the pre-union days. Similarly, immigrant coreligionists from Britain and the United States differed from members of Canada's union church in matters such as hymn selections and the use of lay preaching.

Third, some Methodists viewed Methodism as primarily a religious movement. For example, Nathanael Burwash, the dean of theology at Victoria College (1873–87), was a staunch Methodist, but the church was his second priority. His chief concern, argues his biographer Marguerite Van Die, was to sustain Methodism as an educative and moral force in changing intellectual times. With his religious-movement perspective, he led Victoria College into federation with the secular University of Toronto in 1890 and supported church union with the Presbyterians after 1902.[41]

Fourth, after 1896 Canada's anglo-protestant churches faced demands on their resources that trivialized their differences. Social problems in rapidly growing cities, a massive influx of non–Anglo-Saxon immigrants, and the expansion of home and overseas mission fields pressed protestants to unite their forces.[42] In the prairie region, many communities had small protestant populations that were sufficient to support only one church. Many protestant families in such places saw denominational competition as wasteful.[43]

Methodists responded to these ecumenical pressures by discussing church union with the Presbyterians. Their negotiations for union dated from 1902, when a Presbyterian spokesperson, Principal William Patrick of Manitoba College, invited Methodists to consider the issue.

Methodist support for church union was strong in the prairie region. For the ministers of the three negotiating churches in Winnipeg in 1908, "the most potent reason for union ... [was] the immediate and imperative necessity for the extension of the kingdom of heaven, both in Christian and in heathen lands."[44] In 1906 the lawyer J.A.M. Aikins argued that union was a sensible application of business methods to religious affairs. As he reasoned,

Does one manufacturer or dealer in goods send over the same route and to the same places and at the same time two or three travellers or agents to sell the same goods? Yet that is the principle on which the three denominations have been largely acting ...

The laity say ... wisely, why waste our contributions and money by supporting three sets of churches, three sets of colleges, three sets of church adjuncts, the grand object of which can better be obtained by one. Why this loss of money and expenditure of human effort in senseless and unbusinesslike methods [?] Concentrate, consolidate, combine. Have as much sense in religious matters as in material affairs.[45]

"If the eastern churches, not feeling our physical pressures, decide that nonessentials must keep them apart," exclaimed the pastor in Hartney, Manitoba, in 1905, "then the west by sheer pressure must unite anyway."[46] As the pastor in Alix, Alberta, remarked in 1908, the West had "none of the old settled conditions to stand in the way, no church heritage to bother us."[47] By 1906 Methodists in some prairie and Ontario communities were putting off the construction of church buildings in the belief that church union was imminent.[48]

In 1908 committees of the Methodist, Presbyterian, and Congregational Churches agreed on a draft basis of union. By 1912 the Methodist Church and most congregations of the Congregational church had accepted the basis of union, with Methodists in all but the Newfoundland conference voting massively for it. As table 3.1 shows, the prairie conferences produced the largest Methodist majorities for union.[49] Only the opposition of 30 percent of Presbyterian Church members prevented church union before the First World War.[50]

Although union did not happen, Methodists in several prairie communities joined other protestants in local-union churches. In November 1908, Methodists in Melville, Saskatchewan, helped to form the first local-union congregation. In 1911 protestants of five denominations organized a union church in Kerrobert, Saskatchewan. By 1914 the prairie region had thirteen union churches: six in Manitoba (Wawanesa, McGregor, Beresford, Glenboro, Cypress River, and Oak River); six in Saskatchewan (Melville, Frobisher, Kerrobert, Conquest, Ceylon and Forget); and one in Alberta (Vegreville).[51] In Wolseley, Saskatchewan, Presbyterians and Methodists federated: they shared church facilities and the Methodist minister, but each group kept its denominational affiliation.[52]

Localities organized union congregations in the belief that union of the parent bodies was immanent. Conversely, the parent bodies tried to contain the local union movement with the argument that the larger union was "just around the corner." In April 1913, the three parent churches reached an agreement with the local-union churches. They each received one representative on an interdenominational advisory committee that was to assist and advise them in matters of property, ministerial supply, and the raising of missionary funds. The union congregations, in return, agreed not to agitate for union churches in other communities or to meet to discuss common problems.[53] Meanwhile, after 1911 the Methodist and Presbyterian Churches began to cooperate in their use of resources for the prairie region (see chapter 4).

THE PRAIRIE METHODIST TRADITION

Early prairie Methodism had little influence on the church's regional culture after 1896. The early years had produced two missionary heroes (James Evans and George McDougall), but both were from native missions, now a minor part of the prairie church. In addition, the prairie congregations and pastorate were largely migrants from Ontario. Finally, the spectacular church expansion after 1896 overwhelmed any distinctive features from earlier years.

Table 3.1
Methodist Vote on Union with the Presbyterians, 1912

Conference	Quarterly Board Members		Church Members Age 18 and over		Church Members under Age 18		Adherents	
	VotesCast	In Favour (%)	VotesCast	In Favour (%)	VotesCast	In Favour (%)	VotesCast	In Favour (%)
Newfoundland	991	37	5,776	30	296	33	3,981	30
New Brunswick/Prince Edward Island	1,299	85	8,163	86	579	86	3,306	87
Nova Scotia	1,205	82	7,995	79	514	82	2,775	84
Toronto	3,717	88	28,433	90	3,822	93	5,557	93
London	4,090	89	26,249	87	3,348	89	5,363	89
Hamilton	3,698	84	24,823	86	3,701	81	4,399	87
Quinte	2,926	88	21,668	90	2,408	90	4,840	89
Montreal	3,145	81	21,056	82	2,319	80	6,532	87
Manitoba	2,027	92	11,514	93	1,378	94	4,412	94
Saskatchewan	1,835	95	8,228	94	879	96	4,283	96
Alberta	1,347	96	6,275	95	742	95	2,816	97
British Columbia	1,064	89	5,118	92	541	96	1,085	94
Total	27,344	86	175,298	86	20,527	87	49,349	85

Prairie Methodism did develop a regional character after 1896. It differed from Ontario Methodism in its more rural social profile; its lower population density; its large population of bachelors; its reliance on schoolrooms, poolrooms, and homes, rather than ornate church buildings, for religious services; its widespread use of preachers' shacks and granaries for parsonages; its more youthful clergy and laity; a higher proportion of Britons and probationers in its pastorate; its greater intake of American and British coreligionists; and its above-average support for church union with the Presbyterians. The urgent problems in the region, the prospects for regional greatness, concerns about Methodist progress in the region, and a struggle for regional administrative autonomy caused numbers of prairie Methodists to embrace regional interests.

Even so, other prairie Methodists placed national interests before regional ones. Some distinctive regional features were artifacts of frontier conditions. Compared to the Ontario laity, for example, the prairie laity had higher proportions of farm families, bachelors, and males. Thus, prairie Methodism gave greater representation to religious behaviour of prairie associated with these groups. This did not mean that the religious behaviours of farm families, bachelors, or males differed from the behaviour of those groups in other regions.

Revival Meetings

Many rural and village congregations held protracted meetings or special services annually, often during the winter months.[54] By the 1890s such revival gatherings reportedly were "composed almost entirely of those already directly interested in the church."[55] Even so, noted an Alberta pastor in 1912, many in his congregations were new to Methodism. Stephen Byles, a probationer in Saskatchewan during the years 1908–10, never learned the denominational backgrounds of persons in his congregations.[56] Some revival services focussed on children. As the Reverend G.R. Turk exclaimed in 1903, after special services in Saskatchewan, "it did our hearts good to see the boys and girls, members of Christian households, and our Sunday schools, stand up and declare themselves on the Lord's side."[57]

Methodist studies found that traumatic conversion happened by one's late-teen years or not at all. In 1903 the Reverend C.H. Huestis, a Methodist youth expert who later transferred to the Alberta conference, anticipated conversion at "the dawn of puberty." Also in 1903, the Reverend G.W. Kerby, a Calgary pastor and former evangelist, published a chart that showed the improbability of conversion after age twenty. In 1911 a Manitoba conference committee situated the "natural crisis" at about twelve years of age.[58] An anonymous veteran minister from central Canada fixed the average age of decision at sixteen years and three months for boys and a bit younger for girls. "After that age," he continued, "conversions become less frequent, until, in maturer years ... they almost cease." The problem with adults was that "their notions are set, their ideas formed, their habits settled ... If they are not already Christian ... it is against the law of averages, that anything you say ... will influence them savingly and lead them to religious decision. They have become, many of them, Gospel hardened."[59]

Some revival services aimed at the conversion of fallen children, but others followed the rival approach of Christian nurture, or "salvation through education." The assumption here was that the child was born innocent, not fallen. Thus, the church's task was to keep the child in God's house through Christian education. Christianity, argued the Reverend Robert Milliken, principal of Regina College, before an Epworth League convention in 1912, was "really an educative process whereby the spirit of man may be trained into the hatred of sin and into a corresponding love of righteousness."[60] The *Christian Guardian* published Milliken's address by popular request, as it had for James Speakman's similar address before an Epworth League convention of the Alberta conference four years earlier.[61]

The local pastor conducted the revival services or worked with other local clergy in meetings at several churches. Alternatively the congregation engaged a professional evangelist. A.H. Ranton, a former bartender from Owen Sound, gave several prairie congregations his stock lecture, "From Bar-room to Pulpit."[62] Other Ontario evangelists in the prairie region during the years 1905–7 included the Reverend G.R. Turk, "the singing evangelist"; Millie Magwood of Brantford; the Reverend C.J. Atkinson and Reverend McHardy from Toronto; the veteran team of the Reverends H.T. Crossley and John E. Hunter; and the Reverend G.S. Hunt from Guelph.[63]

In July 1906 the Crossley-Hunter meetings at Souris, Manitoba, reportedly drew people from twenty-five to thirty miles around, destroyed 60 percent of the bar trade, and left one hotel proprietor ready to sell out. Behind such success lay solid promotion by the Methodist and Presbyterian churches, the use of a rink that had been floored and seated to hold two thousand people, and "a large number of capable workers" who accompanied Crossley and Hunter.[64] In 1902 A.H. Ranton's Zion Church revival services involved all Methodist congregations in Winnipeg. Months of prayer and cooperation preceded them. The meetings featured a large choir and up to thirteen ministers on the platform at a time. The enquiry services that followed Ranton's presentation harvested eighty-five new members for Zion Church alone.[65]

In 1906 the famous American evangelists Dr Torrey and Charles Alexander came to Toronto's Massey Hall, and their well-publicized meetings sparked gospel fires in the prairie West. At Calgary's Central Methodist Church, a seventy-five-voice choir sang the famous Alexander gospel songs, and church workers distributed fourteen thousand cards imprinted with Torrey's motto, "Get right with God," among the fifteen thousand people of the city.[66] Moose Jaw Methodists paraded Torrey's motto through the town streets during three weeks of special services. The Epworth League in Grenfell, Saskatchewan, held a Torrey-Alexander meeting with a banner emblazoned with "Get Right with God" stretched across the room. The program consisted of sketches of the lives of Dr Torrey and Mr Alexander and accounts of their "worldwide" tour and Toronto meetings. A message from Dr Torrey, sent upon request to the league, was a highlight.[67]

Methodists held outdoor camp meetings during the summer months. The *Christian Guardian* reported them at Reston, Burnside, and Winnipeg, in Manitoba, and at Edmonton, NWT, in 1896; at McGregor, Manitoba, in 1897; Souris, Manitoba, in 1901 and 1902; Springbank and Youngstown, in Alberta, in 1905; and again at Youngstown in 1912 and 1913.

The 1901 Souris camp meeting was a five-day affair in a local park.[68] To prepare for the event, local Methodists cleared the grounds, erected platforms for the speakers and a forty-voice choir, arranged seating for a thousand people, laid on extra eating and sleeping facilities, and obtained discount railway fares for persons from outside points. The proceedings opened on Wednesday with "Sunday school day." Some ninety persons heard an address on the spiritual side of this work. Missions were the theme on Thursday and Friday evenings. Although rain forced this part of the program indoors, the park ground was usable on Saturday, the most important day. Thus, a substantial crowd partook in Methodist soul-saving, replete with "red-hot" gospel messages and after-meetings. On Sunday, six hundred persons attended morning services; forty-three gave witness at the "love-feast" that followed; and a thousand persons attended the dramatic closing service in the evening.

Sunday Schools and Youth Organizations

Like revival services, the Sunday school, Epworth League, and youth club could support either the traumatic-conversion or Christian-nurture approaches to salvation. The church's ideal was to bring the entire Methodist population, not just children, into its Sunday school classes. In 1914 its elementary, secondary, and adult divisions included 48, 24, and 28 percent respectively of Sabbath scholars in the prairie region; 27 percent of the scholars were church members. At the same time, Methodist Sunday schools and youth organizations were less developed in the prairie region than in Ontario (see chapter 6).

Class and Prayer Meetings

During the years 1898–1914 the number of class leaders for every one thousand Methodist church members dropped from twenty to three in the prairie region and from twenty-six to ten nationally. In 1907 a survey for Hamilton found that 15 percent of the church members were enrolled in classes and only half of these attended.[69] In 1910 the Alberta conference had just fifty class leaders, and a conference committee estimated that only 10 percent of the membership attended class meetings regularly.[70]

In part, the class and midweek prayer meetings fell victim to the rising influence of the social gospel. As a general conference committee observed in 1910, "introspection, with the object of saving the soul of the subject, has in these days, to an almost universal extent, given place to earnest activity for the salvation of one's neighbour."[71] Similarly, many Methodists were uncomfortable giving or listening to testimony in detail.[72]

Even so, Methodist prayer was distinctive, even startling, to outsiders who witnessed it. In 1898 three Ukrainian Protestants found that Methodists at Grace Church, Winnipeg, were "overly pious ... during the prayers, through which they knelt, they sighed loudly, and whenever the preacher made an important point in his prayer, they would exclaim: 'Yes Jesus!' or 'Oh, yes, yes, dear Jesus.' Such conduct on the part of the believers in the church setting did not seem cultivated to us, but rather, as fanatical." At Winnipeg's Knox Presbyterian Church, in contrast, they found "exemplary orderliness, unpretentiousness, and silence ... no one moans aloud during the prayers."[73]

In 1914 Pierre Van Paassen, a Dutch Calvinist student in theology at Victoria College, suffered an abrupt end to his pastoral career in Edmonton. As he explained,

A prayer meeting opened the proceedings the next morning at nine. Everyone present kneeled by the side of a chair in the parlour. My superintendent [T.C. Buchanan], who fulfilled the function of presiding officer, designated the persons who were to lead in prayer by calling the names in turn. My host, the [former] hardware man, came first. To my amazement, he began telling

God details of his own career in the ministry ... He spoke a half an hour and when he said amen at last, I felt ready for breakfast. But now his wife began speaking and continued at great length ... She prayed for eighteen minutes.

I had heard about such Methodist exercises of self-contemplation, but, of course, had never witnessed one. When I say that I did not like what I saw and heard, I put it mildly ... Moreover, since I was extremely uncomfortable kneeling by a rocking chair ... I began to wish for the end of the exercises. How long was this going to last? Did nobody else have sore knees? When were we going to have breakfast? Those were the things that worried me. It soon became evident that we had only started ... I could smell coffee somewhere and I was beginning to feel faint.

[Then] one of the sisters went into action. In a high-pitched sadly lamenting voice she was telling Jesus she had been a vile, contemptible, lascivious sinner. She had spit into the Master's face ... her bosom heaved in anguish as she poured forth a stream of self-accusations ... I felt genuinely sorry for her, for she was in evident distress. I would have risen to wipe her tear-stained face, but was afraid that my gesture might be taken amiss by the congregation. The Spirit had to have its course. She could not find words to express her emotion and started to scream. She threw her head back so far that a button tore off her blouse and her breasts became visible. I thought that the superintendent would cut her slobbering exhibitionism short, but he was encouraging her with loud amens.

Suddenly she stopped on a high note and burst into hysterical sobs. This is the end, I thought ... I quietly rose to leave. "Back on your knees, Brother," came the stentorian voice of the superintendent, and unctuously he added, "Will you lead us next?"

That was too much. If I had spoken to God that moment, I would have apologised for being present in a religious gathering where religion was turned into a mockery, into an outlet for suppressed sex emotions. I was furious at his asking me to pray. "No, Sir," I answered. "I have nothing to say ... I don't feel well" ...

The superintendent was shaking with emotion. I had scandalized the assembly. Nothing like it had happened in the course of twenty-five years in the ministry. I had given offence to my brethren, nay, I had offended the Lord. He placed his hands on my shoulder, and took me aside into the [host's] bedroom ... "We will kneel down together here," he said, "alone with Jesus." "I prefer going out into the fresh air," I said ... A few days later I was on my way back to the East.[74]

Temperance and Prohibition

Nothing so marked a Methodist as his or her opposition to the liquor traffic. Thus, in 1894 the quarterly official board at Medicine Hat,

Alberta, pressed Medicine Hat's MLA to end the sale of liquor by drugstores. In 1897 it asked the Manitoba and Northwest conference to oppose the rumoured appointment of the Duke of Leeds as Canada's governor-general, on account of the duke's "wet" sympathies. In 1905 it named a committee to seek prohibition legislation from Alberta's first provincial government.[75]

Methodist pastors commonly led "dry" campaigns. In 1907 in Wilcox, Saskatchewan, Frank Coop lamented that "only my own people will stand by me in the fight."[76] In 1910 A.E. Smith was determined to keep Neepawa, Manitoba, dry in a local-option vote, despite receiving "an anonymous letter signed 'Railroad Boys' giving him notice to get out of town."[77] In another local-option vote, in Saskatchewan in 1910, C.B. Keenleyside held firm against the liquor interests, who spread rumours that he was an ex-convict, had left Winnipeg in debt, and been exposed for immorality.[78] In 1914 D.R.L. Howarth led the dry opposition to issuance of a liquor license at The Pas, Manitoba.

Sabbath Observance

Sabbath observance was another Methodist signature issue, albeit one shared with the Presbyterians. In 1896 the Manitoba and Northwest conference named a standing committee on the question.[79] In 1901 it warned against Sunday occurrences of worldly conversation, unnecessary work, pleasure visiting, neglect of church services, unnecessary freight train runs, harvesting, the repairing of separators, and desecration by "foreign immigrants" who came "from countries where there prevail very lax ideas."[80] In 1902 the conference, and later the Winnipeg gathering of the general conference, reacted anxiously to rumours that Winnipeg was to hold a plebiscite on Sunday streetcars, as Toronto had in 1897.[81] Despite the Methodist position, in 1906 Winnipeg voted in favour by a large majority.[82]

Elsewhere in the prairie region, in 1904 the Reverend G.W. Kerby denounced Sabbath baseball games and golf matches in Calgary. In 1906 Sabbath observance committees of the Saskatchewan and Alberta conferences warned against legislative concessions to Seventh Day Adventists and Saturday rest-keepers. The Saskatchewan committee also welcomed the appointment of a Western field secretary of the Lord's Day Alliance, "realizing the unsettled condition of the country and the many conflicting opinions and customs prevailing in our western provinces."[83] In 1910 the Alberta conference committee lamented Calgary's acceptance of Sunday streetcars and opposed Sunday activities such as the freighting of settlers' effects, ball games, concerts, harvesting, and threshing.[84]

Amusements

During the years 1886–1910 a Note in the Methodist *Discipline* banned "dancing, playing at games of chance, encouraging lotteries, attending theatres, horse-races, circuses, dancing parties, patronizing dancing schools …[and] taking such other amusements which are obviously of a questionable or misleading moral tendency."[85] Such activities, warned the *Christian Guardian* in 1897, "bring you into undesirable associations, make dangerous acquaintances, stir up evil passions and lead to sinful and dissipated habits."[86]

Prairie Methodists heard the message. In 1905 the Crossley-Hunter evangelist team lectured Brandon, Manitoba, Methodists on "Dancing in the Ballroom," "Personal Purity," "Social Evils," "Mysteries," and "The Model Woman." In 1907 the Reverend Wellington Bridgeman, president of the Manitoba conference, praised them for dealing fearlessly with dance, cards, and strong drink and for calling a sin a sin.[87] In 1904, in a private letter to his family in Ontario, a "clever and devoted minister out west" wrote that Methodists were

unpopular here because we set a higher standard of living than other churches. One of the most flourishing institutions here is the Quadrille Club, something of the wild and woolly character described by Ralph Connor. Every now and then they have a grand dance, keeping the dissipation up all night until five in the morning, with plenty of drinks in between. Our attitude needs no exposition, and as a consequence we have an honourable unpopularity. If we do nothing more here, we are a silent protest against that sort of thing … dancing is most prevalent out in these settlements, and not the refined dance of a respectable eastern home, but a vulgar, low, disreputable, indefensible variety. The long winter gives so much time for relaxation from the strenuous work of summer that those who do not know how to use their heads naturally find an outlet for their energy in their heels. The rough crude conditions of a new country seem to remove all restraint from the animal instincts, while ideals of culture are hardly recognized.[88]

Methodists, wrote Martin Holdom, the Anglican pastor at Castor, Alberta, in 1910,

look upon me as a rather dangerous character for it is generally known that the English preacher occasionally smokes, and it has been reported that he once drank a glass of beer. I came away quite convinced that Methodism cannot save Canada nor the world at large. They lay entire stress on a few petty rules of life: smoking, drinking, dancing, etc. They set up as their standards or ideals a few cut and dried rules instead of that Life, which, if

only men take it as their example, will bring all sides of their beings uncon-
sciously into their natural proposition. How could a man living the Christ-life
allow sin to enter into such things as smoking, drinking, or dancing. Men may
turn them into sin, but there is no sin in the things themselves.[89]

Nevertheless, amusements crept into Methodist tradition. Although
Stephen Byles disapproved, Methodists in Indian Head, Saskatchewan,
indulged in the card game "Lost Hen" in 1907. Byles himself played
fiddle at local square dances while serving as a probationer in Radisson, Saskatchewan, in 1910. In 1912 Dr Christopher Connolly, a
medical assistant at the Pakan hospital mission in Alberta, admitted
to having smoked and played cards in public. In 1910 the general
conference removed the Note from the Discipline.[90]

SUMMARY AND CONCLUSION

Prairie Methodists had a complex, evolving religious tradition. Dating
from 1840 in the prairie region, it was part of Canadian and world
Methodist traditions that originated in the eighteenth century and
came into the prairie region with Methodist migrants and immigrants.
Methodists were members of a religious denomination, and also of a
religious movement whose core beliefs dated from the days of John
Wesley. After 1850, Methodists became socially diverse, and their
religious tradition acquired a pluralist character.

Methodist traditions from outside the region were the chief influence on prairie Methodism. Lesser influences came from the regional
church's pre-1896 foundations and the prairie environment. Much of
the church's regional distinctiveness expressed temporary frontier conditions, not lasting substance. In the meantime, revival services, Sunday
schools, class and prayer meetings, and moral-reform crusades linked
prairie Methodists to national and international Methodist traditions.

4 Money

The prairie region demanded much from Methodist resources during the years 1896–1914. The number of church stations rose almost four-fold, from 163 to 627, and church membership rose three and one-half times, from 16,316 to 56,964. Paradoxically, the Methodist population shrank in southern Manitoba, due to the displacement of farmer-owners by tenants and a trend to larger farms and fewer farmers.

This expansion combined with population contraction cost more than prairie church members were able to raise. In 1914 48 percent of the prairie stations were missions – they were not self-supporting and required grants from the missionary society. In Alberta, where missions made up 77 percent of the stations, Methodists received seventy-five cents in grants for each dollar of salary raised locally. The Missionary Society's chief outlay was for missionaries' salaries. The rest was for expenses of district chairmen and circuits, missionaries' moving costs, half the salaries of student summer supplies, and the salaries and travel bills of conference superintendents of missions.[1] The society issued loans for the construction church and parsonage buildings, and it received requests from district meetings to make up for particular missionaries' salary deficiencies and to pay sickness and funeral expenses. Finally, it spent important sums on non–Anglo-Saxon missions for institutional buildings, hospital buildings and equipment, nurses' residences, school homes, and foreign-language religious tracts.

By 1905 the Missionary Society faced an acute shortage of money for grants and loans to the prairie region. By 1906 it had actually exhausted its church and parsonage loan funds and had begun the practice of borrowing to lend additional sums. In 1911 the department of home missions needed a $100,000 increase in revenues to cover its appropriations and $109,000 for deserving projects that it had not provided for. By 1912 the home department was $30,000 in debt, unable to pay missionaries at the church's minimum salary levels, and swamped by requests for money.[2] In 1913 the department's revenues were up by $50,913, but its appropriations were up by $100,000.[3]

THE METHODIST ORGANIZATION FOR MISSIONS

The Missionary Society was the church's chief agency for missions. Under its rules for 1896, every Methodist who gave one dollar annually was a member. Each station sent its donations by post to the society's general treasurer in Toronto. The society's governing authority, the general board of missions, met annually in October to plan activities for the coming year, while its twenty-one-man executive committee met as needed in the interim. General officers in Toronto managed affairs on a day-to-day basis. Before 1906 the head official was Alexander Sutherland, the general secretary and treasurer. The chief field official was James Woodsworth, the superintendent of missions for western Canada.

In 1906 the general conference created home and foreign departments of missions, gave each department a general secretary and a field secretary, and provided the society with an honorary lay treasurer. It elected Sutherland as general secretary for the foreign department; James Allen as general secretary for the home department; H.H. Fudger, the president of the Robert Simpson Company, as treasurer; and James Woodsworth as the "senior superintendent of missions residing in Winnipeg." The general board then appointed the Reverend C.E. Manning as field secretary of the home department and four "local superintendents," two of them for the prairie region: the Reverend Oliver Darwin for the Manitoba and Saskatchewan conferences and the Reverend Thomas C. Buchanan for the Alberta conference. In 1910 Woodsworth assumed responsibility for the Manitoba conference. In 1912 the general board gave the prairie region two more superintendents: the Reverend Charles H. Cross for northern Saskatchewan and the Reverend Arthur Barner for southern Alberta.

When the general conference of 1906 placed native and oriental missions in Canada in the foreign department, the home department was left with regular English-speaking missions and non–Anglo-Saxon missions. The general conference required the Missionary Society to

give the home department a minimum of 42.5 percent of its appropriations, including half the society's costs of management. In practice, the general board made appropriations in equal amounts to its
two departments until 1910 and then gave home missions the larger
share, due to the "phenomenal development" of church work in
western Canada.[4] In 1914 the general board gave 45 percent of its
appropriations to the home department, 42 percent to the foreign
department, and 13 percent to administration.

The general conference, or the general board of missions acting on
its behalf, set "minimum salaries" for Methodist clergy. In 1910 the
minimum amounts for western Canada were $475 for an unmarried
probationer; $550 for a married probationer; $650 for a single,
ordained man; and $800 for a married minister. The general board
paid the full salaries of missionaries in the foreign department and in
non-Anglo-Saxon missions, except for medical missionaries, who drew
some of their incomes from patients' fees. In regular English-speaking
missions, in contrast, the "people upon the mission" were responsible
for the pastor's minimum salary. Many a missionary received less. Commonly his station had subscribers in arrears or had lost subscribers
through removal. What is more important, the missionary society lacked
the funds to bridge the gap between the amount raised locally and the
minimum, leaving the missionary out of pocket, with no redress.

The *Discipline* required the WMS to work in harmony with the
Missionary Society and avoid competing with it for funds. Nominally
the WMS required the general board's approval for the "employment
or remuneration of missionaries, designation of fields of labour, and
general plans and designs of work." In practice, it had considerable
independence.[5] The WMS did not support regular English-speaking
missions but was deeply involved in non-Anglo-Saxon missions. It paid
the salaries of deaconesses at the All People's Mission in Winnipeg. In
Alberta it ran its own missions and cooperated with the general board
on others.

The general conference of 1906 allowed annual conferences to
create city mission boards to raise and manage money for missions
within city boundaries. The Missionary Society and WMS were to help
out financially with appropriations that the city mission boards deemed
"desirable or necessary." In 1907 James Woodsworth became the chair
of the first city mission board in the West, in Winnipeg. In 1912 the
conferences organized city mission boards for Calgary, Edmonton,
Hamilton, and Toronto.

The Missionary Society was the chief provider of funds for missions
throughout the years 1896–1914, but its share fell from 87 to 76 percent. The WMS's share rose from 12 to 17 percent, and the share

for city mission boards went from zero to 6 percent. Sunday schools consistently furnished 7 percent of the missionary society's funds, while the percentage from Epworth Leagues and other youth organizations rose from 2 to 7.[6] In 1914 the central Canadian conferences held 66 percent of the church's census population and 71 percent of its members, and they raised 75 percent of its donations to missions (table 4.1).

The Missionary Society kept two funds to make low-cost loans for church and parsonage sites and buildings. One fund, the Church and Parsonage Aid fund, issued loans for up to 40 percent of the estimated property value. It was intended to make loans for projects anywhere in Canada, but it was capitalized at only $32,749 in 1906. Despite the society's effort to augment the fund, its capital amount was still just $41,459 in 1914. By 1906 the society had borrowed to lend $10,800 beyond the fund's capitalization, and by 1913 it had borrowed to lend $41,455 beyond the fund's capitalization.[7] The society used these loans from borrowing to cover up to 25 percent more of the property value of the project, to a maximum of $1,000.[8]

In 1902 the general conference authorized the general board to raise an additional emergency fund of $50,000 for northern Ontario and western Canada. In 1903 the Missionary Society raised $29,265 of this amount for its second fund, the North-West Extension Fund, which provided interest-free loans of up to $500 for the erection of churches and purchase of church sites.[9] These small loans were suitable for frontier churches, such as one at Pincher Creek, Alberta, which in 1904 cost $650, including furnishings.[10] The limited capital of the fund, however, was modest, in view of the number of buildings needed. In 1914, for example, 427 of the church's 589 preaching places in Alberta (73 percent) had no church building.[11]

THE PRAIRIES AS A DEBTOR REGION

For the fiscal years 1911–12 and 1912–13, the central Canadian conferences gave nine times more to the Missionary Society than they received back in regular home-mission grants (table 4.2).[12] In contrast, the Alberta conference gave just 34 percent of the amount it received in grants. In addition to regular grants, the Manitoba and Alberta conferences received special-fund grants for buildings on non-Anglo-Saxon and native missions. The prairie region was also responsible for some of the society's administrative costs, which were 13 percent of its budget.

Table 4.3 elaborates on the prairie region's financial relationship with the Missionary Society.[13] During the first three quadrennia, native

Table 4.1
Regional Distribution of Members and Donations to Missions, 1914–15 (Percentages)

	1911 Census	1914 Membership	Donations to Missionary Society			Donations to City Boards	Donations to WMS	Total Donations
			From Congregations	From Sunday School	From Youth Organizations			
Maritimes	10	9	6	5	7	0	13	7
Ontario/Quebec	66	71	78	75	78	73	67	75
Prairies	19	16	14	16	11	23	16	15
British Columbia	5	4	3	4	4	4	4	3
Total	100	100	101[1]	100	100	100	100	100
PRAIRIE REGION								
Manitoba	6	7	6	8	8	18	9	7
Saskatchewan	7	5	5	5	1	0	4	4
Alberta	6	4	3	3	2	5	4	3

[1] Total more than 100 because of discrepancies due to rounding.

Table 4.2
Donations to the Missionary Society, 1911–12, 1912–13

	Donations ($)	As Percentage of Home Mission Grants Received
Maritimes	64,337	116
Ontario/Quebec	872,690	931
Prairies	197,481	107
British Columbia	58,149	70
Within Prairie Region		
Manitoba	90,860	405
Saskatchewan	68,878	130
Alberta	37,743	34

Table 4.3
Missionary Society Receipts and Expenditures for the Prairie Region, by Quadrennia

Quadrennium	Receipts ($)	Receipts Less Expenditures, Regular Missions Only ($)	Receipts Less Expenditures, Including Non-Anglo-Saxon Missions ($)	Receipts Less Expenditures, Including Native Missions ($)
1898–1902	61,231	–3,108	–4,789	–195,298
1902–6	139,162	10,668	–601	–205,663
1906–10	260,516	2,870	–22,252	–227,723
1910–14	349,748	–95,476	–152,282	–270,619

missions accounted for most of the region's net deficit, exclusive of administrative costs. In contrast, English-speaking and non-Anglo-Saxon missions caused much of the net deficit for the quadrennium 1910–14.

Table 4.4 shows prairie regional trends for donations and grants in constant (real) dollars – dollars adjusted for inflation.[14] The real deficit (column 6) was stable before 1910 but then rose to 1.4 times the amount for 1898–1902. Real donations (column 1) rose more rapidly than real expenditures (column 5). After 1910 real expenditures on native missions (column 4) fell sharply while those on English-speaking and non-Anglo-Saxon missions (columns 2 and 3) rose sharply. Thus native missions paid a price for the church's expansion of white settler mission work.

Within the prairie region, Methodist indebtedness for missions was negligible for Manitoba but rose steeply toward Alberta where, in October 1911, 155 of its 200 stations (78 percent) were missions.[15] This geographical pattern mimicked the westward diffusion of white

Table 4.4
Missionary Society Receipts and Grants for the Prairie Region, in Constant Dollars, Relative to the Amounts for the Quadrennium 1898–1902

Quadrennium	Receipts (1)	Grants, Home Department		Grants, Indian Missions (4)	All Grants (5)	Net Deficit (6)
		Anglo-Canadian Missions (2)	Non-Anglo-Saxon Missions (3)			
1898–1902	1.0	1.0	1.0	1.0	1.0	1.0
1902–6	2.1	1.7	6.1	1.0	1.2	0.9
1906–10	3.6	3.3	12.8	0.9	1.6	1.0
1910–14	4.5	6.3	26.5	0.5	2.2	1.4

Table 4.5
Methodist Census Population 1891–1911, as a Percentage of the Methodist Census Population in 1921

	Manitoba	Alberta and Saskatchewan
1891	40	4
1901	70	12
1911	93	74
1921	100	100

settlement. In 1901 Manitoba's Methodist census population was already 70 percent of its size in 1921, compared to 12 percent for the territories (table 4.5). In 1911 Manitoba's Methodist census population was 93 percent of its size in 1921, compared to 74 percent for Saskatchewan and Alberta. Thus the rate of increase was brisk in Manitoba and explosive in Alberta and Saskatchewan.

STRATEGIES FOR INCREASING REVENUES

Education

The church developed two educational movements to stimulate donations to missions. In 1895 the Reverend F.C. Stephenson, a disappointed aspirant for the China mission field, founded the Young People's Forward Movement for Missions. This movement sent college students into meetings of Methodist youth organizations to promote missionary education and systematic giving. The interdenominational Laymen's Missionary Movement (LMM) came to Canada from New York City in 1907. Whereas the Forward Movement focussed on youth, the LMM catered to men.

Table 4.6
Missionaries Supported by the Forward Movement, 1914

	Missionaries	Supported by Prairie Sponsors
China	72	14
Japan	18	2
Canada	22	3
Prairies	13	3
Indian	4	1
Non-Anglo-Saxon	6	2
Mission superintendents	3	0
British Columbia	6	0
Ontario and Quebec	3	0
Total, Canada and overseas	112	19

The Forward Movement became an integral part of the Missionary Society's operations. In 1896 the general board invited Epworth Leagues, Sunday schools, and individuals to sponsor particular missions and missionaries, including WMS missionaries.[16] In 1902 the movement became a department of the Missionary Society, with Stephenson, its secretary, a general officer of the society.[17] The department introduced regular study classes in 1898 and summer schools in 1900. In 1902 it began to publish mission literature in cooperation with thirteen denominations in Canada and the United States.[18] The *Missionary Outlook* (1881–1925), the *Canadian Epworth Era* (1899–1916), and the *Missionary Bulletin* (1903–21) provided youth meetings with information about the church's missions. In the *Missionary Bulletin*, letters from the missionaries in the field took their young sponsors "behind the lines" to see how their money was spent "at the front."[19]

Sponsorship under the Forward Movement suited long-term missions but not regular English-speaking missions that became self-supporting within a few years. Thus in 1914 the movement had sponsors for ninety overseas missionaries, compared to twenty-two for Canada (table 4.6). The nineteen prairie sponsors supported sixteen overseas missionaries but only three for their own region. Within Canada the movement supported five mission superintendents and seventeen pastors on native, oriental, French Canadian, and non-Anglo-Saxon missions.[20]

The LMM promoted missionary education and business ideas and methods in fund-raising. It urged each congregation to adopt the weekly missionary envelope, organize a missionary committee, and practise systematic canvassing.[21] The LMM's interdenominational Canadian council included three Methodists: N.W. Rowell, a Toronto corporation lawyer; H.H. Fudger, president of the Robert Simpson Company and treasurer of the Missionary Society; and A.O. Dawson, a Montreal industrialist. Rowell chaired the Canadian council and was one of two Canadians on the LMM's international executive committee.[22]

In 1908 the Canadian LMM undertook a national missionary campaign. J. Campbell White of New York, the LMM's general secretary, and members of the Canadian council attended banquet meetings of up to three hundred persons in twenty-four cities. Delegates at the city meetings, in turn, took the message to towns.[23] In March 1909, the campaign climaxed with a week-long national missionary congress in Toronto, where speakers challenged four thousand delegates from across Canada to quadruple the nation's protestant missionary donations. As a first step to reaching their long-term goal of $4.5 million annually, they set a target of $1.5 million for 1909 and assigned quotas to each city and province. At both the national and city levels, an interdenominational committee worked through denominational cooperating committees.[24] During the movement's city-wide canvass in Brantford, a Methodist marvelled to see "our lawyers, doctors, merchants, managers, bankers and labourers literally side by side in a house-to-house canvass for the missionary society ... men who had not given an hour's consecutive thought to missions are right in the thick of it ... the whole city is stirred up by missions as it has not been within living memory of this generation."[25]

The LMM did increase donations from wealthy laymen. During the fiscal year 1903–4, for example, just 1 percent of the Missionary Society's revenue came from gifts of $200 or more. By the fiscal year 1913–14 the statistic was 8 percent. Similarly, the maximum gift was $800 in 1903–04 and $3,300 in 1913–14.[26]

Despite its energy for the wealthy few, the LMM had a marginal influence on society revenues, which accumulated primarily from donations in small amounts (less than $200). Although per capita donations in constant dollars (adjusted for inflation) were 10 percent higher in 1914 than in 1909, the year of the congress (table 4.7), the difference expressed a rising trend that dated from the 1890s and that resulted from Canada's economic boom after 1896 and a trend of increasing real wages.[27]

Two prominent prairie laymen, J.H. Ashdown and George W. Brown, shunned the LMM's national campaign in 1909. Ashdown, a Winnipeg hardware-store millionaire, faulted its emphasis on foreign missions when the needs of non-Anglo-Saxon immigrants in Winnipeg were pressing.[28] By the LMM's projections, the Methodist church planned to raise $1 million annually for missions in Asia, but just $500,000 annually for missions in Canada. In 1914 those targets called

Table 4.7
Contributions to the Missionary Society and the WMS, 1898–1914,
in Real Dollars

	Contributions per Church Member ($)	Percentage of Contribution in 1909
1898	0.88	77
1899	0.99	78
1900	1.00	80
1901	0.97	82
1902	0.92	86
1903	1.33	87
1904	1.41	88
1905	1.57	91
1906	1.60	91
1907	1.70	98
1908	1.81	98
1909	1.99	100
1910	2.19	101
1911	2.35	105
1912	2.43	110
1913	2.52	107
1914	2.65	110

for a 286 percent increase in Missionary Society and WMS grants to Asian missions but only a 107 percent increase in grants to missions in Canada. However, despite his sentiments, Ashdown declined to contribute to the church's Winnipeg city mission board during the fiscal year 1913–14.[29]

Brown, a Regina corporation lawyer and future lieutenant-governor of Saskatchewan, refused to contribute to the Missionary Society in protest at its management of prairie mission affairs from Toronto. "The Laymen's Missionary Movement," he advised Albert Carman, the general superintendent,

has been practically a failure in the west. The causes are not so far to seek. Our businessmen have been so repeatedly compelled to contribute in emergencies such as this when the Missionary Board machinery is so slow to move and its management so unacquainted with the real situation (not being able to accept the situation as described to them by their own agents) ... that the businessmen of the Methodist church have not the confidence they should have in the management of the funds, and so prefer to administer what they have to contribute themselves. This is not as it should be but if an advisory council is not established in the west I fear that the break which has begun will continue to widen until serious harm has been done.[30]

Special Funds

The church raised special funds in addition to its regular funds. During the years 1896–1914 three such funds affected prairie church expansion, directly or indirectly.[31] The previously mentioned North-West Extension Fund of 1902 provided interest-free loans for church and parsonage construction. By 1903 the Missionary Society had raised $29,000 of its $50,000 target to the fund. The Wesley Bi-centenary Fund of 1902 was intended to wipe out the society's debt and carrying charges that had accrued from native, French Canadian, and overseas missions. The drive for that fund flopped, raising just $37,564 of its $250,000 goal.[32] In 1910 the Missionary Society launched a $1.5 million Mission Plant and Extension Fund to finance the construction of hospitals, institutional buildings, orphanages, schools, and other capital projects. The society ended its fund drive in January 1914 with pledges of $925,000 (62 percent of the objective) and $203,576 collected.[33]

The general board relied on wealthy laymen for pledges and organizational leadership for its special fund drives. Clearly it missed their support for the Wesley Bi-centennial Fund. The paltry amount raised ($37,564) paled beside Senator George Cox's $35,000 gift to the church's Twentieth-Century Fund in 1899 and Chester Massey's $50,000 gift to the Save St James fund in 1902.

The Mission Plant and Extension Fund was the church's major special fund for missions. In December 1910, the general board proposed to raise the $1.5 million at the rate of $300,000 annually over five years, to be divided equally between home and foreign missions. It appealed "to those who can afford to make a second contribution" and organized banquet meetings in the major cities to reach them.[34]

N.W. Rowell chaired the national committee for the fund drive. The nine provincial vice-chairs included E.R. Wood, the general manager of the Dominion Securities Corporation, for Ontario; G.F. Johnston, the head of a Montreal brokerage house for Quebec; J.A.M. Aikins for Manitoba; the Honourable G.W. Brown, a Regina lawyer, rancher, trust company director and lieutenant-governor of Saskatchewan; W.G. Hunt of Calgary, the Massey-Harris company's manager for the province of Alberta; and T.T. Langlois, a Vancouver businessman. The eighteen-man executive for the campaign included N.W. Rowell; the Honourable E.J. Davis of Newmarket, a former provincial government cabinet minister, one of Canada's largest leather goods manufacturers, and a member of the Toronto board of trade.[35]

In a "private and confidential" letter to principal J.W. Sparling of Wesley College, James Allen opined that

Winnipeg is a strategic point in the campaign ... nor need I say that those who have launched the movement in Toronto are extremely desirous to do everything in their power to forward it in your city. It was understood when we talked together that one method of doing this would be by a meeting of representative Winnipeg and Manitoba men such as was held in Toronto. It was also understood that some of the Eastern men, say the Missionary Secretaries, the Treasurer, N.W. Rowell, E.R. Wood, G.H. Wood, J.D. Flavelle and others might visit Winnipeg and other points and address the meetings in the missionary cause. But you will understand that it will be better if Winnipeg arranged for such a meeting and invite some of the Toronto men to attend it rather than to have the Toronto men urge such a meeting and thrust their visit upon a people who are rather sensitive about government in the East. Our friend Mr Aikins [is] vc [vice-chairman] for Manitoba and I write this, as you will see, in confidence to suggest that you do what you can to arrange for a meeting and to ask for some of us to visit you.[36]

A month later Allen thanked Flavelle for agreeing to attend a complimentary dinner that Aikins was giving in February 1911. He reminded Aikins to invite J.W. Little, the head of a wholesale dry goods firm in London, who was to be in Winnipeg at the time.[37]

By July 1911, the campaign was struggling. As C.E. Manning, the field secretary for home missions, reported, "My trip to the west was not as successful ... as I hoped it would be. I did practically nothing in Manitoba. J.A.M. Aikins was not prepared to subscribe $25,000 and Dr Sparling felt that to go ahead with the canvass without a few of the men promising large amounts, would be to fail in getting as much from Winnipeg as we think that city ought to subscribe ... The feeling is growing upon me that we are making a mistake in depending upon [Aikins] for leadership in church affairs."[38] By October 1912 the fund had pledges of $871,172, just 58 percent of its objective. Some of the richest laymen in Toronto and Winnipeg had given nothing, and this weakened Manning's appeal to men of lesser means.[39]

Indeed, all was not well. In January 1912, six Calgary Methodists – principal G.W. Kerby of Mount Royal College; the Reverend William J. Haggith, chairman of the Calgary district; T.C. Buchanan; W.H. Cushing, who with his brother was the West's largest manufacturer of windows, doors, and sashes; W.G. Hunt, the Massey-Harris company's manager for Alberta; and a Mr Knapp – sought James Allen's assurance that the general board would attend to pressing needs in western

Canada.[40] In Winnipeg, J.H. Ashdown, the hardware store-chain magnate, and H.W. Hutchinson, the vice-president of the John Deere Plow Company of Winnipeg and a director of the parent company in the United States, held the same view. In May 1912, at a meeting of the fund's Winnipeg subcommittee, they moved a resolution to withhold cooperation in raising the city's $200,000 quota, pending an "understanding that no less than two-thirds of the amount subscribed by Winnipegers shall be expended in the city of Winnipeg ... and [that] the remaining third shall be spent in the west."[41] The resolution failed.

At its annual meeting in October 1912, the general board made concessions to prairie Methodist concerns. As before, half the fund was for home missions, but 65 percent of this was now for western Canada, including 50 percent "for church and parsonage sites and buildings and plant for work among European foreigners" in the four western provinces, 30 percent for the same purposes in central and eastern Canada, 15 percent for a reserve fund to meet pastoral salary deficiencies in New Ontario and the western provinces; and 5 percent for an emergency reserve fund.

The general board made $45,750 in immediate appropriations for western Canada, most of it for non-Anglo-Saxon missions. The All People's Mission in Winnipeg got $6,000 toward a new institute building. The Ukrainian mission field in Alberta got $22,500 for parsonages at Chipman and Lamont ($2,500 each), the Lamont hospital ($2,500), and an institute building in Edmonton ($15,000). Other grants for non-Anglo-Saxon missions included $6,000 for "foreigners" in the Crow's Nest Pass, $6,000 for an institute building in Brandon; and $2,750 for small-scale All People's Missions at The Pas, Manitoba, and Taber, Alberta.[42] In 1913 the fund granted the prairie conferences $11,095 for parsonage and church construction, and it granted another $1,672 to the Manitoba conference to pay ministers' salary deficiencies.[43]

The concessions failed to keep the campaign on target. Just $54,000 more in pledges trickled in, and the campaign closed in January 1914 with $925,000 pledged (62 percent of its objective) and $203,576 collected. J.H. Ashdown gave nothing to the fund. J.A.M. Aikins pledged $10,000, not the $25,000 requested from him.

Nevertheless, major donations came from Western men such as H.W. Hutchinson ($15,000); W.G. Hunt ($10,000); W.H. Cushing and his brother and partner, A.B. Cushing ($25,000 and $10,000); and Thomas Ryan, past mayor of Winnipeg and a large wholesaler in boots and shoes ($30,000). As table 4.8 shows, Methodists in the four western provinces pledged more than Methodists in Ontario and Quebec, which had nearly four times as many church members.[44]

Table 4.8
Distribution of Pledges to the Mission Plant and Extension Fund, by October 1912
(Total, $871,072)

Conferences	Percentage of Methodist Census Population, 1911	Percentage of Church Members, 1912	Percentage of Pledges	Contribution per Member($)
Maritimes	10	9	1	1.28
Central Canada	66	72	42	2.04
Prairies	19	16	43	1.92
Manitoba	6	7	14	2.20
Saskatchewan	7	5	12	2.39
Alberta	6	4	16	1.21
British Columbia	5	3	14	2.79

REDUCING WANT

If raising much helped Methodists to make ends meet in the prairie region, then so did wanting little. Mission superintendents bargained hard with congregations over their shares of their pastors' salaries. Working with district chairmen and conference stationing committees, they also rearranged circuit boundaries to eliminate missions. In 1910, for example, one of several adjustments in the Fort Saskatchewan district of the Alberta conference was "that Islay be dropped from the list of stations ... that Trimbleville be detached from Islay & added to the Dewberry mission & that the name of Dewberry be changed to Hazeldean, also that a new appointment be added to be known as Dewberry school, making the mission to consist of the following appointments: Dewberry school, Hazeldean, Irwin, Trimbleville & Lees. Regarding the Wellsdale mission, that Allendale be dropped & the following be added viz. Reeds, McIntosh and Madden from the Dewberry mission."[45] In 1911 Methodists reduced wants by entering into cooperation agreements with the Presbyterians. In 1912 the Missionary Society tried to put conference mission programs on a budget. Finally, city mission boards in the prairie region tried to become self-supporting for the city missions.

A mission could be created either by a mission superintendent during the year or by a conference stationing committee at its annual June meeting. Alberta's superintendent, for example, created eleven missions during the year 1909–10; then the stationing committee added thirty and dropped eight.[46] The superintendent sat on the stationing committee as the general board's representative. This practice allowed the conference and general board to collaborate in the creation and financing of missions. Some missions opened work in newly settled areas. Others arose from the division of a circuit; rearranging appointments on circuits; and upgrading the pastoral supply, thereby raising the minimum salary (for example, sending a married, ordained man to replace an unmarried, ordained man or a probationer).

When creating a mission, the superintendent negotiated with local Methodists the amount that they would pledge toward the pastor's minimum salary. Then he recommended a grant to make up the difference. As superintendent, Oliver Darwin found that his job was to coax money "from men who thought they could not do anything." In 1902, for example, a party of settlers "in the dry belt" between Estevan and Moose Jaw had written to him to request a missionary. When Darwin asked what they would pledge toward the missionary's salary,

One of them said: "We have just arrived here and will not have any income this year: everything is outlay with no income. We shall not be able to give anything this year. Should we have a crop next year we would be able to contribute, but for this year we shall have to ask the Missionary Society to supply us with a missionary." I said to this man ... "My suggestion is that you do not trouble about religion for this year. It does not appear to amount to much: let it go until you have a crop."

A disappointed, and even resentful, look came over their faces on hearing my suggestion. So I went on to say, "When you decided to come West, you knew there were a number of things you were going to need, horses, oxen, and food to sustain them; you would need ploughs, harrows, wagon, and seeder, and other implements with which to cultivate your land. You would also need bread and pork, flour and potatoes, tea and other things, but religion you did not need, and so made no provision for it."

When I got through, I saw a tear start down the cheek of one man, and he rose to say, "Mr Darwin, what you have just said is absolutely true in my case, for I have the paper in my house on which I wrote down the things we were going to need ... but I did not put down anything for my religion. God forgive me! ... You can count on me for at least $25."

The rest of the men continued the discussion and concluded by saying, "Send us a young missionary and we will look after his salary."[47]

During the years 1885–1903, the general board informed the Manitoba and Northwest conference of the amount that it was to receive for missions. The conference's missionary committee then tried to stretch the money, in part by coaxing existing missions toward self-support, as in the Anglican approach of "euthanasia of missions." In 1900, for example, the committee refused a grant for the Pipestone mission and moved to reduce the grant for the Cartwright mission by $5 a year, unless its financial district meeting recommended otherwise.[48]

On some missions the pastor or a layman lightened the committee's load. In 1899 John Lewis, the pastor at Elkhorn, Manitoba, dissuaded his quarterly board from requesting a grant by stating his willingness "to be satisfied with the whole amount raised on the field this year." Although local donations in 1899 produced $107 less than his minimum salary, he refused any money from the society in 1900.[49] In 1902 a farmer in the Battleford area, Ace Hurlburt, subscribed $100 toward a missionary's salary, to be paid out of his coming harvest. When hail destroyed his entire crop of wheat "the day before he intended to cut it," he took out a bank loan to pay his pledge.[50]

With the division of the Manitoba and Northwest conference into three in 1904, the conference missionary committee system ended, which gave mission superintendents the job of trimming the mission list. The Alberta superintendent, T.C. Buchanan, paid visits and wrote letters for the purpose.[51] In 1911 the Irma mission declined his invitation to become self-supporting. In 1912 the Camrose quarterly board responded favourably, despite "not considering the outlook hopeful at this time." In 1913 Buchanan urged Carmangay-Champion Methodists to "try harder" for self-support, given the Missionary Society's embarrassed financial condition and inability to pay the full amount of a salary grant.

Some circuits reverted to mission status due to the removal of Methodist families (Meadow Lea, Manitoba, 1897; New Ottawa, Saskatchewan, 1914; Pincher Creek, Alberta, 1908; Carstairs, Alberta, 1913); fire or crop damage (Sturgeon and Stoney Plain, Alberta, 1903; Carstairs, 1913; Meeting Lake, Saskatchewan, 1910; Carlyle, Manitoba, 1909; Stockton, Manitoba, 1911); the upgrading of ministerial supply and a higher minimum salary (Minitonas-Bowsman, Manitoba, 1907; six Saskatchewan stations, 1914–15); or the reorganization of circuit boundaries (Carstairs, 1913).

Financial misadventure struck Methodists at Sheho, Manitoba, in 1908, and Viking, Alberta, in 1909. Sheho's board of trustees spent $3,500 for a church building, $2,000 more than its authorized budget. To remedy its embarrassment, the quarterly board asked the conference to leave the mission vacant for a year. In 1909 Viking's probationer travelled to the nearest bank, at Wainright, to cash a $600 cheque from the Church and Parsonage Loan Fund. On returning home, reported the probationer, he lost his grip containing the cash while fording the Battle River. This accident forced Viking's quarterly board to borrow another $600 to pay local businessmen for work already completed.[52]

Cooperation with Presbyterians

Informal cooperation was commonplace at the local level. In 1907, recalled Violet Brown, a Methodist parson's daughter and the Presbyterian pastor's wife in Airdrie, Alberta, "the placing of a Presbyterian and a Methodist minister in the same town would look like a bad case of overlapping in home mission work [but it] was not so bad as it seemed. There were four or five country points served by both ministers on alternate Sundays but at no place except in the town did they have both services on the same Sunday as far as I know. Sometimes my husband preached four times on a Sunday." She remembered "no Presbyterian church, but there was a Methodist church and the Presbyterians had the use of it on Sunday afternoons. The Methodist service was in the evenings. It was the same congregation at both services for the most part, but there were several Scottish families who would not attend any but their own service. One old lady, not long out from Scotland, would not attend the Presbyterian service because it was held in a Methodist church."[53]

General cooperation agreements dated from 1899, when the Presbyterian and Methodist mission superintendents agreed to keep out of fields in which the other's church was established. In 1903, when formal discussions about church union were under way, a joint committee of the two churches broadened the superintendents' agreement. Henceforth the churches were to eliminate overlap in existing fields through readjustment; engage in prior consultation to avoid overlap in a newly settled territory; and refrain from entering a field that the other church had occupied for one year.[54]

This arrangement worked poorly due to partisan denominationalism and mutual mistrust. In 1902, on learning of the death of James Robertson, his Presbyterian counterpart as superintendent of missions for western Canada, James Woodsworth opined that

For twenty years Dr Robertson opposed Methodism in this country, both personally and through ministers of his denomination, and often times by disreputable methods. He frequently spoke disparagingly of Methodism in public; and in a variety of ways did he strive to thwart our plans. On two successive occasions I introduced myself to him, yet through all the years following, he never deigned to notice me, though we frequently met in our travels. He acted in the same way to several of our leading ministers. Now the influence of all this cannot be overcome in a day. Our ministers and people are suspicious ...

I would be slow to charge them with misrepresentation, but they seem to possess a strange fancy that if everything is not Presbyterian, it ought to be.

As Dr Gaetz [Methodist] remarked to Dr Herdman [one of Robertson's successors], if a family had some distant relative who was a Presbyterian, they claimed the family.[55]

Methodist superintendents doubted that matters would improve under Robertson's successors: Dr John A. Carmichael for Manitoba and Saskatchewan and Dr J.C. Herdman for Alberta and British Columbia. T.C. Buchanan viewed Carmichael as "the stiffest of the stiff … and he has greatly changed if he desires cooperation of any kind … As I see it the Presbyterian church in its policy is still Robertsonian."[56] Herdman reportedly was open-minded but, as Woodsworth noted, he had accepted his post after a notorious partisan, Dr D.G. McQueen of Edmonton, had turned it down. Cooperation was difficult in any case. "Are we prepared," asked Woodsworth, "to parcel out territory about whose future we know so little? No doubt towns and perhaps cities will spring up when there will not only be room for both churches, but where both will be needed … if by mutual arrangement another church has sole right of way in what afterwards develops into a large centre shall we forever be precluded from entering … If it be said to 'unite only in weak places,' who is to determine where?"[57]

In 1911 the Alberta branches of the two churches drafted a constitution for cooperation agreements, divided the province into nine districts, and gave each district a joint Methodist-Presbyterian committee that was to suggest arrangements for cooperation to a provincial joint committee. Two months later in Toronto, the Methodist, Presbyterian, and Congregational Churches made Alberta the model for a nationwide agreement.[58]

The model applied to two types of situations. One concerned a newly settled territory that was without religious services. Here the Methodists might get settlements along one railway branch line, leaving another branch line to the Presbyterians. Or the denominations might alternate communities along the same branch line. In the second situation, established fields, the Methodists might withdraw from some preaching places if the Presbyterians withdrew from others. In 1911, for example, the Methodists withdrew from eleven places in the High River, Macleod, and Lethbridge districts, and the Presbyterians gave up twelve.

By 1914 cooperation was widespread in Alberta, but rare in Saskatchewan and Manitoba. James Woodsworth believed that Methodists were "losers both numerically and financially" from the cooperation agreements in Manitoba.[59] Similarly, the mission superintendents for northern Saskatchewan and southern Saskatchewan, C.H. Cross and Oliver Darwin, judged that the church lost members in preaching places that it gave to the Presbyterians but failed to gain Presbyterian members in places that it acquired.[60] In 1912 the Reverend W.D. Reid, the Presbyterian superintendent for Alberta, agreed that cooperation was a "complete failure"

where Presbyterians have to become Methodists ... In Carmangay, where we withdrew altogether, we have been told it has only resulted in the unchurching of Presbyterians. In Lunbrek, the Presbyterians, who are in the majority, have practically boycotted the Methodist minister altogether and are asking for Presbyterian services. In Bruce and Viking, where we attempted it, our people rose up in arms and sent in such a petition that we had to go back to them again. In Edison, in the north, the same thing happened and we had to return. In Daysland we have been doing our best to make the people Methodists, but with poor success. This has been our general experience all over Alberta. Presbyterians will not become Methodists ... On the other hand, the Methodists have been more pliable ... Leduc, Nanton, and Granum are places that seem to have amalgamated successfully.[61]

During the years 1912–13, thirteen prairie communities eliminated competition by organizing local union churches. These community churches united members from two or more denominations and were independent of the parent institutions. Compared to Alberta, Saskatchewan and Manitoba had more union churches, but fewer cooperation agreements.

Budgeting Church Expansion

At its annual meetings in October the general board made appropriations based on expected needs for the coming year and then tried to raise the money. In 1912 the board put the conferences on a budget to bring costs under control. To this end, it revived its earlier practice (1885–1903) of working through conference missionary committees. By notifying each committee of the amount of grants that it could expect for the coming year, it hoped to limit the creation of missions to what the society could afford.[62]

Methodist City Mission Boards

In 1912 the Winnipeg city board agreed to pay the entire cost of missions in the city, thereby releasing $7,500 for missionary salaries elsewhere in the west. Methodists in Calgary, Edmonton, Hamilton, and Toronto followed Winnipeg's lead.[63] The Winnipeg board, however, failed to raise the money. Thus, after giving up $4,500 for salaries

Table 4.9
Missions and Salary Grants in the Prairie Region, 1913–15

	Manitoba	Saskatchewan	Alberta	Prairies
NUMBER OF MISSIONS				
Methodists, 1913-14	34	94	133	261
Presbyterians, 1912-13	105	251	163	519
Augmented charges	28	44	27	99
Total (Presbyterians)	133	295	190	618
Anglicans, 1915	84	208	58	350
SALARY GRANTS ($)				
Methodists, 1913-14	37,735	26,117	70,892	134,744
Presbyterians, 1912-13	21,966	57,141	47,168	126,275
Augmentation Fund	3,277	7,740	15,893	20,821
Total (Presbyterians)	25,243	64,881	63,061	156,096
Greek priests				16,399
Total (including Greek priests)				172,095
Anglicans, 1915	5,813	55,224	8,455	69,492

in Saskatchewan and Alberta, it asked the society for a $5,000 grant to meet expenses.[64] In 1912–13 it required a $4,215 grant for its $25,000 budget. The indifference of wealthy laymen had doomed its bid for self-sufficiency. Just one contributor, Captain William Robinson, a millionaire merchant and capitalist, gave as much as $200. Local magnates such as J.A.M. Aikins, Thomas Ryan, and J.H. Ashdown gave nothing.[65]

DENOMINATIONAL COMPARISONS

The comparative data in table 4.9 require a cautious reading. The data for expenses involve estimates and exclude certain overhead costs. The data for revenues mask involuntary contributions from pastors who received less than their "minimum salaries."

The Anglican Church Estimates

In 1915 the Anglican missionary society raised $69,492.33 for missions in Canada. Most of it went in block grants to eleven missionary dioceses in western and northern Canada. Five of these dioceses and 46 percent of the missions were in the prairie region.[66] The estimates assume that the church's entire allocation for home missions went to its missionary dioceses and that the region, and each prairie province, received from the home-mission allocation according to its percentage of the missions in the eleven dioceses.

The Presbyterian Statistics

The Presbyterians and Methodists spent similar sums on prairie missions before 1912. In 1902–3, for example, the Western section of the Presbyterian home mission committee spent $30,130, compared to $24,445 for Methodists. In 1905–6 the Presbyterians spent $52,846, compared to $70,648 for the Methodists. The denominational totals are not comparable, however, because the Presbyterians also issued augmentation-fund grants to augmented charges, which would have been missions in the Methodist system.

Like Methodists before 1912, the Presbyterians made appropriations for the coming year based on expected needs and then tried to raise the money. Contributions from Scottish Presbyterian churches helped. Money from the Old Country peaked at $13,500 in 1900–1, then gradually declined to about $4,000 or $5,000 annually.[67] Like Methodists, the Presbyterians often ran deficits. When receipts fell short of the money spent, they used investment income from their century fund to pay the difference.

The general assembly printed details of its expenditures for the year 1912–13.[68] The amounts shown in table 4.9 exclude the salaries and travel expenses of mission superintendents ($15,941) and missionaries' travel expenses ($14,927). The provincial totals exclude grants to priests of the Independent Greek Church ($16,399), whose geographical distribution was not reported, but the regional total includes them.

The Methodist Church reported the amounts of grants from the missionary society for each station, district, and conference. The data in table 4.9 include the salaries paid by the Winnipeg city mission board and amounts raised by city mission boards in Saskatchewan and Alberta. They exclude allocations from the mission plant and extension fund ($46,749 in 1913), the travel expenses of missionaries and mission superintendents, and the salaries of mission superintendents.

The Denominational Comparison

The Methodists had fewer missions than the Anglicans or the Presbyterians (table 4.9), but they spent more than the Anglicans, although less than the Presbyterians. Compared to the Methodists, the Presbyterians had more stations for the money, because they employed more student summer supplies and homestead missionaries. A disadvantage of this strategy was that a large proportion of their missions closed for part of the year. Interestingly, Saskatchewan was the chief mission province for Anglicans and Presbyterians, whereas Alberta filled this role for Methodists.

SUMMARY AND CONCLUSION

The Missionary Society, the WMS, and prairie congregations raised the money for prairie church expansion. The missionary society divided its money between home and foreign missions. Its home field included ordinary English-speaking missions and missions to non-Anglo-Saxons but not native and oriental missions. The WMS gave primarily to overseas missions. Although it gave nothing to English-speaking missions, it gave considerable support to non-Anglo-Saxon missions.

The Missionary Society cooperated with educational movements to stimulate donations to its regular funds. The real-dollar donations followed a rising trend, though not enough to keep pace with real-dollar expenditures. The society used wealthy laymen to raise special funds, the most important being its $1.5 million Mission Plant and Extension Fund.

Otherwise it relied on small contributions from the masses, rather than large gifts from magnates. Some magnates gave little because they disputed the society's spending priorities (for example, they felt there was too much emphasis on non-Anglo-Saxon missions – or not enough) or its administrative practices (it was too centralized or not centralized enough). What is more important, the church had too few wealthy members to make much of a difference.

Prairie church expansion was partly self-funded but required important sums from central Canada, where two-thirds of the church's members lived. The real-dollar amounts required for English-speaking missions increased slowly until 1906 and then sharply, primarily to meet needs in Alberta and Saskatchewan. The real-dollar amounts spent on non-Anglo-Saxon missions grew explosively. The Missionary Society responded by cutting grants to native missions after 1910, challenging missions to become self-supporting, entering into cooperation agreements with the Presbyterians, and attempting to create self-supporting city mission boards. Its five mission superintendents for the prairies were key officials for directing expansion and finding economies. District chairmen and conference stationing committees also made the Methodist system work.

The Methodists had fewer missions in the prairie region than the Anglicans or the Presbyterians. They spent slightly less than the Presbyterians on salary grants for missions, and both spent more than the Anglicans. Compared to the other churches, the Methodists spent more in Alberta and less in Saskatchewan.

5 Clergy

The Methodists experienced a relentless need for pastors for the prairie region during the years 1896–14. The church increased the number of prairie stations from 163 to 627: in other words, there were 3.9 times as many prairie stations in 1914 as there were in 1896. There were 1.4 times as many in Manitoba, 8.8 times as many in Saskatchewan, and 8.9 times as many in Alberta (table 5.1). Above-average quit rates for prairie clergy exacerbated the demand. The high rates arose from low salaries, harsh living conditions, and large numbers of inexperienced probationers working with little supervision. Various influences dampened the church's supply of pastors, including its requirements for university-educated males, its preference for low-cost bachelors and for Anglo-Canadians, the absence of supply from American Methodist churches, and conditions in the central Canadian conferences before 1896.

GRADES OF MINISTRY

The prairie conferences staffed stations with student summer supplies, lay supplies, probationers, and ordained ministers. Student summer supplies and lay supplies helped to alleviate shortages of clergy at a low cost for cash-strapped missions and to recruit students and laymen for the ministry by giving them experience with the job – and possibly a taste for it.

Student Summer Supplies

In 1907 the church began to hire college students to supply missions during the summer months.[1] The missionary and educational societies

Table 5.1
Methodist Stations in the Prairie Provinces, 1896–1925

	Number of Stations			
	Manitoba	Saskatchewan	Alberta	Prairies
1896	110	28	25	163
1902	137	45	61	243
1906	157	129	120	406
1910	163	200	194	557
1914	157	247	223	627
1919	157	228	214	599
1925	188	260	198	646
	Ratio to Number of Stations in 1896			
1896	1.0	1.0	1.0	1.0
1902	1.2	1.6	2.4	1.5
1906	1.4	4.6	4.8	2.5
1910	1.5	7.1	7.8	3.4
1914	1.4	8.8	8.9	3.8
1919	1.4	8.1	8.6	3.7
1925	1.7	9.3	7.9	4.0
	Distribution of Stations by Province (%)			
1896	67	17	15	99
1902	56	19	25	100
1906	39	32	30	101
1910	29	36	35	100
1914	25	39	36	100
1919	26	38	36	100
1925	29	40	31	100

Note: Because of discrepancies due to rounding percentage totals may be slightly more or less than 100.

jointly paid the student's salary of two hundred dollars, and the local congregation paid his living expenses and travel costs. More than one hundred students served prairie stations annually through to 1914. Sixty-three Ontario students served in 1907. Thereafter, prairie missions preferred students from prairie colleges, to save travel costs.[2]

In 1914 the church hired 157 summer supplies for the prairie conferences – 28 for Manitoba, 66 for Saskatchewan, and 63 for Alberta. This number represented 52 percent of prairie missions and 25 percent of all prairie stations. The Methodist number, however, was just 42 percent of the 370 students on Presbyterian missions – 55 in Manitoba, 191 in Saskatchewan, and 124 in Alberta.[3] With their heavier use of summer supplies, the Presbyterians opened more missions than the Methodists, at small cost. But they also had a greater problem with winter supply. In 1912 they closed 180 missions in Canada on October 1, when the students returned to college.[4]

Lay Supplies

District chairmen could hire lay supplies with a view to bringing them into the ministry. In 1884, for example, Albert R. Aldridge, an English immigrant, "was earning a living using a shovel on the CPR" when James Woodsworth, a district chairman, hired him for the mission at McGregor, Manitoba.[5] He was "received on trial" in 1886, attended Wesley College during the years 1890–92, was "received into full connection and ordained" in 1893, and completed his BA degree requirements in 1894. In 1910 he aid he had "never followed an ordained man at a station and was never preceded by a parsonage."

To approve a candidate for lay supply, the conference ministerial session (or, alternatively, the conference special committee) required him to have been a church member for one year and a local preacher in good standing for six months. The district chairman could renew his appointment indefinitely, but only one year could count toward his term of probation. The prairie conferences approved seventeen men for employment as lay supplies in 1914.[6]

Normally, high school matriculation was a requirement for probation. In 1902 temporary provisions of the general conference allowed James Woodsworth to employ nonmatriculants whom he judged competent for station work. Within a year of his hiring, the lay supply was to undergo examination on Wesley's sermons, the Methodist catechism, and the New Testament. If he passed, then he was eligible for probation. If the conference accepted him as a probationer, then he could proceed to ordination via the regular five-year college training program, except that his program substituted the English Bible for the Greek New Testament.[7] The general conference renewed the temporary provisions in 1906 but dropped them in 1910, ostensibly because few had taken advantage of them.[8]

The Presbyterians had a similar policy during the years 1906–12, when they recruited Scottish catechists who lacked matriculation standing. And like the Methodists, they discarded the practice. In 1912 the church's home mission committee judged that the catechists "rendered good service, but for the most part ... are untrained, inexperienced, without college standing, and enter the work seriously handicapped. After giving the policy a fair trial, your committee does not deem it wise to continue it."[9]

The limited role for lay supplies expressed a widespread Canadian Methodist bias against them and the church's dwindling stock of local preachers (laymen licensed to preach under an ordained supervisor). The number of local preachers per 1,000 prairie church members fell from 15 to 10 during the years 1898–1914. These numbers were higher than the national statistics (which showed a drop from 8 to 7) but notably lower than the statistics for British Methodist churches.[10] In many cases, the local preacher's license was honorific. If the church revoked the licences of those who had not preached in the preceding year, speculated the *Christian Guardian* in 1896, then the local preacher would vanish.[11] By 1914 many of the active local preachers were British immigrants, whose ethnicity was a detraction for Canadian-born Methodists.[12]

Probationers

By the 1890s ordination required college training. Thus the probationer needed high school matriculation and a certificate of having completed the "preliminary course" at college. A lay supply hired under the "temporary provisions" of 1902–10 could meet these requirements during his probation. He also needed recommendations from his quarterly board and district meeting. The district meeting was a key step in the screening process, since the conference officials commonly relied on the district chairman's testimony and gave the candidate only a cursory examination. In 1904 the Moose Jaw district recommended Victor Knowlton who had

been converted to God, has now faith in Christ, is going on to perfection, expects to be made perfect in love in this life, is earnestly striving after it, is resolved to devote himself wholly to God and his work, has been baptized, has correct views on infant baptism and the Lord's supper, knows the rules of the Society and keeps them, does not take snuff or tobacco or intoxicating drinks and will continue to abstain from the same, has read the Discipline and is willing to conform to it. Is not in debt, is 27 of age and has a sound constitution, is not engaged to marry, has been a local preacher for six months and has been unanimously recommended by the Bienfait Q.O. [Quarterly Official] Board as a candidate for the ministry and has stated his call to the work and has sound views on the doctrine of Methodism, has presented a certificate of matriculation and another certificate showing that he has completed the theological preliminary course receiving the following marks.[13]

The probationary term had a minimum length but no maximum. The probationer faced an annual examination by his district ministerial session and was to supply it with "his certificate of standing in his course of study." The examiners queried "his acquaintance with the books recommended to him and a general course of reading which he has pursued during the preceding year." For this purpose he was to deliver to his district chairman "a list of the books which he has read since the preceding annual district meeting, apart from textbooks required in his course of study." A probationer could administer the sacraments if his conference gave him "special ordination" or, alternatively, a one-year license to do so. In 1905 the Saskatchewan conference ordained six men "for special purposes." In 1914 the Manitoba and Alberta conferences gave one-year licenses to eleven probationers and authorized another to perform the marriage ceremony.[14]

In 1903 two veteran Edmonton-district pastors protested the employment of untrained men who lacked common sense: they were dropped after one or two years of employment. Certainly many probationers faltered. In 1893 the Crystal City district sacked J.N. Loach for lack of discretion, ability, and efficiency. A. Rosbach (Deloraine district, 1897) and D.R. Williams and E.J.H. Duncan (Portage La Prairie, 1905) were "dropped in silence" after "withdrawing irregularly" from their work. In 1902 the Moose Jaw district disbelieved W.H. Nugent's claim that he had been disabled for work and dismissed him. In 1906 heresy wrecked the ministry of John Holmes, a lay supply on Manitoba's Binscarth-Foxwarren mission; he did not believe in eternal punishment and insisted on saying so in his preaching.[15] In 1909 J.W. Reynolds of the Saskatoon district failed five first year college subjects. In 1910 R.J. Cox of the Weyburn district passed some subjects, but struggled with circuit work.

Ordained Clergy

By the 1890s the Methodist ideal for the pastorate was an ordained man on a well-organized station. In Ontario the ordinand's job was a busy one. In addition to preaching the word, he had to

meet Official Boards, attend trustee meetings, be present at social gatherings, League socials, Ladies Aid socials, Mission Band and WMS socials, and he must deliver tea-meeting addresses. He must also raise [money to pay] church and parsonage debts, and take supervision of a dozen different church funds ... he must take charge of the prayer meeting and not forget the Sunday school. He must be a prominent figure at all kinds of conventions ... he must conduct Local Option campaigns, and must prosecute a canvas for his church paper. He must visit to the limit of his nervous exhaustion. He must keep abreast of the times by reading one or two daily papers, a Temperance paper, the church paper, one or two theological magazines ... For the sake of his health, he must do a little gardening, a little cycling.[16]

The ordinand's work was busier on prairie circuits, where appointments were more numerous and widely dispersed. In addition to station work, he supervised up to four probationers or lay supplies on nearby circuits. This work entailed periodic visiting, meeting with their official boards, and administering the sacraments (for which lay supplies were unqualified). If the ordinand was district chairman, then he had responsibilities for all stations in his district.

Ordination required a university degree and two years of circuit experience, or three years of residence at college and two years of circuit experience. For men with a BA rather than a BD degree, one of the college years was to be "occupied exclusively with theological studies."[17] The conference could exempt married men without degrees from the residence requirement but not from the examinations. Thus, in 1914 the Saskatchewan conference let Percy Smith at Canora take his "college work on the field."

The church's educational requirement was stiff considering the backgrounds of 192 ordained clergy in the Manitoba and Northwest conference during the years 1881–1902. Twenty-nine percent had never attended college, 43 percent had attended college but had no degree, and 27 percent were college graduates.[18] Although Wesley College awarded honourary DD degrees to three mission superintendents (Woodsworth in 1901, and Buchanan and Darwin in 1916), none was a college man, and Darwin had left public school in Yorkshire "before reaching the end of Grade 1."[19]

Clearly the training for ordination was lengthy, costly, and difficult. Some probationers complained that pressure to study made them ineffective in circuit work.[20] In 1910 an Ontario pastor argued for cheaper, informal education to increase the supply of Canadian-bred ministers and let the church avoid "importing young men from the Old World who know nothing of our country."[21]

A conference received most probationers "into full connection" in the year of their ordination but received some up to three years later.[22] It could "specially ordain" a probationer who did not meet the regular requirements. One such case occurred in 1916, when Tarranty Hannochko, a Ukrainian protestant from Kiev, Russia, was specially ordained. He spoke little English but had attended Alberta College and served on Methodist Ukrainian missions.

Transfers

A transfer committee (consisting of the general superintendent and conference presidents) arranged transfers of clergy from one conference to another. Ministers who transferred at their own request paid their removal costs. Otherwise the general conference fund, Missionary Society, or quarterly official board of a circuit paid the bill, depending on who made the request. The transfer committee could transfer a minister without his consent by a "two-thirds vote of the members present." The committee could also transfer ministers between conferences in the event of "an emergency ... on any missionary field of the North-West or the Pacific Coast."[23]

The Male-Sex Requirements

Women served in the prairie conferences as evangelists, WMS missionaries, deaconesses at city missions, lay delegates at district meetings, and members of quarterly boards.[24] Through its use of male pronouns, however, the *Discipline* blocked women from the ministry and church courts (the annual conferences and general conference). In 1908 a Brantford quarterly board tested the question by recommending Millie Magwood, an evangelist, as a probationer for service in western Canada. Despite its supporting argument that women made up three-quarters of Methodist church members, the district meeting declined to consider her application.[25]

Financial and gender considerations encouraged church leaders to bar women from the pastorate. On the one hand, the Missionary Society sought bachelor probationers to save money. Missions also needed bachelors as church members, given the many bachelors in prairie Methodist populations. On the other hand, the feminine imagery in the church's religious culture, when set against popular notions of bachelor masculinities and of the West as manly space, tended to repel bachelors. In the circumstances, the opening of the pastorate to women would exacerbate the church's low appeal for bachelors. Thus church lore styled rural circuit work as "too rugged for women" and an all-male pastorate as essential to a "powerful, vital church."[26]

Pastor-Homesteaders

In 1908 the Alberta conference stationing committee renounced homesteading for any minister, probationer, or lay supply. The sponsors of the resolution, George Kerby and Austin Richards, recognized the "great temptation for our men to take out homesteads." Drawing on paragraph 260 of the Discipline, however, they warned that pastoral duties and "business entanglements" did not mix.[27]

Although the Missionary Society also refused clergy permission to mix homesteading with pastoral work, it made a few exceptions. In 1912 it allowed two newly ordained married men on Ukrainian missions to homestead. The idea here was that the common experience of farming would help the missionaries to socialize with Ukrainian settlers. Elsewhere, in 1913, it hired four homesteaders to preach for part of the year at untended stations in Saskatchewan's Goose Lake district.[28]

Whereas the Methodist Church "would not stand" for homesteading ministers, the Presbyterian church was merely "down" on them, recalled Violet Brown, a Methodist parson's daughter and Presbyterian parson's wife. In 1907, when her husband John took up a homestead in Alberta's "over the Red Deer" district, the Calgary presbytery's home mission committee agreed to continue his grant on the basis of work done "if he would hold services in the homes of the settlers, or whatever he thought advisable, and report every three months." "Years afterwards," recalled Violet Brown,

a man whose work took him over a large part of Alberta told us that he knew of seven ordained Presbyterian ministers who were living on homesteads and carrying on their work. Of course they did not give full time to their work, but they received only a meagre grant. They solved their own housing problem, which the church was in no position to do, and they brought the gospel services within the reach of communities that would not otherwise have had them. It seems to me that in helping themselves, they also helped the church through very difficult times. No collections were taken up at country points as people did not have money to give.[29]

THE SUPPLY OF PASTORS

Prairie Methodists sought twenty-five additional clergy in 1901, sixty in 1902, and one hundred or more annually after 1907.[30] The shortages rose from east to west. Whereas the Manitoba conference needed eight to twelve new men annually after 1905, vacancies in the Saskatchewan conference numbered forty-six in 1906 and 1909, sixty-two in 1911, and fifty in 1912 and 1914. Vacancies in the Alberta conference numbered fifty in 1909, eighty-two in 1910, and fifty in 1912. In September 1912, the presidents of the Saskatchewan and Alberta conferences used the *Christian Guardian* for a joint "appeal to the people of Canadian Methodism" to deal with "the present emergency ... the most urgent in our history."[31]

Many prairie circuits were without pastors for part or all of the year. In October 1911, when student supplies had returned to college, thirty-five of the sixty-two vacancies in Saskatchewan were still open. In 1914 fifty-eight of the ninety regular missions in northern Alberta had "regularly stationed supplies for the full year," seventeen had student summer supplies, and fifteen had year-round supplies from college students.[32]

Sources of Clergy

The demand for pastors rapidly outstripped the supply from within the region. By 1907 the faculty of theology at Wesley College, Winnipeg, produced about twelve men annually for ordination. The region did not have a second theological faculty until 1909, when Alberta College, Edmonton, opened one.[33] In the circumstances, the society looked to central Canada for men. Few recruits came from the Maritime provinces and Newfoundland, which, like western Canada, were short of pastors.[34]

Two influences dampened the supply of pastors from central Canada. First, the "cream of the crop" chose the glamour of the China and Japan missions over the drudgery of Saskatchewan and Alberta. Compared to home missionaries, the overseas missionaries had more schooling, full pay, better working conditions, higher living standards, and more adventure. Their jobs were attractive and hard to get.[35]

Second, the church had discouraged candidates for the ministry during the 1890s. In 1884 the Methodist church union had glutted the demand for ministers. In 1898 the general conference urged the conferences to accept no probationers during the ensuing quadrennium, and the London and Hamilton conferences complied.[36] The number of local preachers dwindled, and few sermons mentioned "the call."[37] To provide jobs for surplus clergy, the conferences created circuits with fewer preaching places. Thus, when the prairie region became short of men, the undersized circuits in central Canada employed more pastors than the work required.[38]

The church neither sought nor expected pastors from the United States. The American Methodist Episcopal Church (North) had its own shortage of clergy and, compared to the Canadian church, it paid higher salaries and had a lower schooling requirement.[39] Indeed the American church drained pastors from the Canadian church. W.H. Fry, Wesley R. Morrison, and W.E.W. Seller were among the prairie parsons who headed south. Fry, "a colourful character, a good preacher, and an expert canoe man," eventually became the Methodist Episcopal Church's superintendent of missions for the Hawaiian Islands.[40]

Thus the missionary society sought help from British Methodist churches, which had large numbers of experienced local preachers. During the years 1905–12 James Woodsworth, the senior superintendent of missions, made five trips to England and obtained 211 men for prairie service as probationers.[41] "Woodsworth's brigades," in turn, were part of a larger British flood.

Methodist Policy on Recruiting

The society welcomed Englishmen but preferred men who were Canadian-born. After sixty-two British probationers came to the prairie West in 1909, T.C. Buchanan, the Alberta conference mission superintendent, felt "strongly that the Methodist church in Canada should not have to go to England for any more men."[42] Such views resonated with James Allen in Toronto, James Woodsworth in Winnipeg, and Frank Langford in Regina, who became the Western secretary of Sunday schools and young people's societies in 1912.[43] In 1914 Langford worried that "our young men from England are in danger of remaining entirely out of touch with the great movements of our church. Conditions in these rural communities are so radically different from what they have been accustomed to that they have to acquire somehow entirely new conceptions of the familiar words 'missions,' 'social reform,' [and] 'Sunday schools.' It is amazing how little they have in common with those movements which are so familiar to us."

The preference for Canadians over Britons was evident too in the pastoral ranks. As "one of the many" English probationers found, "Canadians dislike a preacher from England ... [Thus] amongst other advice my chairman gave me on my arrival ... from the Old Country was: 'You had better get a Canadian-cut suit as soon as possible or you'll be recognized as an Englishman.'"[44] "Another of the many" believed that many Canadian clergy treated his countrymen "with no small measure of contempt" and that superintendents and others took every opportunity to ridicule "Green Englishmen."[45] An Ontario pastor counselled the Englishmen to "forget where you were born, do as the Romans do."[46]

To minimize the need for British clergy, the missionary society's mission superintendents canvassed the Ontario conferences for men at every opportunity. During July and August of 1905 Oliver Darwin visited seven Methodist summer schools in Ontario and gave thirty addresses "bearing upon the conditions and needs of the North West."[47] In 1909 T.C. Buchanan appealed for men in fourteen municipalities in eastern Ontario.[48] In 1909, after the Saskatchewan conference recommended that Oliver Darwin visit Ontario and England, the general board's executive committee authorized an Ontario tour but not an English one.[49]

For financial reasons, the superintendents recruited more bachelors than married men and more probationers than ministers. Both marriage and ordination increased the minimum salary that the Discipline required for clergy. If the pastor was a probationer or a bachelor, then the mission could pay more of his salary, and the society could issue a smaller grant.[50] Thus the probationer who married without the consent of his conference was "dropped in silence." Similarly, the conferences refused married men as probationers unless the man or the circumstances were extraordinary. Oliver Darwin had been one such case in 1884.

PASTORAL CASUALTIES

The resignations, dismissals, and deaths of clergy exacerbated the problem of supply. During the years 1896–1914 pastoral resignations and dismissals in the prairie region occurred at three times the rate for the conferences of central Canada (table 5.2).[51] During the years 1905–14 the *actual* number of losses in the region was higher, despite its having just 20 percent as many clergy. Within the region the rates and numbers of loss rose sharply from Manitoba westward to Alberta.

The Reverend A. Mosely of Calgary reviewed the church's experience in Alberta. Of the eighty-five probationers brought into the conference during the years 1908–10, just fifty-two (61 percent) remained by 1912. Of seventy-nine lay supplies who had declared their intention to become probationers, just thirty-two (41 percent) had done so. "Only those who have done it," continued Mosely,

know what a disheartening thing it is to succeed men who have left the work disappointed, disillusioned, or perhaps bitter. The people have a certain indefinable attitude to him which is difficult to overcome ... To give one instance: A certain mission in Alberta saw five different Methodist probationers and supplies within a single year. Is it necessary to say that the people of that place looked upon this interesting little panorama with increasing indifference and probably with contempt for the church that suffered such things.

Then, sir, what is the effect upon the men who escape this slaughter of innocents – the men who remain with us? Can it be possible that they are totally unaffected by the causes – whatever they are – of this lamentable condition of things ... These men see continually their brethren dropping out, men who were just as eager and full of promise as themselves. They feel the stress of the same conditions which forced those brethren out of the work.

The church which cannot produce or keep ministers cannot produce or keep members. And if a church cannot do these things it cannot have an adequate influence upon the life of those members it retains.[52]

Table 5.2
Pastoral Casualties in the Ontario and Prairie Conferences, 1896–1904, 1905–14

Conference	Number of Clergy in 1903	Dismissals and Resignations 1896–1904	Dismissals and Resignations as Percentage of 1903 Total	Losses 1896–1904, Including Deaths < Age 65	Losses as Percentage of 1903 Total
Toronto	318	16	5	25	8
Hamilton	275	10	4	18	7
London	269	14	5	24	9
Quinte	224	14	6	28	13
Montreal	267	33	12	45	17
Ontario/Quebec	1,353	86	6	140	10
Manitoba and Northwest	267	50	19	59	22

Conference	Number of Clergy in 1910	Dismissals and Resignations 1905–14	Dismissals and Resignations as Percentage of 1910 Total	Losses 1905–11, Including Deaths < Age 65	Losses as Percentage of 1910 Total
Toronto	363	40	11	48	13
Hamilton	287	20	7	31	11
London	273	24	9	46	17
Quinte	211	10	5	21	10
Montreal	285	21	7	32	11
Ontario/Quebec	1,419	115	8	178	13
Manitoba	184	25	14	33	18
Saskatchewan	230	65	28	73	32
Alberta	231	77	33	87	38
Prairies	645	167	26	193	30

The high pastoral quit rate in the prairie conferences had many causes. Low incomes and the church's loose supervision of "green" supplies were two of them.

Pastoral Salaries

The general conference set minimum salaries for categories of clergy, exclusive of horse-keep (not to exceed $100), housing (the rent or free use of a parsonage), removal expenses, and incidentals. Thus, in August a mission's quarterly official board set its budget by the minimum amount for the pastor's salary, and sums for housing, horse-keep, and incidentals. It then gave each of its appointments an appropriation (amount to be raised) and asked the Missionary Society to bridge the difference between its total for appropriations and the target sum.[53]

The general conferences of 1906 and 1910 raised the minimum amounts to keep pace with inflation (table 5.3). The changes in 1910 provided extra-large raises for western Canada to allow for the high cost of living there.[54] Although the raises were adequate for the inflation influence, the minimum amounts compared poorly with business incomes in Canada and pastoral salaries in the United States.[55] As the Edmonton district meeting noted in 1906, pastors earned less than ordinary labourers, lived in dugouts and shanties, cooked their own meals, depended on businessmen for favours and privileges as ministers, and did "things as ministers which they would scorn to do as men."[56]

What is more important, neither the church nor any of its boards and committees had "any legal obligation ... for payment of any minimum amount mentioned in the *Discipline.*" In theory the Missionary Society's grant made up the difference between the minimum salary and the amount pledged by the circuit. In practice, the circuit and/or the society commonly failed to pay its share, leaving the pastor out of pocket, with no redress. For want of funds, noted an Edmonton district resolution in 1910, the general board of missions paid a "variable proportion" of the grants needed for minimum salary levels. In 1900, for example, the board issued grants on the basis of 76 percent of the minimums; in 1901 the basis was 75.5 percent of the minimum for married men and 78 percent of that for single men.[57] In 1907 the Reverend B.W.J. Clements of Wessington, Alberta, was "compelled to borrow money to keep straight with the world." "I don't believe," stated Clements, that "you will ever get our men to think the missionary society not responsible for the full salary according to the Discipline."[58] Men newly arrived from England and Ontario, noted the

Table 5.3
Minimum Salaries Set by the General Conference ($)

Year	Married Ordained	Unmarried Ordained	UnmarriedProbationer
1894–1906	600	350	300
1907–10	750	600	400
1910–14			
Western Canada	1,000	800	600
Eastern Canada	900	700	500

Table 5.4
Average Salaries Paid to Missionaries in the Home Field, 1895–1905 ($)

Year	Married Ordained	UnmarriedOrdained	UnmarriedProbationer
1895–96	500	267	234
1896–97	500	267	234
1897–98	540	288	252
1898–99	540	288	252
1899–1900	480	280	240
1900–1	456	266	228
1901–2	468	273	234
1902–3	492	287	246
1903–4	540	315	270
1904–5	558	326	279
Disciplinary Minimum, 1895-1906	600	350	300

Note: Salaries are exclusive of horse keep, moving expenses and a furnished parsonage.

Alberta conference probationers' association in 1912, naively planned their budgets on the basis of the minimum salary, not knowing that it was merely "an ideal to be aimed at."[59]

On average, home missionaries received less than their minimum salary during the decade 1895–1905 (table 5.4).[60] The average salaries paid reached the minimum amounts in 1906 but then fell behind in 1907, when higher minimum amounts came into force. In 1910 they again reached the minimum amounts when, once again, higher minimum amounts came into force. At the end of the church year 1910–11, 250 home missionaries had received $50 to $200 less than their minimum salaries. In 1914 the average salary paid once again reached the minimum amount.[61] This was too late for Harry H. Cragg of Taber, Alberta, who quit the ministry to enter business in 1912, having "found it impossible to live on the salary he was getting, and support his wife and family."[62]

Cragg offered two explanations for the low salaries in the mission fields. First, the conference stationing committee continually added new fields, even though the church could not provide sustenance for existing fields. Second, the society paid administrators and foreign missionaries their full salaries. This left the home missionaries to absorb the society's financial shortages.[63]

The slowing of church expansion was one remedy for the salary problem. In 1911 the conferences entered into cooperation agreements with the Presbyterians to divide work in established fields and newly settled territories. In 1912 the general board of missions began to notify each conference of the total amount of grants available to it for the coming year and hence the number of missions it could afford.[64] Special funds provided a second remedy. In 1907 the Saskatchewan conference established a sustentation fund to pay salary deficiencies; in 1914 the fund paid $971 of $4,371 in unpaid salaries from the previous year. The Manitoba conference contingency fund paid $735 of $1,500 in salary deficiencies for 1911–12 and $1,275 to eleven pastors with deficiencies in 1913–14. The Missionary Society's Mission Plant and Extension Fund issued $5,422 toward salary deficiencies in Manitoba and Saskatchewan for 1912–13.[65] In 1904 the Minitonas-Bowsman, Manitoba, mission took out a bank loan to pay its pastor his $190 salary deficiency.[66]

Irregular payments, as well as deficiencies, of salary were an issue. Thus the clergy pressed quarterly boards for "regular payments, weekly, monthly, or at least quarterly, so that a pastor does not need to wait until the end of year for the larger part of his salary." In 1903 the Sidney, Manitoba, board urged the trustees at its four appointments to collect the whole of the pastor's salary in the fall and pay him in full, not less often than quarterly. In 1912 the Durban, Manitoba, board agreed to draw money from the bank when necessary to pay up for the quarter. Also in 1912 the Elm Creek, Manitoba, board arranged a $400 line of credit with a bank, so that it could pay its pastor monthly.[67] Sooner or later, most prairie boards adopted the weekly envelope system to regularize revenues and salary payments. In 1914 the Fort Macleod quarterly board appointed one Mr Briggs to visit members in arrears and allowed him 5 percent of the amount collected.[68]

Family medical bills and funeral costs could shock a pastor's finances. When they did, district meetings and circuit quarterly boards sought relief from conference funds (contingency funds, sustentation funds) or the Missionary Society. One hardship case, in the district of Carman, Manitoba, in 1898, was that of Menotti C. Flatt whose prolonged illness brought bills of $400. When Septimus E. Colwill suffered typhoid fever for eight weeks in 1896, his Oakville, Manitoba, circuit secured a replacement supply at Colwill's expense. In Manitoba's Birtle district in 1904, the death of Walter Adamson's child saddled him with medical and funeral costs. In Alberta's Stettler district in 1908, R.W.J. Clements had $300 in medical bills, as did Percy Morecombe in the Olds district in 1912. In the Manitoba conference's Carman district in 1912, W.R. Hughes had medical and funeral costs for his wife's fatal illness, and Walter Adamson faced bills for sickness in his family and for surgery in Winnipeg.[69]

Misadventures jolted pastoral pocketbooks in other cases. W.E. James of the Calgary district lost his horse "by accident" in 1902. In the Moose Jaw, Saskatchewan district, in 1905, George Marshall and J.E. Spencer each lost their horse to the disease of glanders. In Saskatchewan's Yorkton district in 1914, Percy Smith lost two horses and C.W. Topping another.[70] In 1912 probationers in Alberta suffered when the Missionary Society failed to reimburse them, as promised, for all or part of their rail fares to the prairies.[71]

The Supervision of "Green Hands"

The prairie conferences had above-average numbers of inexperienced, young clergy. During the years 1902–10, the percentage of prairie stations with probationers rose from 16 to 34, compared to an increase from 7 to 10 per cent for central Canada (table 5.5).[72] These data exclude probationers who were at college or "left without station at their own request." If one counts all probationers, then they were a majority. In 1911, for example, probationers made up 54 percent of 256 clergy in Alberta and 51 percent of 148 clergy in Saskatchewan.[73]

Compared to an ordained man, the probationer had few resources. He lived alone and was more likely to serve on a mission than a self-supporting station. He preached in schoolhouses and poolrooms, not churches. He lived in granaries and preachers' shacks, not manses. "A very large percentage of them," observed a "westerner," did "not know how to preach, and have done little or no preliminary theological study. Under the difficulties of their work they lose their enthusiasm; the people are tired of their attempts to preach, and do not pay all the salary, so the young man quits the work."[74]

To guide the "green hands" on missions, the church had supervisors at the local, district, and conference levels. At the local level, an ordained man supervised one to four probationers on stations proximate to his own. The conference stationing committee made the arrangements. In Saskatchewan's Battleford district during the church year 1908–9, for example, Thomas Lawson, a veteran ordinand at Radisson, supervised the probationers at Lashburn, Maidstone, and

Table 5.5
Ministers and Probationers on Stations

	Prairie Conferences			Ontario Conferences		
	Ordained Clergy	Probationers	Probationers (%)	Ordained Clergy	Probationers	Probationers (%)
1902	154	29	16	903	67	7
1906	213	89	29	839	69	8
1910	267	137	34	840	91	10
1914	365	87	19	845	94	10

Note: The figures are for years that the general conference met.

Borden. As Stephen Byles at Lashburn recalled, "the custom was for the students, every three months or so, to go to the centre where the senior supervisor lived and take his services, and the supervisor would come out to the student's field for the weekend and meet the men and have communion services on Sunday."[75]

The frequency of contact depended on how far the supervisor was from the probationer's station and the number of men under his supervision. In 1911 ordinands in the Saskatchewan conference oversaw up to six circuits, some 125 miles distant from their own.[76] During eight months at the isolated Lashburn mission, Byles met his supervisor once. At his next mission he met regularly with his supervisor, whose parsonage was a two-hour buggy trip away.

The district chairman oversaw the clergy in his district. The conference required him to settle disputes, hear appeals, and visit a circuit when its local supervisor so requested. His capacity to supervise was limited, however. Due to the Methodist itinerancy system, he often was new to his district and unfamiliar with local conditions.[77] In some cases, he was also new to the position of district chairman. In the newly created Alberta conference in 1904, "four of our six chairmen are filling that position for the first time. Another is putting in his second year, and only one, the president of the conference, is an old hand at the game."[78] In many cases, the chairman's own circuit was large and poorly organized and made heavy demands on his time.[79] Conversely, the chairman's congregations paid a price for his district responsibilities. In 1899 the Moose Jaw quarterly board went "on record," unsuccessfully, "that they did not wish their minister to be chairman of the district."[80]

The superintendent of missions gave guidance at the conference level. Indeed the church had created this position in 1882 to relieve "the chairmen of districts of heavy responsibility and put the oversight of missions in general in the hands of one man, who could under limitations mobilize the financial resources of the missionary society of which he was the immediate agent."[81] During the years 1887–1902, James Woodsworth supervised missions in the Manitoba and Northwest and British Columbia conferences. His report to the general conference in 1898 conceded his inability "to give adequate supervision to so large an area," despite having travelled ninety thousand miles in the quadrennium.[82] Thus, in 1902 the general conference provided for five superintendents: one for each of New Ontario and British Columbia and three for the prairie region. The society named Thomas C. Buchanan for the Alberta conference, Oliver Darwin for the Saskatchewan and Manitoba conferences, and James Woodsworth as senior superintendent for western Canada.

Oliver Darwin made a vivid impression on probationers. To his fellow Yorkshireman, Stephen Byles, Darwin was "the most outstanding character in the Methodist church in Saskatchewan in the days when I was on that field." George Dorey, Woodsworth's recruit from England's Channel Islands, saluted Darwin as "a true friend" to all who served under him, especially to those "in difficulties not of their own making." When Dorey's band of "bewildered English recruits" got to Winnipeg, "we had no difficulty finding Dr Darwin. He found us … From that day until his retirement in 1928, he was the authentic voice of authority as far as Home Mission work was concerned."

Dorey also remembered Darwin as "a rather grim figure – greatly demanding" to some of the recruits.[83] As Stephen Byles recalled, Darwin "was a big man and had the voice to equal the size and he was aggressive and dominating in a way." He was "an authoritarian with these young fellows. Some of them were quite afraid of him," though Byles himself "hadn't the same background and hadn't the same fear."

Although the prairie superintendents were more numerous after 1902, the coverage area grew. During the year 1905–6, Darwin "travelled 21,291 miles; visited 77 circuits and missions; delivered 126 sermons and addresses; attended 25 Board meetings; 7 District meetings and 2 Annual Conferences" in Manitoba and Saskatchewan.[84] Despite his effort, each district held circuits that he had not seen, to say nothing of newly settled areas that he "might have visited on a prospecting tour."[85]

In 1910 Woodsworth relieved Darwin of responsibility for the Manitoba conference, and the Missionary Society furnished Darwin with an $800, twenty-horsepower Ford Runabout for his work in Saskatchewan.[86] In 1912 the society added two superintendents.[87] It assigned Charles H. Cross to northern Saskatchewan and left Darwin with the south; and it assigned Arthur Barner to southern Alberta (75 percent of the territory) and left Thomas Buchanan with the north. Despite these additions, the prairie superintendents had a mean number of 10.6 districts to supervise in 1914, up from 5.0 in 1902.

To summarize, the prairie conferences had great numbers of novice clergy who needed supervision. The distances between circuits, the itinerancy system, and the inexperience of supervisors hampered supervision at the local, district, and conference levels. In the circumstances, the high quit rate among "green hands" was hardly surprising.

STEPHEN BYLES: A PROBATIONER'S PROGRESS

Byles was a lay supply in Saskatchewan in 1908–9 and a probationer during the years 1909–16. His career exemplified the "green Englishman's" inexperience with prairie church life, his need for supervision, and his mixed success in getting it.[88] It showed the challenge that the church's educational requirements presented. Reading between the lines, it exposed the special difficulties that a green Englishman encountered – Byles's surprising difficulty finding a station and his callous treatment from certain fellow pastors.

Byles, a younger son of a Yorkshire newspaper proprietor, was born in 1887 and left school at age 15. In 1905, at age 18, he immigrated to Saskatchewan to work as a farmhand. By 1908, at age 21, he lacked savings to take up homesteading and wondered what to do with his life. He enjoyed teaching Sunday school, and the ministry interested him, but finding a position was difficult. His own Congregationalist Church had few openings in the Canadian West, and he lacked the high-school matriculation requirement for probationers in the Presbyterian and Methodist Churches. The Methodist pastor at Wide Awake enquired on Byles's behalf, discovered the temporary provisions of 1902–10 for hiring nonmatriculants, and put Byles in touch with Thomas Lawson, the chairman of the Battleford district. In October 1908 Lawson sent him to Lumsden for assignment to one of the four stations under the Reverend William Arnett's local supervision. Arnett, however, dispatched him to Davidson, in the Saskatoon district,

to replace a probationer who was due, actually *overdue*, to return to Wesley College, Winnipeg, the Theological centre for all Methodist students in the Manitoba and Saskatchewan conferences. On arrival at Davidson I left everything at the station, for I had brought along all my goods, the sea-dust included, and set off to locate the young student and/or his lodgings. Somehow I found both the lodgings and the lodger, had a good lunch and then matters took a strange turn. Asking me to stick around for a while, he went off by himself and left me to wander around the town. Presently he turned up to inform me that the Committee of the church had persuaded him to stay on at Davidson and not return to Wesley College that fall. The message was clear and instant. I would not be wanted in Davidson, and the sooner I could get on the train and back to Lumsden, baggage and all, the better. The Davidson people certainly knew a good bargain when they saw one, for the young man was very capable; but they could not know the dejection of one passenger on the CNR train that afternoon as it crawled back to Lumsden.

My arrival at Lumsden the same day that I had left was a bit of a shock to Mr Arnett. He now had two problems; one, of course was what to do with a would-be preacher; and the other was the matter of disciplining the man we left at Davidson. As to the second, I believe no action was taken; as to the first, it is probable that Mr Arnott would have been better pleased if I had stayed on the farm. Mr Arnott had no other appointment available under his jurisdiction and further arrangements had to be made through the Superintendent of Missions for Saskatchewan, the Rev. Oliver Darwin. After a tiresome wait of nearly a week, I received word that I was to proceed to Lashburn, about as far away as I could get by train and still be in the Province. Early next morning I was on the train again bound for Lashburn, a busy town some sixty-five miles west of N. Battleford. This time there was a real vacancy, with no student to replace. The congregation had no option. It had to be me!

Lashburn, a three-point circuit in the Battleford district, was under the local supervision of the Reverend E.A. Davis at North Battleford.[89] Byles arrived there in November and

found lodgings with a bachelor Presbyterian minister, well on in years, whose ideas and capabilities for housekeeping left much, very much to be desired. The place was a large one-roomed "shack" with dark unfinished walls, uncovered floor boards, which were never cleaned; and the only heat depending on a kitchen stove, and the only light a coal-oil lamp. Altogether it was the gloomiest lodging imaginable ...

We had other difficulties too. He considered that my violin was an "instrument of the devil," in just those words, and just as bluntly declared that I should get rid of the scholarly commentaries on the Major and Minor Prophets recently published by [his] fellow Scotchman, Dr George Adam Smith.

Byles's worst memory, however, was

the agonizing nights that I endured. The double bed itself was abhorrent, the only coverings being dark grey woollen blankets almost begging for a visit to the Chinese laundry, and the uncovered pillows were even worse. Added to this was the sheer discomfort of being used as a bed-warmer after the fire had died down and the mean winter chill penetrated the place. Pressing his chubby body against mine as hard as possible he would call out with a thick Scottish burr, "More heat! More heat!" My only escape would have been to fall out of the bed on the other side.

The horses that Byles could afford were no prize winners. His first was a "wall-eyed bronco with his own ideas of service to the ministry. No doubt he was quite accustomed and amenable to being ridden but the idea of hauling a sleigh was beneath his contempt." The horse "just balked" unless Byles ran alongside the sleigh, then jumped in as the sleigh gained speed. His second horse was a veteran trotter and former racehorse from Boissevain, sprained in the hind leg, whose stride had a peculiar rhythm like "one, two, three, *up* – one, two, three, *up*."

"What I did for preaching," he recalled, "I don't know, I must have read a lot of other people's sermons I think because it was all new to me. I knew nothing about Methodist administration and I did not see my supervisor until the following May. I struggled along but the people were wonderfully patient and I enjoyed my year there." Byles used his skills as a hired man to court favour with church members, most of whom were farmers. What probably saved him was that his church services were "the chief social event of the week, and I say social event because the people liked to stay around and [get] all the latest reports of how the families were doing."

In addition to preaching and visiting, Byles had to study for his examination to become a probationer under the temporary provisions of 1902–10. Byles's memoirs recalled:

some required study set for probationers by some department of the Methodist administration. Among the set assignments were John Wesley's Sermons, some fifty of them, and John Wesley's Doctrine of Christian perfection. Not long before the spring break up I was directed to Lloydminster to write my examinations. The questions on the book of Wesley's sermons were tough for this beginner … the examination on the doctrine was particularly baffling as it was my first confrontation with anything of the sort … the last question on the Doctrine was: "How does this Doctrine compare with your own view?" After not too much though I wrote, "Since this was my first acquaintance with the Doctrine and I had no previous theological instruction, it agreed very well! … Fortunately, I passed all three sections of the examination at Lloydminster and, therefore, was acceptable as a probationer in the Methodist ministry. What my classification was prior to that point I never learned."[90]

Before Byles could become a probationer, the not so small matter of his work in the field required his local supervisor's approval. Thus, in May Byles met the Rev. E.A. Davis of North Battleford, for the first time. Up to that time, I had been left entirely on my own. I knew nothing of the church's machinery or administration. The visit of Mr. Davis was, therefore, somewhat of an initiation, and a most welcome one. This was my first experience with the Official Board of the charge, [with] representatives coming from all four preaching places. The main concern, naturally, was the condition of the work under its present "beginner." A second equally important concern was the state of the membership and finances. The third was arrangements for communion services. All those matters were beyond the jurisdiction of the probationer, who could only claim that he had done his best.

Byles passed muster. In June 1909, the conference "received him on trial" and stationed him at Maymount and New Ottawa, a four-point station. The Lashburn station had a church building at one of its preaching places. At this station he held services in a small hall above the town's poolroom at Maymount and in one-room schools at the other points. The parsonage was owned by the previous probationer, William Keall, one of Woodsworth's English recruits, "who asked the fantastic price of $90 for it." Byles hired himself out to area farmers to pay it off, but at the year's end the church bought it at the same price.

Compared to Lashburn, this station was closer to his supervisor, the Reverend Meno Culp at Radisson, just a two-hour buggy drive away. Byles came to know Culp's family and made their parsonage a second home. During one winter visit, he was "storm-stayed" with some distinguished visitors. Indeed he "had the rare privilege of sharing both room and bed with the general superintendent of the Methodist church of Canada, Dr S. Chown ... one of the great spiritual leaders in Canada at the time, but as with most men who can be truly called 'great' he was one of the most humble of men and a gentle spirit. My memory recalls this brief association with the head of the Methodist church as one of the most uplifting experiences in a long life."

During 1910–11 Byles was stationed at Radisson, "a distinct promotion, for the town was only second in size to North Battleford and the Methodist church had been regularly served for a number of years by ordained ministers. But promotion did not bring any of the privileges of ordination, [such as the use of] the commodious and well-appointed parsonage." This remained the residence of Mr Culp who, because of his fluency in German, had been assigned to special work among some twelve Mennonite villages north of the town.[91]

Byles found board and lodging, and his year at Radisson became the highlight of his probation years. "Never once during my twelve months," recalled Byles, "did I hear an unkind word or receive criticism of my pastoral performance, or lack of it. Instead the good folk gave every encouragement and were generous in their hospitality." What is more important, his musical background in England came into play. The unassuming Byles was an expert violinist (he was later to win a gold medal at the Saskatchewan festival, "but, of course, there was no competition then"). With two "very fine pianists" to accompany him, he delighted in using "music that I hadn't touched since I came to Canada. It also opened many doors for me, not just Methodist doors either." Denominationalism in those towns, he recalled, ended with the church service. "So the whole town was open ... Life took on new meaning." The Radisson church also had a choir, which provided another opening for Byles's musical talents. His school in England had sung the Messiah every year, so he had learned "to sing those choruses in practice, unaccompanied."

He passed the years 1910–12 at Regina College getting his junior and senior matriculation "while in full charge of an appointment" (Craven one year, Richardson the next). He had no money, so he sold books for a Chicago company that gave him a bicycle on credit for transportation. In 1912 the conference left him without a station so that he could attend Wesley College for his theological studies. However, he withdrew from Wesley College within a week of his arrival in Winnipeg. He was there on the understanding that he would be a part-time assistant for a sick pastor, but on Byles's arrival, the pastor announced that he did not need him and also disclaimed responsibility for him. Destitute and discouraged, Byles returned to Saskatchewan, where his chairman found him a station near Saskatoon.

In 1916 the conference gave him leave to enter war service with the YMCA. In 1918 he married, with the blessing of his mission superintendent (C.H. Cross). Only then did he learn that Wesley College was closed to him due to its lack of accommodations for married students. So he stayed in the YMCA's employ, gradually tired of his annual probationer's examination, and quit the ministry.

ENGLISH PROBATIONERS AND CANADIAN METHODIST CULTURE

Some 1,200 ministers and probationers served prairie stations during the years 1896–1914. Table 5.6 reports places of birth for 663 of them.[92] Ninety-eight percent were born in Canada or Britain, and 89 percent were born in Ontario or England. However, the figures for place of birth are misleading about where some of them had passed their formative years. Six of the Ontario-born men had in fact moved to the prairie region as children under age eleven. Thirteen British-

Table 5.6
Places of Birth of Ministers and Probationers in the Prairie Conferences, 1896–1914

	Number	*Percentage*
Canada	377	57
Ontario	317	48
Quebec	11	2
Atlantic	38	6
Prairies	9	1
"Canadian"	2	<1
Britain	273	41
England	238	36
Scotland	10	2
Ireland	15	2
Wales	8	1
"British"	1	<1
Other dominions	5	1
Europe	5	1
United States	3	<1
Total	663	

born men had moved to Ontario as children or spent more than twenty years there before coming to the prairies. Although English-born, the Bone brothers, J.T. and W.H. ("there are no dry bones"), were recruited in Toronto. All three American-born men were Canadian except in birth. F.M. Wootten was born in Ohio to English parents but raised as an orphan in St Thomas, Ontario; Manley Eby was of "U.E.L. stock" and a graduate of Victoria College; and M.C. Brunton moved west from Ontario and had parents in Saskatchewan.

The prairie conferences clearly received a huge influx of clergy from England. The men in "Woodsworth's brigades" alone made up 18 percent of the 1,200 prairie pastors. The percentage was lower in Manitoba, where the church's expansion was largely over when the first brigade arrived, but they were higher for Saskatchewan and Alberta.[93] Twenty of thirty men in Woodsworth's first brigade located in Saskatchewan and, once there, attracted friends from later brigades. As James Allen noted in 1912, Saskatchewan was the only conference that was "almost entirely dependent upon Britain to fill its vacancies."[94] Britons made up 58 percent of Saskatchewan's 190 pastors who had arrived since 1905 and were still active in 1913.[95] The Alberta clergy were only slightly less British. In 1907 "the large majority" of the 81 members of the Alberta conference probationers' association were "Englishmen by birth."[96]

The British clergy changed the Canadian Methodist tradition less than their numbers suggest. First, a British presence was part of the

Canadian tradition. During the years 1897–98, for example, 41 percent of the death notices in the *Christian Guardian* involved British-born descendents. In 1910 the presidents of the Montreal and Bay of Quinte conferences were British-born.

Second, acculturation worked among the Britons. Yes, the probationer Fred Passmore reportedly "was British and remained so," and Stephen Byles "never lost" the Congregationalist ideas from his Yorkshire upbringing. Even so, Byles entitled his memoir "The Canadianization of a Yorkshire Lad." Like A.E. Whiteside in 1911, he was "British-born, but Canadian by adoption." In 1912 Oliver Darwin visited England, after eighteen years away. His prairie-grown daughter laughed at the "toy engines" on England's branch-line railways, and his eldest sister burst into tears on realizing that she had taken him for a "foreigner." In the Sunderland football stadium Darwin, now the "man from the Canadian prairie," watched "the English" at their national game.[97]

Third, except for a few "old hands" like Darwin, the Britons were junior men. Although more than half of the Saskatchewan clergy, Britons made up just 23 percent of forty-four district chairmen for the years 1909–12.[98] Although "the great majority" in the Alberta conference probationers' association were "Englishmen by birth," G.D. Misener, "an old Ontario boy," was the association's president in 1907, and Charles Bishop, another Ontarian, was its secretary.

The prairie Methodist colleges were another Canadian influence on junior men from Britain. Twelve of thirteen faculty members for whom the writer has information were from central Canada, and the other, the Irish-born Robert Milliken, had immigrated to Ontario in 1885, at age 24.[99] Apart from their educational role, the Canadian-born faculty gave Methodists continuity of leadership. These academic clergy were exempt from the itineracy and resided permanently in the prairie cities where their colleges were situated. College principals, in particular, were key contacts for James Allen when he was arranging matters in the prairie region.

SUMMARY AND CONCLUSION

The church used student summer supplies, lay supplies, probationers, and ordained men to staff stations. It insisted on male clergy, preferred bachelors (to save money), and gave its pastorate stiff schooling requirements. It generally barred clergy from homesteading to supplement their meagre incomes. Compared to Presbyterians, Methodists made less use of student summer supplies and homestead missionaries who were married. Consequently, they had fewer stations but supplied a higher proportion of them with regular services through the year.

By 1905 the rapidly developing prairie conferences experienced massive shortages of men, especially in Alberta and Saskatchewan. Conferences in central and eastern Canada were unable to meet the demand in western Canada, and American Methodist clergy were unavailable. Thus Britain, especially England, became a major supplier of men for prairie service. The missionary society's officials appreciated their British recruits but favoured Canadian men.

The high quit rate for prairie clergy exacerbated the shortages of men. Low, uncertain salaries were one cause. Another was the large number of inexperienced probationers with little supervision. Stephen Byles's career exemplified the travails of these "green Englishmen."

Of 663 clergy for whom the writer has information, 57 percent were Canadian-born and 41 percent were born in Britain. The percentage of British-born was below average in Manitoba but above average in Saskatchewan and Alberta. The British influence on prairie Methodist traditions, however, was less than the numbers suggest. Canadian-born men held most of the senior positions, and young Britons learned Canadian ways.

6 Laity

Prairie church statistics encouraged Methodists, yet caused them concern. Certainly Methodists had big gains in membership and in the population identified as Methodist in the census. Compared to Presbyterians and Anglicans, they reported more church members and a higher ratio of church members to the population identified as Methodist. Nevertheless, increases in Methodist Church membership and census population lagged behind population growth. The denominational counts in the 1911 census enumeration, moreover, showed more Presbyterians and Anglicans than Methodists. For all three churches, the ratio of church members to the denominational census population was lower than in central Canada and declined westward from Manitoba. This trend appeared to show that protestant church life weakened as one travelled west.

A scrutiny of the statistics leads to a different story, however. Protestant church life was not unusually weak in the prairie West. Methodist and Presbyterians had comparable church expansion programs and achievements in the region, with the Anglicans trailing behind. The protestant achievements in church membership were impressive considering the difficulties that the churches faced.

CENSUS POPULATIONS AND REPORTED MEMBERSHIPS

Methodists fared poorly in censuses for the prairie region. During the years 1908–9, denominational censuses for Winnipeg, Regina, and

Calgary showed more Presbyterians than Methodists in each city. Anglicans, too, outnumbered Methodists in Winnipeg and Regina, and Roman Catholics were also more numerous in Regina.[1] "My own impressions, after more than 30 years in the west," stated the Reverend John Maclean in Winnipeg in 1911, "are that Methodism is not holding its own, and that there is a considerable leakage which is not altogether due to the inadequacy of our immigration department ... In regard to the city of Winnipeg, there is not the growth in our churches which there ought to be when we consider the hundreds of members and adherents who have gone there from other parts of the Province, without reckoning those who have come from the old country."[2] The Reverend David Kennedy of High Bluff, Manitoba, despaired of the "overshadowing influence" of the Presbyterians who "*seem* to be forging ahead and outstripping us in this race."[3] In Portage la Prairie the Reverend Wellington Bridgeman was disgusted at "Methodism holding a sickly third place in the city of Winnipeg, and a poor second place in the other cities of the most progressive province in Confederation. In all the annals of history did Methodism ever make such a record?"[4]

The publication of Canada's census of 1911 (in 1913) appeared to substantiate the Methodist nightmare. It showed that Presbyterians had surpassed Methodists as Canada's largest protestant confession, and that Anglicans also surpassed them in the prairie region (table 6.1). The Methodist showing was especially weak in Manitoba, where 14 percent of the population was Methodist, compared to 19 percent for Anglicans and 23 percent for Presbyterians.

Methodists blamed their "awful census" on the shortage of clergy, the itinerancy system, a decline of Methodist spiritual power and denominational loyalty, and the church's emphasis on overseas foreign missions and non-Anglo-Saxon home missions.[5] Immigration was another influence. The editor of the *Christian Guardian* attributed Presbyterian strength in Saskatchewan to the "well known fact that recently Scotch people have constituted no small part of the newcomers to this province." A Hespeler, Ontario, Methodist reasoned that his church had done well, considering that it had no nationality to draw upon.[6]

The Methodist census population lagged behind population growth in the prairie region. During the years 1901–21, it increased 3.6 times, compared to 4.7 times for the population as a whole (table 6.2). It also lagged behind other confessional census populations. Manitoba, however, was the heartland of the "awful Methodist census." Thus, relative to other confessional census populations, Methodist strength increased from east to west.

Table 6.1
Denominational Populations as a Percentage of Total Population, Census, 1891–1921

	Manitoba	Saskatchewan	Alberta	Prairies	Ontario	Canada
1891						
Methodist	19	–	–	17	31	18
Presbyterian	26	–	–	23	21	16
Anglican	20	–	–	21	18	13
Baptist	11	–	–	8	5	6
Roman Catholic	13	–	–	15	17	41
1901						
Methodist	20	–	–	17	31	17
Presbyterian	26	–	–	22	22	16
Anglican	18	–	–	17	17	13
Baptist	4	–	–	4	5	6
Roman Catholic	14	–	–	16	18	42
1911						
Methodist	14	16	17	16	27	15
Presbyterian	23	20	18	20	21	15
Anglican	19	15	15	16	19	14
Baptist	3	4	5	4	5	5
Roman Catholic	16	18	17	17	19	39
1916[1]						
Methodist	13	15	16	15		
Presbyterian	22	20	18	20		
Anglican	19	15	15	17		
Baptist	2	4	5	4		
Roman Catholic	18	19	16	18		
1921						
Methodist	12	13	15	13	23	13
Presbyterian	23	21	21	22	21	16
Anglican	20	15	17	17	22	16
Baptist	2	3	5	3	5	5
Roman Catholic	17	19	17	18	20	39

Note: The provinces of Saskatchewan and Alberta were created in 1905.
[1] Census of prairie provinces.

Table 6.2
Prairie Denominational Populations as Ratios of Corresponding Census Population in 1901

	Total Population	Denominational Populations				
		Methodist	Presbyterian	Anglican	Baptist	Roman Catholic
1901	1.0	1.0	1.0	1.0	1.0	1.0
1911	3.2	2.9	2.9	3.1	3.6	3.4
1921	4.7	3.6	4.5	4.8	4.5	5.3

Table 6.3
Church Members as a Percentage of Methodist Census Populations

	1871	1881	1891	1901	1911	1921
Canada	21	22	27	33	30	33
Maritimes	23	25	24	28	29	31
Ontario/Quebec	21	22	27	31	34	38
Prairies			20	31	22·	21
Manitoba					29	33
Saskatchewan					17	20
Alberta					19	18
British Columbia					24	24

REPORTED CHURCH MEMBERSHIP STATISTICS

During the years 1901–21, the church's reported membership for the prairie region increased 2.8 times, compared to 3.6 times for the Methodist census population, mentioned in the previous section, and 4.7 times for the regional population. The membership statistics appear to show that Methodist attachment to church life weakened as one travelled west (table 6.3). In 1911 church members, as reported, made up 22 percent of the prairie Methodist census population, compared to 34 percent of the Ontario Methodist census population. Within the prairie region, the percentages were notably lower for Saskatchewan and Alberta than for Manitoba.[7] Finally, the percentage for the prairie region declined from 31 to 21 during the two decades 1901–21. This pattern contrasted with the rising trends in the percentages for central and eastern Canada.

These findings have intuitive appeal. With lower rural population densities than central Canadian Methodists, prairie Methodists had less access to church services. They had a higher percentage of persons who were too young to be church members and a higher percentage of bachelors who, everywhere, tended not to be members.[8] Finally, the apparent weakness of Methodism in the prairie region fitted pastoral complaints about rampant materialism and religious indifference during the prairie region's post-1896 wheat boom.

Even so, prairie Methodist church life appeared to compare favourably to Presbyterian and Anglican church life in the region. Methodists reported more church members than Presbyterians and Anglicans in 1914 (table 6.4). They managed this despite ranking third in census population in 1911 and having fewer church stations than the Presbyterians.

Table 6.4
Reported Church Members, Prairie Region, 1914

	Manitoba	Saskatchewan	Alberta	Prairies
Methodist	21,339	17,996	15,585	54,920
Presbyterian	26,001	15,168	13,283	54,452
Anglican (1915)	13,075	14,155	7,533	34,763

Table 6.5
Nonresident and Inactive Methodist Members (Percentages)

	Nonresident Church Members		1 June 1914 to 31 May 1915		
	1919 (1)	1925 (2)	Joined by Letter (3)	Left by Letter (4)	Ceased (5)
Canada	4	8	5	4	2
Maritimes	9	15	2	2	1
Ontario/Quebec	3	6	4	4	2
Prairies	5	9	7	6	4
Manitoba	5	8	5	5	4
Saskatchewan	6	7	8	5	3
Alberta	6	11	9	7	4
British Columbia	10	10	8	9	3

THE DENOMINATIONAL STATISTICS UNDER SCRUTINY

What is more important, the reported statistics for church membership are inaccurate, regionally biassed, and misleading for comparison. In addition, the criteria for membership differ somewhat between the Anglicans and the two other churches.

High Counts of Methodists

The inclusion of nonresidents inflated the reported membership. In May, quarterly boards revised their membership lists, in order to forward year-end statistics to their district meetings. Their revisions purged some, but not all, of their nonresident or inactive members. Members who "left by letter" to join other congregations were obvious purges (6 percent of prairie members in 1915; table 6.5, column 4). In addition, the quarterly boards "ceased" 2 percent of the national membership and 4 percent of the prairie membership (column 5).[9] In 1902, however, many of the 95 names on the revised roll for Elkhorn, Manitoba, were not "in very close touch with the church."

In 1910 the Boissevain circuit listed 191 members, of whom just 175 were "still here and attend church." In 1912 the Sintaluta quarterly board directed its pastor to write to some members "who have been away some time." In 1914 the Fort MacLeod quarterly board purged its membership of two men, but only after they had been "absent for over two years."[10]

In 1919 the conferences began to report subtotals for nonresident members. The percentage of nonresident members rose in all regions except British Columbia between 1919 and 1925. For both years, the percentage varied regionally (table 6.5, columns 1, 2). Given the unstable trend after 1919, it is tricky to speculate about the percentage for 1914.

Low Counts of Methodists

Missions were less likely than self-supporting circuits to keep accurate records, since they were not as well organized and were more likely to be without a pastor for part of the year. Their clergy were apt to be lay supplies or probationers, rather than ordained men. Thus the large number of missions among the stations in the three far-western provinces (table 6.6) deflated counts of their members. Reflective of this, above-average percentages of circuits in Saskatchewan, Alberta, and British Columbia gave no information about members in 1915 or reported no change from 1914. In 1910 the Moose Jaw district urged "that a record be kept of missions that have not kept the registration of membership and vital statistics." In the Souris district in 1904 good record keeping was unlikely on the Hope mission, which had four pastoral supplies during the year, with breaks between their times of work.[11] In 1909 the Lashburn, Saskatchewan, quarterly board "read the membership" and instructed its probationer, Stephen Byles, to revise it before the Battleford district meeting.[12] As Byles later recalled, however,

On the circuits that I served [1908–16] there was very little organization as far as I know or remember, in any way. I do not recall being responsible for a membership roll in any of the fields, except possibly the Radisson field, which was highly organized, having had an ordained minister, but on the others, no. What denominational background these people had in a sense was no concern of mine. They came to church and I took the service and that was that. I suppose most of them had a Methodist background but there was, as far as I know, no proof and I do not recall having to keep many records of the enrolment of people according to their denomination or church background.[13]

Table 6.6
Methodist Stations, 1914–15

	Stations	Stations That Were Missions (%)	Membership Statistics	
			No Data (%)	No Change Over Previous Year (%)
All Conferences	2,025	30	4	11
Maritime	200	37	0	7
Ontario	1,013	12	1	7
Prairies	649	48	8	16
Manitoba	173	22	10	11
Saskatchewan	245	38	8	18
Alberta	231	77	8	19
British Columbia	163	64	7	14

Finally, cooperation agreements with the Presbyterians and the organization of local union churches lowered the counts. Under cooperation agreements, the church lost members at preaching places from which it had withdrawn. At the same time, it reportedly failed to gain many Presbyterians as members at preaching places from which the Presbyterians had withdrawn. The church also tended to lose members who entered into union churches. In 1914 the prairie region had thirteen local unions involving Methodists. Within a year or two of their organization, the conferences dropped five from their lists of stations and gave no information about members for seven more.

The Church Union Count of Methodists

In February and March 1912, Methodist circuits polled their "qualified" church members on church union with the Presbyterians.[14] In May 1912 they reported their membership numbers for the annual conference statistics. The two counts of members differ (table 6.7, columns 1, 2). The conference count is notably higher for central and Maritime Canada and Saskatchewan; moderately higher for Manitoba and British Columbia; and notably lower for Alberta (column 3). Columns 4 and 5 report church members as a percentage of the Methodist census populations. If one uses the qualified-voter count for calculation, then the striking declining trend as one moves from east to west disappears. The percentages for the prairie and Maritime regions match (24 percent), and the percentages for Alberta and British Columbia surpass the percentage for Saskatchewan.

The circuits made no special census of members for the union vote, and their local arrangements varied.[15] The quarterly board at High

Table 6.7
Conference Counts of Church Members and Qualified Voters on Church Union, 1912

Conference/Region	March 1912 Qualified Voter Count (1)	15 May 1912 Conference Count (2)	1912 Conference Count as Percentage of List Count (3)	Members as a Percentage of Methodist Census Population	
				1912 Conference Count (4)	1912 Voter Count (5)
Canada	287,994	337,627	117	31	27
Maritimes	24,827	30,621	123	29	24
Ontario/Quebec	203,760	244,530	120	34	29
Prairies	48,504	50,022	103	24	24
Manitoba	19,978	21,750	109	33	30
Saskatchewan	12,593	15,424	122	20	16
Alberta	15,933	12,848	81	21	26
British Columbia	10,903	12,454	114	24	21

River, Alberta, simply directed the pastor to distribute ballots to the congregation. At Boissevain, Manitoba, circuit officials gave out ballots with annual membership cards for two consecutive Sundays and then mailed these documents to other eligible persons. Methodists in Manitou, Manitoba, held a Wednesday evening congregational meeting to get as many of the votes as possible and then made a personal canvass of nonattending members. The Minnesdosa, Manitoba, circuit held a congregational meeting for the vote but allowed members to submit ballots earlier to the circuit's superintendent or recording steward.

The writer treats the qualified-voter count as the more reliable of the two. It is less likely to include lapsed members and nonresidents. And as the lower count, it provides a sterner test of the church's expansion program.

The Presbyterian Statistics

Presbyterians and Methodists had similar requirements for membership, but their reporting practices differed. Unlike Methodists, Presbyterians listed nonresident and inactive members on a reserve roll and excluded them from their statistics for members.[16] Also unlike Methodists, Presbyterians tended to omit information about members for student missions. In Saskatchewan in 1914, for example, they reported the information for 95 percent of their self-supporting stations and "ordained mission fields" but did so for only 45 percent of their student missions. In that year Presbyterian student missions in the prairie region numbered 370: 2.4 times the Methodist total. Thus

Table 6.8
Reported and Revised Church Membership Statistics for the Prairies, 1914–15

	Manitoba	Saskatchewan	Alberta	Prairies
REPORTED				
Methodist	21,339	17,996	15,585	54,920
Presbyterian	26,001	15,168	13,283	54,452
Anglican	13,075	14,155	7,533	34,763
REVISED				
Methodist	20,313	17,139	21,061	58,523
Presbyterian	26,477	20,051	15,315	61,843

Presbyterians lacked information about members for 20 percent of their stations, compared to 8 percent for Methodists.

The Denominational Comparison

Table 6.8 shows the reported Methodist, Presbyterian, and Anglican memberships and also revised totals for the Methodists and Presbyterians. The revised Methodist totals take the 1911 voter list totals as accurate and assume that the conference counts for 1914 were high or low by the same percentage as in 1911. The revised Presbyterian totals assume that the number of church members per family for self-supporting and ordained mission stations also obtained for student missions that did not report information about members.

In contrast to the reported memberships, the revised totals show more Presbyterians than Methodists, but the difference is small. Methodists had the higher total in Alberta, a finding consistent with other evidence. Alberta, for example, was the chief mission province for the Methodists, but not for the Presbyterians. As expected, the Anglican membership ranked a distant third. Differences in the criteria for membership are at best a partial explanation for the lower Anglican totals.

THE RECRUITMENT OF MEMBERS

Methodists acquired members in five basic ways. First, they opened missions to reach Methodists in newly settled areas and in the process attracted protestants who were without services of their own confession. Second, they used Sunday schools, youth organizations, and revival meetings to bring the children of Methodists into membership. Third, they appointed immigration chaplains to contact British Methodist immigrants and distributed pamphlets about the Canadian Methodist Church to American Methodist immigrants.[17] Fourth, they gained (but also lost) members through marriages between Methodists and persons of other denominations. Fifth, Methodist missionaries tried to convert non–Anglo-Saxon immigrants to protestant values. In a few cases they turned their converts into Methodists.

This section examines the three major influences on Methodist, Presbyterian, and Anglican membership growth: their church expansion programs, their resources for bringing children into membership, and immigration and migration into the prairie region.

Protestant Church Expansion Programs

A church had to reach its own people in newly settled areas. In the process, it could attract protestants who lacked access to services of their own confession. Conversely, a church could lose supporters in a settlement if a rival moved in first. As the Anglican pastor Martin Holdom noted of Gatsby, Alberta, in 1911, "We certainly ought to have a resident man in this place; there must be 400 people around the town. The Methodists have quite a large church, and, of course, they get practically all the people."[18]

Population turnover complicated church expansion. The pioneers of Vulcan, Alberta, notes Paul Voisey, commonly had moved several times before coming to Vulcan and often did not stay long. High rates of geographic mobility obtained for the European-born and for American immigrants and Canadians. Bachelors and also whole families moved regularly. One woman "remembered packing five times in her first five years of marriage."[19] Thus Methodists could expect regular gains and losses of members in places where they committed resources. To hold members who moved, Methodists clearly needed a regional network of church service sites that touched as many communities as possible.

Even so, a church's commitment of resources in a town involved some risks. A confession could lose its following through out-migration or defection to another confession. Erskine, Alberta, reported Holdom in 1910, started with "a large number of Methodists and Presbyterians," but "A certain minister belonging to the 'Christian Church' came in from the States. He converted both the Presbyterian and Methodist ministers, and swept the whole place, except of Church [of England] people ... We use the Methodist church as they haven't a congregation."[20] In any case, prairie towns went from boom to bust when their settlement rushes ended. The boom in Castor, Alberta, broke in 1912, and the town lost 57 percent of its population over the next decade. In Paul Voisey's vivid prose, "Many towns shared Castor's fate. Built on exuberant expectations fired by settlement

Table 6.9
Church Expansion in the Prairie Region, 1914

	Manitoba	Saskatchewan	Alberta	Prairies
STATIONS (CIRCUITS)				
Methodist	157	247	223	627
Percentage that were missions	22	38	77	48
Presbyterian	207	353	232	792
Percentage that were missions	42	65	72	61
With augmented charges	53	82	85	76
Anglican	136[1]	253[1]	87[1]	476
Percentage that were missions	62	82	67	74
PREACHING PLACES				
Methodist	354	550	583	1,487
Presbyterian	453	894	536	1,883
Anglican	250[1]	465[1]	160[1]	875[1]
CLERGY				
Methodist	116	134	114	364
Presbyterian	137	153	98	388
MISSION SUPERINTENDENTS				
Methodist	1	2	2	5
Presbyterian	1	3	3	7

[1] Estimate.

booms, they shimmered briefly in the prairie sun and faded in the ensuing twilight."[21]

If Presbyterians had an edge over Methodists in church expansion, then it was a small one. By 1914, the Presbyterians had more circuits, more preaching places, and more mission superintendents in the prairie region (table 6.9).[22] The Presbyterian advantage in circuits and preaching places, however, came entirely from greater numbers of student missions: 370 compared to 157 for the Methodists. For want of replacement supplies, the church closed most of these stations when the students returned to college.

The Anglican church expansion program was weaker than the Methodist and Presbyterian programs. In 1905, on the completion of his tour of the diocese of Saskatchewan, Bishop Jervois Arthur Newnham reported "churches closed, missions vacant, the support of your clergy promised by the people, yet withheld; congregations far smaller than they should be, while our own people go to other churches."[23] By 1914 the Anglicans had fewer stations and preaching places than the other two churches.[24]

As Marilyn Barber notes, prairie Anglicans were more British than their Methodist and Presbyterian counterparts, since they were apt to be British immigrants rather than migrants from Ontario. They ranked the imperial tie ahead of the Canadian national tie. Their bishops were Britons who looked to Britain for clergy and financial support. Similarly, prairie laymen gave money to British missionary societies.[25] Unlike Methodists and Presbyterians, Anglicans kept their prairie operations administratively separate from central Canada at the level of the national polity (see chapter 2).

During the 1890s the British missionary societies emphasized native missions and were slow to appreciate white-settler missions as a priority. They also believed in the "euthanasia of missions," whereby they would reduce grants to make the mission fields self-supporting. Canada's Anglicans moved slowly to take up the developing British slack. Their bishops first met in a national general synod in 1893. In 1896, right at the start of the Laurier wheat boom, the second general synod decided not to reconvene for six years. Although the general synod of 1896 agreed in principle to organize a national missionary society, resistance form the central Canadian dioceses made the agreement a dead letter. The proposed missionary society of the Canadian church was finally organized in 1902 and became effective about 1905. In the circumstances, observes John Webster Grant, Anglicans had to "contemplate retrenchment rather than advance ... during the most crucial years of western development."[26] British Anglicans helped with their archbishops' Western Canada Fund in 1909. Even so, the Anglican pastor at Castor, Alberta, judged in 1911, "we are easily the last Christian body with regard to enterprise and missionary spirit. The Romans, Methodists, and Presbyterians are far ahead of us."[27]

The Nurture of Children

By 1896 children were the principal source of new members in the central and eastern Canadian conferences of the Methodist Church. Thus Sunday schools and youth organizations occupied a central place in church work. The formal policy of the general conference board of Sunday schools and young people's societies was "a Sunday school in every preaching place ... all the members of the church and the community in the Sunday school ... [and] every member of the Sunday school in the church."[28]

Methodists grouped sabbath scholars into elementary, secondary, and adult divisions (table 6.10). Compared to Ontario, the prairie Sunday schools held a larger percentage of their scholars in the

Table 6.10
Regional Development of Methodist Sunday Schools and Youth Organizations, 1914
(Percentages)

	Preaching Place with Sunday Schools	Including Union Sunday Schools	Preaching Places with Youth Organizations	Distribution of Sunday School Members		
				Elementary	Secondary	Adult
Maritimes	56	73	18	46	25	29
Ontario/Quebec	88	95	61	42	28	30
Prairies	52	68	27	48	24	28
Manitoba	64	90	51	47	26	28
Saskatchewan	49	65	19	48	24	28
Alberta	48	57	20	50	23	27
British Columbia	75	87	52	57	24	18
Canada	72	83	44	44	27	29

elementary division. In part, this expressed the more youthful age profile for the prairie Methodist population.

Compared to Ontario, Methodist Sunday schools and youth organizations were less developed in the prairie region. In 1914 just 27 percent of prairie preaching places had a youth organization, compared to 61 percent for central Canada (table 6.10). Just 52 percent of prairie preaching places had a Sunday school, compared to 88 percent for central Canada. If the calculation includes union Sunday schools, then the percentage was 68 for the prairie region and 95 for central Canada. Within the prairie region, the percentage of preaching places with Sunday schools and youth organizations was lower for Saskatchewan and Alberta than for Manitoba.

The percentage of preaching places with Sunday schools was similar in the Methodist and Presbyterian Churches (table 6.11).[29] Like the Methodist percentages, the Presbyterian percentages were lower for the prairie region than for central Canada and declined from east to west within the prairie region. The same patterns obtain for the percentages of preaching places with youth organizations.

The Anglican statistics for Sunday schools are for parishes, which were like stations or circuits, rather than preaching places. In addition, the Anglican diocesan boundaries differed from provincial boundaries. Even so, the Anglican statistics show patterns similar to those of the other churches. Prairie parishes were less likely than central Canadian parishes to have a Sunday school, and the percentage of parishes with Sunday schools declined from east to west within the prairie region.

Simply put, all three denominations had difficulty establishing Sunday schools and youth organizations in the prairie region. As

Table 6.11
Sunday Schools and Youth Organizations, by Denomination, 1914–15

	Preaching Places with Sunday Schools, Including Union Schools (%)		Preaching Places with Youth Organizations (%)		Sunday Schools perParish
	Methodist	Presbyterian	Methodist	Presbyterian	Anglican [1]
Maritimes	73	99	18	42	1.76
Ontario/Quebec	95	97	61	66	1.46
Prairies	68	65	27	27	0.91
Manitoba	90	73	51	41	1.18
Saskatchewan	65	63	19	23	0.79
Alberta	57	61	20	22	0.78
British Columbia	87	70	52	49	1.05
Canada	83	82	44	44	

[1] Omits dioceses with no data.

Presbyterian probationers in Saskatchewan found at various stations, "(1) There are no children, we preach mostly to bachelors; (2) we cannot get anybody to act as superintendent; (3) The service is at 7 o'clock in the evening, and most of the children are so far away that the parents cannot bring them during the day to Sunday school and attend the service in the evening."[30] Stephen Byles, the Methodist probationer in the province quoted earlier, did

not recollect much organized Sunday school work in any of the circuits I served ... In those places, especially in the rural parts out in the country, there was only one opportunity for the children to come to service and that was the regular church service. So, I always spent some little time to speak to them ... the number of children seemed to grow as I went along because I had a close association with them through the week ... It was the kind of approach that I was accustomed to in my own childhood. I never went to Sunday school until I was quite a grown boy and yet we always had some part in the service and we were always acknowledged. So it was not a new enterprise for me. It was carrying on with a tradition that I had known in the Old Country."[31]

All things considered, Methodists had a slight edge over Presbyterians in Sunday school work in the prairie region. They had just 83 percent of the Presbyterian total for Sunday schools, but 106 percent of the Presbyterian total for sabbath scholars. Their advantage over the Presbyterians, however, was less than they enjoyed in central Canada – 154 percent for schools and 200 percent for scholars.

Finally, if the calculation includes union schools, then Methodists and Presbyterians each had twice the Anglican totals for Sunday schools and Sabbath scholars.

Immigration and Church Membership

Stephen Byles recalled great differences among his Saskatchewan congregations. At Lashburn, near the Barr Colony, the people "were mostly English, and only some of them would be leaning towards the Methodists." At Maymount they were mostly "Canadians with a mixture of the people from the United States [who were] quite different from people with a more conservative background." At New Ottawa (later renamed to Speers), thirteen miles distant from Maymount, "a whole group of people had moved from Ottawa, even a retired minister among them." The people at Radisson "were almost entirely from Ontario and of Methodist extraction."

Clearly, immigration and migration played on the census populations and memberships of churches in the prairie region. Migrants from Ontario were the best source of prairie Methodists. As table 6.12 shows, Ontario natives made up three-quarters of the 296 Methodist laymen who were listed in biographical dictionaries (an elitist selection).[32] For every Ontario-born person in the prairies, however, three persons who were born in other provinces or in Britain, the United States, or Europe by 1911 (table 6.13). British, American, and European immigrants, in turn, consisted of fewer Methodists than Presbyterians and Anglicans.

British Immigrants

By 1931, when published censuses first reported denominational affiliation by place of birth, the United Church of Canada had absorbed the Methodist Church and two-thirds of the Presbyterian Church. Even so, 47 percent of British-born residents of the prairies were Anglicans (table 6.14). By the writer's estimate, 27 percent had been Presbyterian before coming to Canada and 15 percent had been Methodist.[33] Thus British immigration brought 3.1 Anglicans and 1.8 Presbyterians for each Methodist.

Clearly, the Presbyterians benefited from the Scottish immigration. As table 6.14 shows, few Scots were Roman Catholic, and most of the non-Catholics were Presbyterian. The Presbyterians, no fools, had an immigration chaplain at Glasgow, but not at other British ports. The Reverend John Chisholm, the Presbyterian immigration chaplain at Montreal, met all passenger ships. As he noted, however, "the number of Presbyterians coming from countries other than Scotland and the North of Ireland is relatively small."[34]

Table 6.12
Birthplaces of Prairie Methodist Laymen

Birthplace	Manitoba N	Manitoba %	Saskatchewan N	Saskatchewan %	Alberta N	Alberta %	Prairies N	Prairies %
Ontario	132	78	45	74	45	69	222	75
Other provinces	9	5	5	8	11	17	25	8
Prairies	15	9	1	2	1	2	17	6
Britain	9	5	6	10	5	8	20	7
United States	5	3	4	7	3	5	12	4
Total	170	100	61	101	65	101	296	100

Note: The figures are for laymen listed in biographical dictionaries, 1896–1914.

Table 6.13
Birthplaces of Prairie Residents in 1911, as a Multiple of Ontario-Born Prairie Residents

Birthplace	Manitoba	Saskatchewan	Alberta	Prairies
Ontario	1.0	1.0	1.0	1.0
Other Provinces	0.3	0.5	0.5	0.4
Britain	1.2	0.8	1.1	1.0
Europe	1.1	0.9	1.0	1.0
United States	0.2	0.7	1.4	0.7
Total Non-Ontario	2.8	2.9	4.0	3.1

Table 6.14
Denominational Affiliation in the Prairie Provinces, by Place of Birth, 1931 Census
(Percentages)

Place of Birth	Anglican	Presbyterian	United Church	Roman Catholic	Lutheran
Ontario	14	26	42	8	–
Britain	47	17	25	5	–
England/Wales (66)	67	4	19	3	–
Scotland (26)	7	47	38	3	–
Ireland (9)	27	21	26	21	–
United States	5	8	34	18	18
Europe	–	1	3	45	26

American Immigrants

"Then there are the American settlers," remarked N.W. Rowell, at the Methodist general conference in Winnipeg in 1902. "We are used to reading of the great Boer trek," continued Rowell, "but this deals with the marvellous flow of population from the States of Nebraska, Iowa, Minnesota, and the Dakotas to the Canadian West. The movement started in 1897, and from 700 in that year has progressed to over 30,000 for the first six months of 1902. You see the trains of these people with their effects at almost every station in Alberta and Saskatchewan. A fine class of settlers they are, energetic and enterprising. They need churches, and it is our duty to occupy the ground."[35]

By the writer's estimates, American immigration to the prairie region brought 2.3 Methodists for each Presbyterian and 4.8 Methodists for each Episcopalian (Anglican). The data for estimation are for American immigrants to western Canada during the years 1907–9. Nine states near the international border supplied 92 percent of the immigrants. The estimates assume that all 110,656 immigrants from the nine states came to the prairie region.

The American Bureau of the Census reports the numbers of Methodist, Presbyterian, and Protestant Episcopalian (Anglican) church members by state in 1906. For each of the nine states of emigration, one calculates each denomination's church members as a percentage of all church members. The estimates assume that each denomination's percentage obtains for emigrants from the state, that the three denominations have similar criteria for church membership, and that their counts of church members are equally complete (or incomplete).[36]

In terms of Methodist-Presbyterian-Anglican rivalry, the relative strength of Methodists among American immigrants failed to compensate for their relative weakness among British immigrants. First, the British immigrants were more numerous than the American immigrants. In 1911 there were 1.4 British-born residents on the prairies for each American-born resident. Second, more American than British immigrants belonged to denominations other than Methodist, Presbyterian, and Anglican. Thus in 1931 the United Church, Presbyterian, and Anglican census populations made up 89 percent of British-born residents of the prairie region, compared to 47 percent of its American-born residents.

The British and American immigrants had contrasting distributions within the prairie region, however. In 1911 the distribution for British-born residents was as follows: Manitoba, 39 percent; Saskatchewan, 33 percent; and Alberta, 28 percent. The distribution for American-born residents was Manitoba, 10 percent; Saskatchewan, 42 percent; and

Alberta, 49 percent. Thus the ratio of British-born to American-born residents was 5.6 in Manitoba, 1.1 in Saskatchewan, and 0.8 in Alberta. These ratios help to explain why the denominational census of 1911 was more "awful" for Methodists in Manitoba than in Saskatchewan and Alberta. They also explain why Alberta was the chief mission province for Methodists, whereas Saskatchewan filled that role for Presbyterians.

Continental European Immigrants

Except for Baptists, the Anglo-Canadian Protestant churches had little to gain from the non-Anglo-Saxon immigration. Some of the immigrants, however, had Calvinist Protestant traditions and hence an affinity with Presbyterians. In 1911 the Presbyterian mission superintendent for Manitoba and Saskatchewan estimated that "one-third of the 17,000 Hungarians west of the Great Lakes" were "Presbyterian." In 1912 the Presbyterian superintendent for Alberta believed that German, Dutch, and Norwegian immigrants with Reform Church backgrounds were ripe to become Presbyterians.[37]

Immigrant Co-religionists as Church Members

British and American immigrants clearly added to the Methodist, Presbyterian, and Anglican census populations. Although all three churches appointed immigration chaplains in a bid to turn their immigrant co-religionists into church members, the results disappointed them.

In 1906 the Methodist general conference appointed the Reverend Melvin Taylor as immigration chaplain at Montreal. Taylor was to devise a method of communicating with prospective Methodist emigrants in Britain, meet Methodist immigrants who disembarked at Canadian ocean ports, furnish the immigrants with a letter of introduction to the pastor at their intended destination, and inform the said pastors that the immigrants were coming. Armed with a budget of two thousand dollars, Taylor organized immigration committees at Montreal, Halifax, Quebec City and St John. The Missionary Society gave the conferences small grants to appoint part-time chaplains in these cities and in Ottawa, Toronto, Hamilton, and Winnipeg.[38] It sent letters to two thousand British Methodist clergy in 1906–7 and 1909–10 and five thousand British Methodist clergy in 1913–14. The letters warned about the Roman Catholic immigration service and asked British pastors to support the Methodists.[39]

The work was more difficult than meets the eye. The British and American immigrants came from Wesleyan Methodist, Bible Christian,

Primitive Methodist, and Methodist Episcopal Churches: denominations that had vanished in Canada through the church unions of 1874 and 1884. Thus Methodist immigrants often found the Canadian service strange. British Wesleyans, for example, discovered that some of their favourite songs were missing in the Canadian hymn book or that Canadian Methodists disparaged them for their accents and dress, for appearing to put on airs, or for being misfits.[40]

Few British and American Methodists seemed to have joined the Canadian church. During the quadrennium 1906–10 the chaplains met 19,771 Methodist immigrants. As far as the church could determine, 441 became members and 813 became adherents.[41] During the single church year 1912–13, the chaplains gave letters of introduction to 15,399 immigrants.[42] To discover how many of the immigrants used the letters, the Missionary Society wrote to every pastor of a Methodist church in Canada. Replies from 1,058 pastors (a 50 percent response) reported that 2,171 British immigrants, 126 American immigrants, and 102 other immigrants had joined the Canadian church. As J.H. Riddell and other Methodists judged, "the Methodist church gained very small additions to its membership" from the "tens of thousands who found a new home in Canada."[43]

The Presbyterians had immigration chaplains in Glasgow, Quebec City, Toronto, Winnipeg, and Vancouver. The Glasgow chaplain collected information on Presbyterian families in Scottish ports, then forwarded it to Canada on faster lines by way of New York. With the detailed information in hand, chaplains at the Canadian ports could approach bewildered Scottish families by name ("Good-morning Mrs Anderson, Welcome to Canada!") and ensure that their belongings were transported to the railway station, free of charge (the cost was included in the price of the railway ticket).

Despite their well-organized program, the Presbyterians fared little better than Methodists in turning Old Country co-religionists into church members. Many Scots reported themselves as Presbyterian out of convention and were inactive in the church.[44] Presbyterian immigrants from Scotland and northern Ireland, noted the church's mission superintendent for Manitoba in 1914, "hold aloof for many reasons. The process of being transplanted into new soil has disturbed their relations to the church. New surroundings are taken advantage of to express old prejudices. Inability to support ordinances keeps others away for a time."[45]

Anglicans had chaplains at British ports of departure, chaplains for the voyage across the Atlantic, and chaplains in Canada at Quebec, Montreal, Toronto, Hamilton, Winnipeg, and Vancouver. They also had deaconesses at Toronto, Montreal, Calgary, Moose Jaw, Hamilton, and Edmonton to watch out for "Church girls" who had come out for domestic service. During the years 1911–13 the chaplains met 871 ships and gave 87,838 letters of introduction. Nevertheless, "the old plan of obtaining names and addresses of our incoming Church people by personal visitation has been discontinued ... not more than five percent of those who receive letters of introduction present them to the clergy [at their Canadian destinations], though they are always urged to do so. The clergy must be enabled to find those who fail to report themselves."[46]

European immigrants added little to Anglo-Protestant church memberships in the prairie region by 1914. The Methodist Church had some fifty members from its non-Anglo-Saxon missions in Winnipeg and east-central Alberta. In 1908 the Presbyterian Church had four Hungarian Calvinist missions. It also subsidized the Independent Greek Church, a Ukrainian Protestant denomination, during the years 1903–13. In 1913 the Presbyterians cut off funds for the Independent Greek Church and ordained nineteen of its clergy. As Presbyterians, however, the Ukrainian pastors were unable to hold their congregations. Thus just 2 percent of prairie Ukrainians reported themselves as Presbyterian or United Church supporters in the 1931 census.

THE METHODIST ACHIEVEMENT ON THE PRAIRIES

"Poor attendance, meagre financial support, and spiritual apathy [and] demand for interdenominational universalism," argues Paul Voisey, indicated "that neither church nor religion mattered much to the population" in Vulcan, Alberta.[47] Nevertheless, as Voisey appreciates, low population densities and crude transportation discouraged attendance at religious services. Going anywhere "usually meant wrestling with horses, harness, and hitches first." Conversely, rural ministers on the prairies were to see "a dramatic upsurge in church membership with the arrival of the inexpensive Ford" automobile in 1919.[48]

A second issue is whether "just 50 percent of membership" constituted "poor attendance" at Vulcan's Presbyterian-Methodist union services in 1914. Lynne Marks found that "churchgoing was a far from universal practice" in Ontario small towns during the 1880s. As the *Campbellford Herald* reported, "no more than one-fifth of the inhabitants of the village could be found in church on a Sunday morning." Less than half the Protestant families in Campbellford and Thorold included church members.[49] In Brantford, Ontario, in 1852, just 44 percent of Methodist adults were church members.[50] What is more important, the Vulcan area had three large, overlapping population groups who were especially difficult for the Methodist Church to reach: immigrant co-religionists from the United States and Britain, bachelors, and newcomers who left the area after a short stay.[51]

Perhaps the "meagre" financial contributions from Vulcan's Methodist settlers expressed penury rather than religious indifference. As Violet Brown, a Methodist pastor's daughter and Presbyterian parson's wife, recalled of Alberta's "over the Red Deer" country in 1907, "no collections were taken up at country points as people did not have money to give." In their correspondence with the home mission department, three Methodist pastors in Alberta argued the same point.[52]

Finally, the rejection of theology, doctrine, and denominationalism (what Voisey calls "a diluted Christian universalism") is problematic as evidence of spiritual apathy. As Voisey appreciates, avoidance of denominationalism was practical in the denominationally mixed congregations of prairie communities. In Protestantism at the national level, moreover, cross-denominational theological differences had displaced confessional alignments. What is more important, as Christie and Gauvreau argue, the rejection of theology and attraction to the social gospel marked a return to experience in the Methodist evangelical tradition, not irreligion.[53] The social activist Nellie McClung, for example, was impatient with theology and other-worldly evangelism, yet looked to the social gospel for "spiritual exercise."[54]

Voisey's evidence for religion in Vulcan raises questions about his theory, a modernized version of the frontier thesis. A community, reasons Voisey, results from the interplay of four basic forces: environment, tradition, frontier, and metropolis.[55] Other influences, such as demography and technology, are secondary. Vulcan's population had many bachelors, for example, because frontiers attract bachelors.

In this context, how is one to interpret the religious behaviour of Vulcan bachelors? Did low church attendance arise from frontier demography (frontiers have bachelors and bachelors have low church attendance), the frontier itself (bachelors have lower church attendance in frontier conditions in their communities of origin), or bachelor tradition (bachelors everywhere felt masculine alienation from feminized religious culture)? Similarly, did "diluted Christian universalism" in Vulcan religious services express a weak tradition in frontier conditions (Voisey) or the emulation of a metropolitan trend (Christie and Gauvreau)? Simply put, Voisey's theory is a useful heuristic but tricky to apply.

SUMMARY AND CONCLUSION

During the years 1896–1914, both the prairie Methodist census population and church membership rose, but both also lagged behind population growth. In census population, the Methodists placed a "sickly third" behind the Anglicans and Presbyterians. In church membership, they ranked second, slightly behind the Presbyterians.

Compared to Ontario, Methodist Church members made up a lower percentage of the Methodist census population in the prairie region. The small regional difference arose primarily from the severity of the rural problem and the large numbers of bachelors and immigrant co-religionists in the prairie region.

Methodists and Presbyterians were comparable in terms of their agencies for nurturing children into church membership and church expansion programs. Presbyterians had more Sunday schools but fewer Sabbath scholars. They had more circuits, but the difference came from student missions, which commonly closed for the winter months. Both churches fared better than the Anglicans in the development of Sunday schools and church expansion.

Immigration added more Anglicans and Presbyterians than Methodists to denominational census populations. It had a small influence on Anglo-Canadian church memberships, however, because many of the immigrant co-religionists declined to join the Canadian churches. Similarly, denominational census populations included many immigrant co-religionists who were inactive in Canadian church life. Thus, contemporaries erred in using census data to measure their competitive success.

Effectively, the Methodist and Presbyterian achievements on the prairies were impressive given the difficulties that the churches faced – the rural problem, the weak response from immigrant co-religionists, the extreme version of the bachelor problem, and the high level of non-Anglo-Saxon immigration. The revised church membership statistics, not the census statistics, measure their accomplishments better. On that basis, the Anglo-Protestant rivalry was a horse race, ending in a Methodist-Presbyterian photo-finish, with the Anglican mount trailing.

7 Methodists and Non-Anglo-Saxon Immigrants

During the years 1901–11 the non-Anglo-Saxon percentage of the prairie population rose from 26 to 38. Methodists widely perceived non-Anglo-Saxons as a threat to Canada's moral standards and standard of living as to its cultural homogeneity and national identity. Accordingly, they pressed the government to assimilate Canada's non-Anglo-Saxon residents and discourage non-Anglo-Saxon immigration. Where the government's role ended, the role of the Protestant missions began. Along the way, these missions met with resistance from the Roman Catholic and ethnic Old World churches, ethnic nationalists, and the non-Anglo-Saxon settlers themselves, so that by 1914 prairie society differed considerably from Methodist ideals.

This chapter gives background for chapters 8 and 9, which examine Methodist missions to non-Anglo-Saxon immigrants in the prairie region. It reviews Methodist opinion on Canada's immigration policy, Methodist views on public schooling as an instrument of Anglo-Canadianization; and the questions of why prairie public schooling differed from the Methodist model and how Ukrainians, in particular, resisted public schooling along Methodist lines. It also considers Ukrainians as composing a mission field for Anglo-Protestant, Roman Catholic, and Ukrainian-ethnic churches.

The hundred thousand Ukrainians were the prairie region's largest non-Anglo-Saxon group of immigrants. Their example illustrates vividly the complexity of public schooling and Protestant mission work among these immigrants. What is more important, Ukrainians formed prairie Methodism's chief non-Anglo-Saxon mission field before the First World War.

METHODISTS AND CANADA'S IMMIGRATION POLICY

Methodists commonly took a dim view of Canada's immigrants from central Europe. "The general opinion of the people in this country," reported the Reverend John Maclean, the *Christian Guardian*'s reporter for the Manitoba and Northwest conference, in 1901, "is that we do not want any more of these people in the west. The quality of the immigrants is more important to us than the quantity. We cannot afford to have the refuse of Europe dumped into our western country, as an ignorant foreign population can work a great deal of harm."[1] In 1908 the Reverend Wellington Bridgeman, president of the Manitoba conference, noticed "a strong and growing feeling here that the Ottawa authorities should shut down on foreign immigrants altogether and aim to fill our lands with English-speaking people."[2]

A second viewpoint tolerated the immigration of nonpreferred groups but asked government to stop promoting it. As the *Christian Guardian* commented in 1898, "we cannot see why any extraordinary fuss and effort should be put forward to bring out the foreigners to Canada."[3] "We love our ain the best," exclaimed another Methodist.[4] A third perspective endorsed Canada's use of medical inspections to screen out immigrants who were physically or mentally unfit. In 1909 J.S. Woodsworth, the superintendent of the All People's Mission in Winnipeg, urged government to strengthen the screening process by doing the inspections in Europe rather than Canada.[5]

The dominion minister of the interior was responsible for immigration. Interestingly, Methodists from the prairie region filled this position in Wilfrid Laurier's governments (1896–1911). Clifford Sifton (minister from 1896 to 1905) was a Methodist lawyer from Brandon, Manitoba, and Frank Oliver (minister from 1905 to 1911) was the Methodist owner of the *Edmonton Bulletin*.[6]

In 1896 Sifton became famous for his vigorous promotion of immigration, settlement, and "stalwart peasants in sheepskin coats." Behind the scenes, his openness to central European immigrants was short-lived. In 1899 he ended bonus payments to steamship companies in a bid to reduce their numbers, but in 1904 pressures from the Austro-Hungarian government caused him to restore the bonuses retroactively to 1901.[7] Although Sifton failed to end the bonuses, his efforts foreshadowed policy under his successor.

Frank Oliver largely ended recruiting in central Europe while increasing settlement bonuses to British booking agents. At the same time, the government adopted new restrictive provisions for the Immigration Act in 1906 and 1910.[8] As Oliver explained, the central European's cultural peculiarities were "a drag on [Canadian] civilization and progress," whereas the Briton arrived in Canada "practically a ready-made citizen."[9]

Despite Methodist nativism, neither the general conference nor any of the annual conferences demanded an end to the immigration of non-Anglo-Saxons, and neither of Laurier's Methodist interior ministers entertained such a course of action. Simply put, Methodists accepted that "foreigners" were coming. Bolstered by a militant view of British civilization, Methodists were confident that Anglo-Canadian society could assimilate the newcomers.[10] Anglo-Canadians on the prairies were not alone but were the vanguard of an ascendant Anglo-Saxon dominion and an outpost of a vast British Empire. From the perspective of the Anglo-Protestant world mission, Canada's non-Anglo-Saxons presented Methodists with a providential opportunity. Through their church's Japan and West China missions, they were helping to "evangelize the world in this generation." Through immigration, part of the world – the "foreigners" – was coming to them.[11]

PUBLIC SCHOOLS AND ANGLO-CANADIANIZATION

Public schooling, judged a Methodist Church commission in 1909, was the chief instrument for turning non-Anglo-Saxon immigrants into Anglo-Canadians.[12] "The church can do a great deal," opined the *Christian Guardian* in 1910, "but at the most she can only touch the fringe of the matter. The public school is the place where the foundations of good citizenship must be laid broad and deep."[13] In 1911 a special committee of the general board of missions reaffirmed "that the education and conversion into good citizens of the foreign population of Canada is primarily a responsibility resting upon the state."[14]

Methodists intended the public school to assimilate the children of "foreigners." First, it was to make them literate in English. Without the language barrier, the children would be accessible to Anglo-Protestant missionaries, would be able to read the Bible, and would become liberated from the religious authority of "decadent" liturgical churches. Second, the school was to impart Anglo-Canadian knowledge, such as an Anglo-Canadian version of Canadian and world history and world geography from an Anglo-Canadian perspective.

School teaching was like mission work to young Methodists in the Star colony, a Ukrainian bloc settlement northeast of Edmonton.

Around 1907, when public schools first opened, recalled the Reverend William Pike,

the first teachers in some of them were from Methodist parsonages in the East. At Wostok, Miss Eva Duke and her sister taught in two schools. At Kiseliw, Miss Mary Howard taught and lived alone in an 8 × 10 shack behind the school. In nearby schools taught a Miss Dawson and Nan Whittaker – all from ministers' homes. There were also a number of young men from Universities in the East who spent their summers teaching in the 'Colony.' Among them were Fred Tilson, Robert Stewart, and J.K. Smith. All of them did good work and found the missionaries cooperative, for they all had similar ideals. Thus missionaries, teachers, doctors, and nurses – all dedicated – tended "The Flame," kindling it in many young hearts. Many persons of Ukrainian descent have felt the warmth of it.

One of the university men, J.K. Smith, became a missionary in the Star colony. Two young graduates of Victoria College, Ethelwyn Chace and Ella McLean, became WMS missionaries in the colony after teaching Ukrainian children in the public school at Bavilla. On his tour of Ukrainian schools in 1919, J.K. Smith met one teacher who was a missionary's wife (Mrs P.G. Sutton, formerly Miss Phoebe Code of the WMS ranks) and another who had "served for a term under the WMS and is now in close touch with the society though working independently of them." At a third school, possibly Bavilla, the WMS had supplied the teacher "for some years."[15]

The Methodist ideal for prairie schools had several elements. First, each province was to have a single public system to which all landowners paid tax. This provision allowed separate schools but exposed their supporters to double taxation. Second, English was to be the sole language of instruction. Third, the teachers, texts, curriculum, and length of the school year were to meet Anglo-Canadian standards. Fourth, school attendance was to be compulsory for children of a legally defined school age. Fifth, government was to hire school inspectors and truant officers to enforce the law. Sixth, Anglo-Canadian men and women made the ideal teachers.

The Methodist design encountered problems in application. Anglo-Canadians who were willing to teach in remote "foreign" districts were in short supply. Anglo-Canadian teachers had difficulty communicating with children and parents who spoke no English.

The Anglo-Canadian–trained, ethnic-bilingual teacher was a possible solution to the problem. Indeed, all three provincial governments on the prairies opened Anglo-Canadian–run normal schools to train male teachers from Ukrainian settlements. In theory the ethnic-bilingual teacher could ease ethnic unilingual students into full-blown English-language, Anglo-Canadian education in the senior grades. In one fanciful scenario, an ethnic Ukrainian teacher gave way to an Anglo-Canadian replacement once the groundwork was done. As a Saskatchewan school inspector reported in 1910, "Excellent results appeared for one school, Ukraina, after two summers' work; and the Ruthenian teacher in charge, an exceptionally bright student, positively affirmed that he would not return to the school for another year on the ground that his pupils were ready for a skilful English-speaking teacher. His idea was that the Ruthenian pupils should acquire the Canadian outlook under the same sort of stimulus he was receiving himself as a student of the university."[16]

Similarly, the Anglo-Protestant–trained bilingual ethnic missionary was a possible solution to Methodist staffing problems on non-Anglo-Saxon missions. In schools, as on missions, however, Methodists distrusted the ethnic recruit's ability and willingness to impart Anglo-Canadian values to the ethnic community. An added risk in schooling was that bilingual instruction in theory would be foreign-language instruction in practice.

In every prairie province, the school system diverged markedly from the Methodist model. Manitoba had no compulsory attendance law during the years 1897–1916. In the circumstances, speculated Methodists, some "foreign" districts would decline to tax themselves in order to open a public school. They had little tradition of schooling in the Old Country, and in Canada they were poor.[17] In 1909 government statistics indicated that 30 to 40 percent of the province's school-age children were out of school.[18] In 1913 attendance was notably low in the Ukrainian and northern districts. In one district with forty school-aged children, the average attendance during November was two. Officials found that 11 schools they believed to be open were closed.[19]

The Manitoba law permitted bilingual instruction in public schools with ten or more students whose mother tongue was not English. In 1908 the government opened a Ruthenian Training School at Brandon to prepare qualified ethnic Ukrainian teachers for bilingual schools. By 1913, reported J.S. Woodsworth, Manitoba had 42 German, 33 Ukrainian, and 110 French bilingual schools.[20] In 1916 it had 61 German, 111 Ukrainian and Polish, and 120 French bilingual public schools; 1 school in 5 offered bilingual instruction.

Woodsworth believed that so-called bilingual instruction was foreign-language instruction in practice. The bilingual school boards could not find Anglo-Canadian teachers who were fluent in the foreign language. Consequently, they staffed their schools with ethnic Canadians who knew little English. By his estimate in 1913, 25 percent of the province's 268 bilingual school teachers were illiterate in English.[21]

Saskatchewan and Alberta each had a compulsory attendance law but could not enforce it. According to J.T.M. Anderson, a school inspector and future premier, Saskatchewan left enforcement to the discretion of the local boards, which did nothing.[22] In 1911 a third of Alberta's Ukrainians had schools, the attendance rate was 50 percent where schools were open, and just four Ukrainian children in rural Alberta had gone beyond the fourth grade.[23] In 1919 a missionary in the Star colony, W.H. Pike, met a thirteen-year-old girl who had never attended a day school, even though one was within a mile of her farm home.[24]

Saskatchewan and Alberta permitted foreign-language instruction between 3:00 and 4:00 PM, and after 4:00 PM at parental expense.[25] Like Manitoba, they established Anglo-Canadian–run teacher-training schools for "foreigners" (at Regina in 1909 and Vegreville, Alberta, in 1913), but the schools produced few teachers. Thus ethnic Ukrainian school boards in Saskatchewan and Alberta hired permit teachers from Manitoba, which had a fully developed bilingual system.[26] The permit teachers – 97 in Saskatchewan in 1915 and 13 in Alberta in 1913 – had attended the Ukrainian normal school in Brandon but had not yet graduated.

Several influences underlay the failure of the Methodist model in prairie provincial law. First, the school laws for Manitoba in 1897 and Saskatchewan and Alberta in 1905 were national political compromises between Anglo-Canadian and French Canadian interest groups. Just as national politics produced the compromises, so it discouraged efforts to revise them.

Second, the archbishop of St Boniface, Adélard Langevin (1895–1915), opposed school laws that would help to assimilate non-Anglo-Saxons into Anglo-Canadian society. Their assimilation might turn them into protestants. Worse, it would turn them into English-speaking Roman Catholics and wreck francophone control of the church's prairie dioceses, where four bishops and 78 percent of the clergy were francophone in 1911.[27] Thus in 1902, and again in 1909, Langevin thwarted efforts by Anglo-Manitobans to obtain a compulsory school law and a repeal of bilingual school privileges for languages other than French.[28]

Third, all three provincial governments made concessions in school laws to court the ethnic vote. Liberal party administrations followed this course in Saskatchewan and Alberta, and in Manitoba a Conservative administration did so, with support from Langevin and his clergy.[29]

Fourth, central European ethnic groups, such as Ukrainians, tended to oppose any type of publicly funded schools. Schools cost time, and Ukrainian families needed their children for labour. Schools cost money, and the Ukrainian settlers were poor. Schools taught skills that had little application in the subsistence farm economy. With their large bloc settlements and insular local economies, the settler families sensed that Ukrainian, not English, was the more functional language. In the Old Country many rural districts had a 95 percent illiteracy rates among men – proof that literacy was a frill.[30] The settlers' long-term objective, moreover, was to carry on the subsistence farming of the Old Country, not to become commercial grain farmers. That objective, and the attraction of friends and relatives nearby, explained why they chose homesteads in the park belt rather than on the prairie.

Fifth, a small educated class of Ukrainians worked against the Methodist design for schools. Some were peasants' sons who had had enough schooling in the Old Country to find employment as government agents and newspaper editors.[31] Others had taken courses at government training schools for "foreign" teachers. Either way, the absence of priests from the Old Country churches enhanced their standing in the largely illiterate peasants' settlements. The school teachers in particular were damaging to the Methodist cause. They gave Ukrainian language instruction to the extent that provincial law or local conditions allowed. By 1907 they were nationalists whose teaching valued Ukrainian rather than Anglo-Canadian knowledge. Above all, suggests Orest Martynowych, the educated class challenged the proprietary claim that was the basis for the Anglo-Canadian content. Canada was not an "English" country and never had been. It belonged to all who laboured in it. The ideal of English unilingualism promoted hegemony for an Anglo-Canadian elite, not national unity.[32]

Even so, countervailing influences undermined the insularity of peasant communities. After 1905 prairie Ukrainians were a diverse group that included commercial grain farmers, urban workers, and labourers in resource industries, as well as peasant settler families. Railway branch-line construction brought the Anglo-Canadian world into hitherto remote sections of the bloc settlements. Ukrainian settlers in the bloc settlements discovered that literacy in English helped one to get along. In 1903, John Bodrug, a Manitoba Ukrainian with lower-gymnasium and teacher's seminary education from Galicia, compiled a Ukrainian-English dictionary of three thousand most-needed words. "Everywhere I went," explained Bodrug, "our immigrants begged me to write them a manual of the English language with a lexicon, as they were finding it difficult to get along in Canada without such a handbook."[33]

PRAIRIE UKRAINIANS AND
THE FUTURE OF CANADA

Methodists expected the protestant churches to take up the task of assimilation where the public school left off. They wanted the "foreigners" to have Anglo-Canadian religious values, social values, and culture. The Methodists and Presbyterians opened missions to get the job done. In each case, Ukrainians were the primary ethnic target in the prairie region.

From the Methodist perspective, the Ukrainians were ripe for protestant picking. They arrived without priests from their Old Country churches. Nationalism, potentially a source of resistance, was weakly developed in their peasant culture. Methodists believed that the immigrants had reason to be grateful to Anglo-Canadians. Canada's free lands had liberated them economically from an Old Country landed class. As they acquired literacy and knowledge of protestant Bible truths in Canada, they could break definitively from their "decadent," authoritarian, Old Country churches.

In reality the Ukrainians presented a complex, three-dimensional challenge for missionaries. First, they attracted competition. The number of rival missionary churches increased, as did their resources for mission work. By 1912 the Ukrainian settlements formed a mission field for seven denominations – the Russian Orthodox Church, an Old Country Ukrainian branch of the Canadian Baptist Church, Canada's Roman Catholic Church, with its rival francophone and anglophone branches, a Canadian-Ukrainian Catholic Church, the Independent Greek Church, and the Presbyterian and Methodist Churches.[34]

Second, Ukrainian ethnic nationalism surged on both sides of the Atlantic Ocean about 1907, when the term "Ukrainian" came into use.[35] In Canada its promoters were the small but growing class of educated peasants' sons who were emerging as local leaders. With careers as married priests closed to them (discussed below), they became Ukrainian bilingual school teachers. Here nationalism helped to empower them in a peasant culture that traditionally saw teachers as "loafers." Ukrainians, they insisted, needed an educated class to withstand the nationalist agenda of the anglophone host society.

As nationalism gained popular support, it affected missions. It promoted ethnic churches, Ukrainian priests, and Old Country religious traditions. At the same time, it undermined Old Country liturgical traditions by promoting laymen in the management of church affairs. Ironically, Anglo-Canadians helped to diffuse ethnic nationalism. Their school policies trained the Ukrainian bilingual teachers who inspired the nationalist movement, and their intrusive, assimilative agenda provided a sounding board for an ethnic nationalist reaction.

Third, the Ukrainian peasant's social and economic insularity and the language barrier dampened the Anglo-Protestant missionary's influence. The Ukrainian settlements presented the protestant missionary with dense thickets of relatives and neighbours from Old Country villages who were suspicious of outsiders. The peasant's resistance to protestant persuasion was especially telling during the early years of settlement, when the other dampening influences – competition from the Old Country churches and ethnic nationalism – were negligible.

The Old Country Churches

Of the hundred thousand Ukrainians who had immigrated to the prairie region by 1914, the Austrian provinces of Galicia and Bukovynia supplied 94 percent. Five percent came from Transcarpathia, Hungary, and 1 percent came from the Russian Empire. The 70,500 Galicians outnumbered the 23,500 Bukovynians by three to one.[36] In religion, the Galicians were Greek Catholic, and the Bukovynians were Greek Orthodox. The Bukovynians were the majority in the Star colony in Alberta, where the Methodists opened missions.

The Greek Catholic Church worked under Rome but practised the Eastern rite, not Rome's Latin rite. Its priests were worldly married men who were active in politics and village institutional life. They were the key local leaders in Galician villages in the Ukrainian districts, where 95 percent of the Ukrainians were peasants and 90 percent were illiterate. "Ruthenian priests," explains John-Paul Himka,

did not see their role as limited to preaching the Gospel and administering the sacraments; they felt instead that they owed the community in which they were stationed a more rounded form of service. Many priests instructed their parishioners in agricultural techniques ... Father Naumovych administered homeopathic treatments and fostered beekeeping. On this level of pastoral activity the priest's wife was often a great help. She might set herself up as an amateur apothecary and visit the sick, or ... organize a church sorority or women's club where she taught better ways to sew and cook. The priest thus saw himself as an all-around elevating force in the village, and it was only a natural extension of this self-image to see himself as an activist of the national movement, especially where organizations associated with the movement were so patently beneficial to his parishioners: reading clubs encouraged literacy, cooperatives encouraged thrift and saved peasants from unnecessary exploitation, insurance companies and volunteer fire departments protected the peasants' property, gymnasium clubs built a strong body, and so forth.[37]

Old Country experience shaped the Galician immigrant's response to the Anglo-Canadian and francophone Roman Catholic agendas in Canada.[38] In Galicia in 1910, Ukrainians made up 40 percent of the population, and Poles, including the landed elite, made up 47 percent. Historically the Polish elite aimed to assimilate the Ukrainians into Polish society. They pressed the Greek Catholic Church to Latinize – to become Roman Catholic – and provided schools with Polish-language instruction, a Polish curriculum, and a compulsory-attendance law in 1873. The government did not enforce the law, however, and in 1900 36 percent of the Ukrainian children were not in school. To summarize, the Polish agenda in Galicia gave Ukrainian emigrants a template for the Anglo-Protestant and Franco-Roman-Catholic agendas that awaited them in Canada.

American experience reinforced the Polish experience. During the 1880s Irish American bishops of the Roman Catholic church tried to Latinize the religious life of Ukrainian immigrants. During the 1890s, Rome assisted the bishops with measures that barred married priests from service in North America. This largely ended the supply of Greek Catholic priests, 95 percent of whom were married.

Even without the Roman measures, Canada's prairie region held little attraction for Old Country Greek Catholic priests. In Galicia the Greek Catholic Church was a state church whose priests drew their livings from government subsidies (a government salary, a parish farm) and user fees for church ceremonies. Canada had no state churches. Thus, priests in the prairie region would have needed subsidies from the Austrian state church or contributions from the pioneer peasants' families, who had little money and no experience with a voluntary system of church finance. As it happened, the state church declined to "send" (support financially) bachelor priests to Canada. Thus, Galician Ukrainians in Canada had no Greek Catholic priests, and they had a marked distaste for Roman Catholic substitutes.

In 1910 Ukrainians made up 38 percent of Bukovynia's population, and they were the largest of its ethnic groups. The priests of their Greek Orthodox Church were Ukrainian but worked under an ethnic Rumanian hierarchy. The Bukovynian church declined to send priests to North America, which was under the Russian Orthodox Church's authority. Thus, like Galicians, Bukovynians in Canada were without their traditional Old Country priests.

By 1900 Russia's tsarist regime, in a bid to undermine support for Austria's Hapsburg regime, was spending eighty thousand dollars annually on a Russian Orthodox mission to North America, and in 1905 the Russian mission began a major push in the prairie region. By 1906 it had five (self-supporting) parishes, nineteen missions, and

6,748 adherents. By 1910 it had twenty-seven parishes in Manitoba.[39] With its Russian Ukrainian priests, the mission attracted Bukovynian Ukrainians and also some Galician Ukrainian Catholics.

The supply of priests was modest for the need, however. In 1914 many parishes had religious services only irregularly. Financial improprieties and public drunkenness tarnished the reputation of several priests. Moreover, the peasants' families resented them for demanding large fees, payable in advance, for church ceremonies. Methodist observers viewed the priests as opportunists, but an alternative possibility was that the Russian state salary was too small for a living and the settlers were too short of money to make up the difference.[40]

The Roman Catholic Mission

Like the Polish bishops in Galicia and the Irish-American bishops in the United States, Archbishop Langevin intended to turn Galician Ukrainians into Roman Catholics. The Galician immigrants, however, rejected his celibate French Canadian priests who followed the Latin rite and could not speak Ukrainian. Many of them turned to the Independent Greek Church, a Protestant denomination that immigrants from Galicia founded in Canada in 1903 (see the next section).

Langevin responded by putting a Ukrainian gloss on his Roman mission. First, he recruited priests who spoke Ukrainian.[41] In 1899 he obtained the first of four Belgian Redemptorist monks who undertook language study in central Europe before coming to Canada. Second, with Rome's permission in 1906 he allowed the Redemptorist monks and four French Canadian secular clergy to transfer from the Latin to the Greek rite. In the meantime, Langevin's suffragan bishops in Alberta and Saskatchewan acquired six Ukrainian monks from the Jesuit-reformed Basilian order of the Greek Catholic Church in Galicia.

The changes failed to appease the Galician settlers. The Redemptorist monks and French Canadian priests were celibate ethnic outsiders who lacked fluency in Ukrainian. The Basilian monks, although Ukrainian, were celibate and pious, poor substitutes for the married, worldly secular clergy who organized Galician village life.[42] In 1912 Langevin bowed to the inevitable. Rome gave the Galicians a Ukrainian Catholic diocese under a Galician Ukrainian bishop, Nykyta Budka. Eight secular priests from Galicia bolstered Budka's pastoral staff.

Roman roots in the Galician settlements, however, were shallow. Budka's clergy, for example, had little attraction for Galicians. By Roman dictate, the eight Galician secular priests were bachelors, not married men. The six Basilians from Galicia were not the worldly community leaders that the settlers wanted. The eight others – the four Redemptorist monks and four French Canadian secular priests – were ethnic outsiders who spoke Ukrainian haltingly.[43] In any case, Budka had too few priests to supply some of the settlements with regular services.

In addition, the settlers had acquired a taste for a lay voice in church affairs that Budka refused to recognize. Under Langevin's regime, the settlers had built churches but refused to transfer the ownership of local property to the synod and Langevin's control. When Budka, like Langevin before him, pressed for the transfer of ownership, the settlers refused him.

The Independent Greek Church, 1903–13

As mentioned previously, the Independent Greek Church was founded in 1903. By agreement, the Ukrainians managed the church and supplied it with clergy. The Presbyterian Church paid salaries to its clergy, gave them theological training at Manitoba College, and supported *bursas* (residences) so that Ukrainians could attend high school and college. Presbyterian records show fifteen to twenty thousand supporters of the new church in 1907 and then a declining trend. The support was prairie-wide but declined westward from Manitoba.[44]

The new church arose from unusual conditions in the prairie region.[45] The Galician settlers had no Greek Catholic priests, their traditional community leaders, and they rejected Roman Catholic substitutes. The few Galician men who had had schooling in the Old Country moved into the vacuum of local leadership. Three of them – John Bodrug, Cyril Genik, and John Negrich, all from the village of Bereziv, Galicia, – founded the church. Protestants with the equivalent of high-school matriculation were rare in Galician peasant society, so the Presbyterians jumped at the chance to sponsor them.

Bodrug later described himself and his colleagues as self-taught protestants. After reading the New Testament, they wanted to return the Galician Ukrainian people to the simplicity of the Apostolic Church. Conversely, they rejected popes and liturgy and disliked the Anglican service that the three attended in Winnipeg on account of its "Roman Catholic form of ritual."

Even so, their protestant convictions were convenient, since they attracted Presbyterian sponsorship and provided a religious justification for rejecting Roman Catholicism, in addition to ethnic-nationalist and social-class motives (the Roman priests were an obstacle to the careers of educated Ukrainians as married priests and lay leaders). Finally, the protestant apostolic model of church governance played to Galician popular sentiment by empowering laymen. Under the Independent

Greek Church's constitution, laymen kept ownership of local church property, and the governing body was the *consistory*, which had equal numbers of clergy and laymen: it was not an assembly of bishops.

The new church rejected Roman authority but retained elements of Greek Catholic tradition and otherwise was transitional to protestantism. The consistory form of government was like the Presbyterian form, and priests could marry. The church offered a short service that was Bible-centred, not liturgical, rather than the traditional Greek Catholic long service. Its auricular confession was optional, and its leaders agreed on phasing out traditional rituals that clashed with the Bible.

By 1912 the church's progress toward protestantism was too slow for its Presbyterian sponsors, and in 1913 the Presbyterian general assembly cut off funds for the church and ordained twenty-one of its priests as Presbyterian pastors. Like the Roman Catholics, the Presbyterians were ethnic outsiders, however, and by swallowing the ethnic church, they lost most of its following.

SUMMARY AND CONCLUSION

Methodists regarded non–Anglo-Saxons as less desireable immigrants. They tolerated immigration from the European continent but discouraged government from promoting it, and they favoured the use of medical inspections to screen out the unfit.

Methodists looked chiefly to the public school to turn the non-Anglo-Saxon immigrants into Anglo-Canadians. But to their dismay the provincial governments on the prairies failed to develop their schools to Methodist specifications. Opposition from Archbishop Langevin, a shortage of Anglo-Canadian teachers, the emergence of ethnic bilingual teachers and ethnic nationalism, and resistance from Slavic immigrant groups influenced the outcome. At the same time, countervailing influences were integrating the ethnic communities with the larger society and undermining resistance to the Methodist design.

The Methodist and Presbyterian Churches opened missions among the "foreigners" to continue the work of assimilation where the public school left off. The Ukrainians were the chief ethnic target of the protestant missions. These peasant people had arrived in the prairie region without their priests, their local leaders in the Old Country. Nevertheless, competition from several churches, the emergence of educated laymen as ethnic leaders, the beginnings of ethnic nationalism, and peasant distrust of outsiders made protestant mission work difficult.

From the Methodist standpoint, Ukrainian religious life on the prairies gave rise to three key developments during the years 1896–1914. One was the failure of the francophone Roman Catholic mission and its transformation into a pseudo–Greek Catholic diocese in 1912. The second was the rise and fall of the Independent Greek Church, a failed protestant experiment for Ukrainian lay leaders and their Presbyterian sponsors. The third was the slow diffusion of the Russian Orthodox mission among Bukovynians and some disgruntled Galician Greek Catholics. Bukovynians, however, were the heart of the Russian Orthodox constituency. Bukovynians, in turn, were a majority in the Star colony, where the Methodists located their missions.

The two chapters that follow read like case studies, but they cover 98 percent of the church's non-Anglo-Saxon missions in the prairie region. Chapter 8 treats the All People's Mission in Winnipeg – the prairie region's gateway city, in which ethnic groups intermingled. Chapter 9 examines Methodist missions in Alberta's Star colony, the largest Ukrainian bloc settlement in Canada.

8 All People's Mission, Winnipeg

Winnipeg was the metropolis and the gateway city for non-Anglo-Saxons in the prairie region. In 1911 "foreigners" made up a third of its population of 136,000. Clustered on the north side of the CPR tracks were 37,000 Hebrews, Germans, Ukrainians, Poles, and Scandinavians. Each group was a transient population with personal and institutional ties to the homogeneous bloc settlements in rural districts. For Ukrainians, Winnipeg was "the seat of Latin- and Eastern-rite Catholic bishops, headquarters of the Independent Greek Church and its Presbyterian sponsors, home base for most nationalist school teachers and socialist organizers, who carried their ideas into the rural and frontier regions of Canada, and the address of practically every Ukrainian newspaper in Canada."[1]

Winnipeg Methodists viewed the city's non-Anglo-Saxons as part of "a great national problem." Their "foreign" cultures and rural, peasant backgrounds and their transiency exacerbated the social problems of Winnipeg's lower-class urban life. Thirty "specimen cases," wrote the Reverend S.P. Rose in 1908, would

bring the blush to the face of a young person. Our first visit is to a woman of twenty-eight, by no means repulsive and not in appearance bad. She is morally sound asleep. She is separated from her husband, and has two children, infants, which are not his. Three beds, one table, one bench, two chairs, a stove, which draws badly, a few dishes, never too clean, constitute the furniture. A barrel, with a generous supply of liquor, is prominently in evidence. Smoke fills the house all the time. Eight boarders, all men, share this miserable accommodation with this woman and her two sickly children. Nine adults, three beds and two rooms! And probably these men will help to determine, at the next general election, who shall be Canada's first minister!²

Conversely, the city's north end showed immigrants the worst of Anglo-Canadian culture: the liquor seller, the ward boss, and the capitalist employer who despised them. Methodists responded with the All People's Mission.

THE EARLY YEARS, 1889–1906

In 1889 Dollie Mcguire, "a warmhearted Irish girl," founded Sunday school classes in McDougall Methodist Church for children of German and other nationalities.³ With her outgoing personality and gifts of food and clothing, she overcame language barriers between herself and immigrant families. In 1890 she moved her work to a tent and then to a cheap addition at the rear of McDougall Church, to accommodate the one hundred or more children who attended her classes. The move protected the immigrant's children, with their ethnic dress, from the ridicule of Anglo-Canadian children. In 1891, when the McDougall Church congregation moved to a new building, Mcguire began renting halls, and each move brought her closer to the CPR station and the dominion immigration building, where the immigrants disembarked.⁴

Dollie Mcguire's mission acquired its own building in 1893, when the Methodist Sunday school association of Winnipeg purchased the original McDougall Church building and moved it to a rented lot just north of the CPR station. To mark the occasion, the mission's staff printed the last seven words of Isaiah 5:7 – "My house shall be called a house of prayer for all people" – on a sign in eight languages. Henceforth All People's became the popular name for the mission. In 1902 the Methodists purchased the Maple Street Congregational Church to house it.

Three German-speaking teachers and a series of pastors served the mission during the years 1893–1905. The pastors included Thomas E. Morden from Ontario, formerly a missionary to Germans in Ontario and Manitoba; Manitoba-born Thomas Eli Taylor; Richard L. Morrison, MD, a medical missionary; and Alfred A. Thompson from Ontario. The mission held Sunday school classes, prayer meetings three nights a week, mothers' meetings, and house visitations. It gave relief to the poor and sick, distributed English-language periodicals, assisted men in finding employment, and operated a reading room with newspapers in several languages.

Despite the busyness at All People's, most Winnipeg Methodists were unaware of it until 1898, when the expected arrival of 12,000 Ukrainians drew attention to the immigration question.[5] Officials of Zion Methodist Church urged the construction of a large building to replace both All People's and Zion church. As Thomas Morden explained,

In the part of the city ... which is first seen by strangers arriving there, Methodism ... is not well represented. Zion church is out of sight, a block away from Main Street and hidden by buildings ... All People's is directly in front of the CPR passenger station, [but] it is a little, unpretentious building which does not at all accord with the idea of Europeans who have heard of the Methodist church as the largest Christian body in America. The question has now been raised whether it is not possible to ... erect ... a building of which the denomination need not be ashamed. The carrying out of this plan would mean the placing of a large church in the populous part of the city, where there are now numerous hotels, many temporary residents and a large proportion of citizens who are not of the wealthy class. The energy of the different denominations has, in the past, been directed away from this part of the city, every new church, with the exception of the small mission buildings having been erected some distance to the south ... there is ... a danger of putting up too many small buildings where a smaller number of the better class would be a greater source of strength ... a large and respectable church, with an active membership meaning business, situated right in the main thoroughfare ... surrounded by the rush of travellers and immigrants, would have a field of usefulness well worth cultivating.

"It is just at this stage," he added, "that a little personal interest taken, and a friendly handshake given for Christ's sake would tell for good for all time to come."[6]

In 1899 All People's became a mission and was therefore eligible for a Missionary Society grant, instead of being simply a private venture of Winnipeg's Methodist churches. The status of mission required church members, so the All People's staff reported themselves as such to meet the requirement.[7] By January 1904 British immigrants were replacing non-Anglo-Saxon immigrants in the mission's catchment area.[8] Thus the mission's superintendent, Alfred Thompson, judged that the non-Anglo-Saxon work was in an "unprogressive state" and called for a "complete change of policy with a new location, different equipment, and an increase of supervision."[9]

In 1905 the Missionary Society opened a second mission, Bethlehem Slavic, on Stella Avenue and placed it under the Reverend Jaromir V. Kovar, an Austrian-born protestant. Kovar held services in German, Slavic, and Bohemian, and an Austrian protestant woman, a Miss Kochella, held Sunday school classes. An Austrian-Czech protestant, Frank Dojacek, served the mission as a colporteur, selling thousands of Bibles and religious tracts below cost, advising immigrants about Canada, and giving comfort and lunches to the distressed.

By 1907 the Bethlehem Slavic Mission reached four hundred immigrants of sixteen nationalities. Kovar held cottage meetings in Polish and Austrian homes for some 220 adults, including 22 families and their boarders.[10] He and Dojacek also held biweekly religious services and distributed religious tracts in a rural Ukrainian settlement north of the city, at Beauséjour and Brokenhead.[11] On average, 48 children attended the mission's Sunday school and 41 attended its night school classes.[12]

Dojacek spoke to the people in their native tongue but found that "they do not like [it] if I refer to their personal need of salvation. At one they say, 'I have and keep my own religion.'"[13] The high turnover of the immigrant population made gains difficult. As Kovar discovered, 80 percent of the adults to whom he ministered were boarders. Much of his progress was among the few immigrants who were already protestant. In 1906 he formed a separate mothers' meeting for German protestants, whom he found easier to reach than Polish Roman Catholics and Lithuanians.

The original Maple Street mission catered increasingly to British immigrants. Nevertheless, its superintendent during the year 1905–6, the Reverend Hamilton Wigle from Ontario, reported that only 8 of his 45 Sabbath scholars had English as their mother tongue. At his special children's service in January 1906, "a striking feature of the program was a national representative chorus by thirteen girls of thirteen nationalities. It was most impressive to hear them singing in one tongue and one faith ... we need hardly draw the attention of our thinking readers that this children's work means the Protestantizing and Canadianizing of 215 mothers and homes in the near future."[14]

In December 1905 Wigle wrote to every pastor in the prairie conferences that "these people are soon to be a part of us, and we ought to be doing something to mould their religious life, and to bring them to the social, educational and religious status of our Canadian civilization."[15] He urged each pastor to count the "foreigners" in his area and secure young men from each nationality for theological instruction at Wesley College. Wigle believed that the immigrants would respond better to missionaries from their own ranks than to Anglo-Canadians. Wigle's approach also would free Canadian-born missionaries for the undermanned Anglo-Canadian mission work. Whatever its merit, Wigle's idea was not to prevail.

In 1907 Winnipeg's Methodist city mission board turned the Maple Street and Bethlehem Slavic Missions into branches of a multiple-site

All People's Mission. It named the Reverend James Shaver Woodsworth as the first superintendent of the consolidated mission. J.S. Woodsworth's family connections helped him to land the job. His father, James, was the chair of the city mission board, a member of the Wesley College board, and the senior superintendent of missions for western Canada.

MISSION IDEOLOGY DURING THE WOODSWORTH ERA

The literature for All People's focuses on Woodsworth, but the mission was more than its superintendent. Wesley College and Winnipeg's Methodist churches supported it. In 1911 its staff included fifteen full-time workers, two probationers from Wesley College during the summer months, and one hundred volunteers from Wesley College and city churches. The staff, in turn, commonly differed from Woodsworth in their views of immigrants and Methodist religion.

Woodsworth's Views of Immigrants

Woodsworth saw humanity as a hierarchy of biological and cultural "races," headed by Anglo-Saxons and Northern European peoples. Asians, blacks, natives, and Slavs were at the bottom.[16] "In his own mind," observes Mills, Woodsworth sought "the betterment of his inferiors. The foreigners were a "problem." They were arriving in too large numbers and their customs, unless altered, were likely to be a deadweight upon the superior standards of the Anglo-Canadian way of life."[17]

Although Woodsworth was later to appreciate immigrant traditions, in 1909 his *Strangers within Our Gates* sounded a nativist note. Whereas immigrants from northern Europe were "able to care for themselves," those from southeastern Europe posed "an entirely different problem. Most of these are Roman or Greek Catholic or Jews. They, too, bring their religions, but often these are not of a very high order." Even Jewish immigrants (nine thousand strong in Winnipeg in 1911) came largely "from Russia, Austria and Roumania, and constitute an entirely different class from those who come from England or Germany." With eastern-European Jews, explained Woodsworth in 1911, nationality more than religion bound the younger generations to their synagogues. In Canada, however, without the persecution of their homelands (pogroms, police repression), their nationalism and their attachment to synagogues, was likely to fade.[18]

Anglo-Protestant experience in Quebec coloured Woodsworth's views of Roman Catholicism as a religion for immigrants.[19] The Word of God was a closed book in many francophone homes in Quebec. Rome was the sworn enemy of British liberties and principles: it aimed for nothing less than a restoration of Roman Catholic orthodoxy, backed by force. Regional circumstances on the prairies possibly reinforced the Quebec analogy in Woodsworth's thinking. Mgr Adélard Langevin, the francophone Roman Catholic archbishop of St Boniface vigorously opposed the assimilation of prairie immigrants into Anglo-Canadian society.

Even so, "the Catholic peoples of southern and eastern Europe" were not "the French Catholic question over again. So different are the two that if we declined absolutely to establish missions among the French, we still might consider the advisability of missions among these peoples." First, many of the immigrants were without any religious services. "In Winnipeg," noted Woodsworth,

there is a large Polish church with missions in outlying points, and a Ruthenian (Greek Catholic) church with several missions. There are also a number of scattered missions among Poles and Hungarians. But a study of the *Catholic Directory* reveals a surprisingly small number of distinctively foreign churches. The Redemptorist Fathers at Brandon and Yorkton, and the Benedictine Sisters at Winnipeg devote themselves largely to work among the Poles. The Basilian Fathers of the Greek United Rite at Winnipeg and the Sisters, Little Servants of Mary, are working among the Ruthenians.[20]

Second, Roman Catholicism was not a national religion for the immigrants, as it was for French Canadians. Galician Slavs were Roman Catholic because Polish overlords had forced the religion on them "three hundred years ago." Polish immigrants were solidly Roman Catholic, but the hierarchy in the prairie region was French Canadian, not Polish.

Third, poverty, ethnic hatred, ignorance, and authoritarian churches had kept the Slavic immigrants outside the pale of Austrian and Russian civilization. "The great majority" were

Roman or Greek Catholics. They are peasants, the majority illiterate and superstitious; some of them bigoted fanatics, some of them poor, dumb, driven cattle, some intensely patriotic, some embittered by years of wrong and oppression, some anarchists – the sworn enemies alike of church and State. The Slav is essentially religious, but his religious instincts have never found true expression. The move to a new land means a shaking of the very foundations of belief. The old associations are left behind, the mind is prepared for new impressions, the individual is thrown into an entirely different social life, and is enveloped by a different religious atmosphere. Sometimes he may cling tenaciously, desperately, to the old beliefs; often he renounces them entirely. Modifications must take place. The desire for light and liberty lies behind even the excesses into which some plunge. Light and liberty – these are what are needed.[21]

In 1907 a Polish woman, Mrs Vasafrshki, exemplified the problem in Winnipeg. As she told Woodsworth, "I went to confession a few times. The priest began to ask me some awful questions ... In the church he points to a picture of the Virgin Mary and says 'There she stands, asking you to give her money. She wants to buy a new dress.'" "There are people who believe that," observed Woodsworth, "but Mrs Vasafrshki is more enlightened."[22]

The immigrant threat to Anglo-Canadian religious culture was a subtle one. As Woodsworth explained,

We shall inevitably become more or less a part of all we meet ... we hear of Greek Catholics, Syrian Catholics ... and a score of other sects of whom we had not even read in our histories ... They are here to stay ... [and] we are forced to live and let live. We are coming to realize that they have been brought up in a certain way, and we sometimes grudgingly admit that their religion is perhaps good enough for them. In doing so, our old exclusive conceptions are broken down ... Here, indeed, lies a most important question. Will the broadening of our ideal and the breaking down of our bigotry carry with it the lowering of our own moral standards?[23]

Paradoxically, the immigrants threatened Canada with atheism as well as Old World religious tradition. "As time goes on," continued Woodsworth, "better education and frequent intercourse with English-speaking Protestants and the prevailing spirit of the new world tend inevitably to weaken the power of the church. Men especially refuse to be guided by those whom they regard as their exploiters.[24] In the circumstances, he detected "a danger that these people may do as they have in the United States – break away from the bondage of Rome and yet not enter into the liberty of the children of God."[25]

Finally, the heterogenous immigration militated against "that one-ness of purpose without which true national life is impossible."[26] "How much more serious the question is with us," Woodsworth added, "when we consider that we are not as yet a united nation, but that again and again in various forms we are forced to recognize the cleavage between French and English."[27]

Woodsworth's *My Neighbor* (1911) added a sociological critique to the immigration problem. His starting point was urbanization. Within a few years, he predicted, "half our population will be living in cities and large towns." Based on British and American experience, Woodsworth worried that Canada's cities would develop slums and "whole foreign wards with their mixed population from Southeastern Europe." The "foreigners," with their ignorance and inexperience with democracy, were easy prey for corrupt ward bosses.[28] In their willingness to work for low wages, they undermined the living standards of Anglo-Canadian labourers and contributed to slum conditions.[29] Meanwhile, their "conditions of living and standards of morality were not such as to qualify them for becoming good Canadian citizens without a good deal of educating and refining."[30]

In 1908 Woodsworth doubted that "the danger in the city is great at the present time. We haven't the pauper class of the old land."[31] The poor were new arrivals in Canada who accepted substandard living conditions temporarily in order to win a foothold in Canadian life. Their poverty would end once they had paid their transportation bill and had saved enough to bring out their families.[32] Moreover, unemployment and crowded living conditions were to some extent a seasonal problem.[33] What worried Woodsworth was the future. With British and American experience in mind, he feared that the temporary conditions in Winnipeg could become permanent.[34]

The question for protestant Canadians, insisted Woodsworth, was how best to "help their Catholic and Jewish neighbors" who had "become part of our community; we cannot ignore their presence; we cannot be indifferent about their welfare. Here we encounter one of the most serious problems that has ever faced our Canadian People. The Protestant church ... is on trial."[35] Each age assigned its specific task to the church, which in Woodsworth's age was "the establishment of the Kingdom of God on the earth. The new conception of the missionary enterprise is not only the salvation of individuals but the uplifting and redemption of nations and races."[36] "As Christians" Methodists owed the immigrants "all that has purified and elevated and enriched our lives. We owe it to them to convince them that religion is not mere ecclesiasticism, nor faith superstition, nor worship ritualism."[37]

Woodsworth's nativism gradually mellowed.[38] By 1913 he saw the "foreigner" as "our equal, in some respects our superior, and ... if he becomes a menace to our civilization the fault is not really his, but is due to the peculiar conditions surrounding him in a new land and our general indifference to his welfare." Woodsworth saw value in immigrant languages, subject to the "unifying influences of the school" and the thorough teaching of English.

Woodsworth's Evangelicalism

By 1907 Woodsworth was embracing a radical social gospel, one with a moderate program for social reform but a radical expression of the Methodist evangelical tradition. Whereas the church's mainstream held that social and personal salvation were complementary goals, Woodsworth had lost faith in personal salvation and saw its quest as competitive with the social gospel. As he argued in 1906, "Jesus said little about saving souls [but] spoke often about the establishment of the Kingdom."[39] "We want more to save our age than our nervous dying souls," he exclaimed in 1910.[40] In 1914 a "Lover of Zion" praised Woodsworth for having "done a good work," but called on him to stop giving "hard knocks" to a church that had "great patience with him" and had given him "plenty of scope to air his peculiar notions." Time and again in "summer schools, League and Sunday school conventions," Woodsworth had "held up to scorn the idea of getting souls converted, and magnified institutional work." Far from opposing self-ishness in the church, Woodsworth had promoted it by "making light of personal religious experience, and making more of the football club than of the prayer meeting in the church."[41]

In 1907 Woodsworth claimed that he had never experienced conversion. Although this was common for Methodists of his age, Christie and Gauvreau dispute his claim – Woodsworth's diary entry for 10 August 1896 reported that he "gave himself to Christ."[42] In any case, if Woodsworth had found faith in 1896, then he had lost it by 1907. He dismissed Biblical descriptions of supernatural events as "superstitions" or "mere traditions." He no longer accepted standard Methodist doctrines such as original sin, Christ's atonement, the virgin birth, the physical resurrection and ascension into heaven, and the authority of the scriptures. Thus Woodsworth tendered his resignation from the ministry, stating that "un-Methodist" beliefs made him unsuitable for pastoral work. How could he help others find personal salvation when he could not help himself?

Out of respect for his father, neither Woodsworth nor the church wanted his resignation, so he withdrew it when the conference refused it, found his beliefs acceptable, and gave him an alternative to pastoral work – the superintendency of All People's, now a multiple-branch city mission. His new job was heavily administrative. He was "a sort of business manager, promoter, publicity agent, collector, clerk and messenger boy all rolled into one."[43] At the same time, he had the conference's blessing to engage the social gospel, while avoiding the issue of personal salvation.

Woodsworth is controversial in the literature. Mills makes the conventional argument that Woodsworth blundered by entering the ministry. His "religious experience had been a hollow and superficial one, a second-hand habit passed down from his parents." It consisted of belief in "good works" (personal purity) but was lacking in a spiritual experience of God. For Woodsworth, "God was present in nature and the world but mainly he was *out there* and at a distance."[44]

In contrast, Christie and Gauvreau locate Woodsworth's religious journey in the Methodist mainstream.[45] His rejection of Methodist doctrinal standards expressed a popular rejection of an elitist, theologically laden evangelicalism of the (late) nineteenth century. Conversely, his social gospel marked a return to the emotional, experiential religion of the early nineteenth-century North American frontier. Contrary to his claim in 1907, Woodsworth had experienced conversion. His persistent religious doubt expressed a traditional Methodist quest for holiness, not a descent into unbelief. At the same time, Woodsworth was ambitious and manipulative. His attempted resignations expressed an "unfulfilled ambition to replicate his father's status as a prominent church leader" and "extreme individualism and restiveness" in the face of church strictures upon the freedom of individual ministers. His letter of resignation in 1907 was a "ploy to get a permanent appointment at All Peoples."

The revisionist Christie-Gauvreau portrait is the more persuasive, but it is overdrawn. Its ambitious, manipulative Woodsworth fits uneasily with its idealistic interpretation of his religious culture. It dismisses Woodsworth's statements about his religious experience and attempted resignations, and it obscures what Woodsworth saw as the central development in his religious journey. That is, it turns his explicit testimony about loss of faith in personal salvation into routine "religious doubt" during a quest for holiness. It attributes evangelical activities at the mission, incorrectly, to Woodsworth.[46]

In contrast to Woodsworth, many of the one hundred or so full-time staff and volunteers were out to save souls and used social services to "bait the gospel hook." The Maple Street and Bethlehem Slavic branches regularly held revival meetings and won converts because this suited their congregations of English Methodist immigrants. During his years at All People's (1911–14), the Reverend Edmund Chambers acknowledged a need for "social work ... to acquaint [the immigrants] with their duties and privileges as citizens of a democratic country." He also noted "a deeper and more important effort to be made to change the heart and point them to the glorious liberty of the children of God ... confident in the power and prayers of His people, we can go forward knowing that His kingdom will come in the hearts and lives of men as well as in their social environment.[47] In 1911 Arthur Rose, a probationer at All People's and Woodsworth's successor as superintendent in 1913, urged his colleagues to "preach salvation" to Polish immigrants rather than the "Gospel of Canadian citizenship."[48] "Instead of trying to cover a lot of ground as in the past," opined the Reverend William Somerville in 1912, at the opening of an All People's settlement house, "workers will go out after individuals – and send converts out after others."[49] Simply put, Woodsworth's radical social gospel did not define All People's. It was unusual among his colleagues at the mission, and some of them disputed it.

DEVELOPMENTS AT THE MISSION, 1907–13

During Woodsworth's superintendency, the mission expanded its facilities, increased its staff, and emphasized "work among non-English-speaking peoples."[50] The missionaries commonly sought to sway the values of the immigrants but not to turn them into Methodists. Major developments were the resignations of the mission's three Austrian protestant workers (1907), the opening of two institutional buildings (1908–9), the attempted capture of a Polish Catholic congregation (1908–12), the introduction of People's Forum meetings (1910), and the opening of two social settlements (1912).

The Austrian Protestant Staff

None of the Austrian protestant workers at Bethlehem Slavic Mission survived the centralization of Winnipeg's city missions in 1907. The development was curious, given Hamilton Wigle's endorsement of convert missionaries for non-Anglo-Saxon mission work. In February 1906, moreover, James H. Morgan, the president of the Manitoba conference, had recommended Dojacek for "special ordination."[51]

Perhaps the Austrians had moved on. By February 1906, Jaromir Kovar had received calls from two protestant Bohemian congregations in Saskatchewan.[52] During the years 1905–14, Frank Dojacek evolved from a distributor of Methodist religious tracts into Winnipeg's pre-eminent ethnic publisher and bookseller, starting with a "suitcase full of books" and selling "farm to farm, house to house."[53]

Alternatively, the Austrians were pushed. In this scenario, the church's city mission board preferred "one their own" for the key appointment, or perhaps nepotism was at work, or both. So, as mentioned, it chose Woodsworth, a unilingual Anglo-Canadian and the board chair's son, to superintend the consolidated mission, and it passed over the foreign-born, multilingual Kovar. With Woodsworth in charge, Dojacek was expendable, and so the Manitoba conference refused him "special ordination." These are speculations, however. The writer's sources do not show whether the Austrians were pushed or moved on.

The Institutes

All People's added two new institute buildings: a $15,000 building on Sutherland Avenue in 1908 and a twelve-thousand-dollar building on

Stella Avenue in 1909. In both cases, the missionary society contributed five thousand dollars, and Winnipeg Methodists paid the balance. Each building furnished a swimming tank, a reading room, gymnasium equipment, and a library, as alternatives to unsavoury recreational outlets.[54]

The institutes were signatures of Woodsworth's approach to missions. He lived with his family beside the Stella Avenue facility, with his home "open to the people" and functioning, effectively, as the mission's first settlement house. Meanwhile, two older centres (Maple Street and Bethlehem Slavic) catered primarily to Old Country English Methodists.

The full-time staff increased from nine to fifteen between 1908 and 1911. In 1909 it consisted of Woodsworth, a second ordained clergyman, three deaconesses, and four kindergarten teachers. By 1911 it had another four deaconesses and a boys' worker. Two probationers from Wesley College joined the mission during the summer months, and one hundred volunteers from Wesley College and city churches assisted the full-time staff. In 1909 local churches paid half the mission's ten-thousand-dollar annual budget. The balance came from the Missionary Society and the WMS.

The mission reached hundreds of immigrants through its varied activities. In 1908 it contacted 138 children and 200 homes through kindergarten work, largely because the city's public schools did not offer it. It also enroled 300 girls in sewing and kitchen garden classes, taught English to 100 persons in night classes, attracted 70 women to mothers' meetings, and reached others through house visitation.[55]

The Polish Catholic Project

Woodsworth sought to sway the values of immigrants but not to make them Methodists. As he reasoned, peasant peoples could not suddenly embrace Methodist beliefs and forms. By race and temperament, they required the warmth and colour of their traditional ritualistic service and could change only gradually to protestantism.[56] One strategy was to reform ethnic national churches that had broken free of their Old World parent denominations. The Presbyterians attempted this by supporting the Independent Greek Church, and Woodsworth approved. The Ukrainian adherents of the Independent Greek Church were "Ignorant – yes, but eager for knowledge. Superstitious, yes – but breaking the bonds that have held them for centuries. Peasants – yes, but a people who are becoming Canadian citizens."[57]

In 1908 Woodsworth spotted an opportunity with the Polish Independent Church. This immigrant Catholic church rejected Roman authority and claimed two hundred thousand members in North America in 1904, when Poles in Winnipeg organized its first Canadian congregation.[58] In 1908 a financial crisis forced the Winnipeg congregation to default on the mortgage of its Burrows Avenue church. Winnipeg Methodists bought the building but allowed the Poles to use it. In a letter to his cousin C.B. Sissons, Woodsworth marvelled at the

Methodist church with altar and crucifixes and candles and holy water and confessional, etc. A Methodist Catholic church. Well, it is a ticklish business but we intend to keep the congregation with the church. They claim to have about 200 families in the parish. An old priest has been ministering to them. We will permit them to carry on their services in much their own way. We don't appear in the matter. Simply give them the privilege to continue to use the church which they built but which is now controlled by us. Then our man will preach the Gospel to them, distribute the Bible among them and induce them to send their children to the Public Schools. Our hope is that if the light is given and the truth implemented that the useless forms will slough off. Independence from Rome is not necessarily Reformation but affords the opportunity for Reformation.[59]

Meanwhile, the Methodists made the building a branch of All People's and used it for Polish mission work. Two of the branch's staff, B. Baligrodzki and A. Sosnowski, were young Poles who attended Wesley College on $150 scholarships from the Missionary Society. Baligrodzki served as interpreter for Methodist Sunday school classes and mothers' meetings, held Methodist religious services, and helped to reform the Polish congregation by "taking down pictures of the Polish saint and changing the name of the church from that of St Mary of —— (Polish tradition) to the Church of Our Saviour, at the same time getting rid of the statue of the Virgin. This is a big step. They ask why. He explains. They are thinking about it and talking about it. These illiterate peasants have never questioned [their religious practices] before."[60]

In 1909 Woodsworth regretted his mission's inability "to secure satisfactory foreign workers" for work among older immigrant boys.[61] To remedy the deficiency, students at Wesley College sponsored a probationer, Edmund Chambers, for two years in Poland, to learn the Polish language and customs. In 1911 Chambers took a Polish bride.[62] In 1910 a second probationer, Arthur Rose, left for three years in Poland, and a Polish protestant, Paul Kupka, joined the staff at the Burrows Avenue branch.

In Europe, Arthur Rose learned that German and Russian efforts to denationalize Poles had in fact hardened them against assimilation. "This knowledge," opined Rose, "should somewhat change our tactics in mission work. We have preached too much, through the press at least, the Gospel of Canadian citizenship. The result has been that these people, driven to us by denationalizing forces, have scented danger and have avoided us. We must therefore preach salvation to *Polish people*, and we shall find that not only will they more readily accept our teaching, but [they] will sooner become Canadian citizens and better ones."[63]

In 1912 the Polish Independent congregation closed the Burrows Avenue branch by buying back their building.[64] A year later the Presbyterian experiment with the Independent Greek church ended badly. These outcomes helped to discredit the strategy of using ethnic convert clergy to protestantize and Canadianize non-Anglo-Saxons.

With the outbreak of the First World War, Methodist specialists in Polish mission work moved on. Paul Kupka became a probationer at Wesley College in 1914 but left the ministry within two years. Edmund Chambers enlisted in the armed forces and then did YMCA work in Poland, his wife's homeland, after the war. Thomas E. Welsh trained for Polish mission work at All People's by attending college in Przymsi, Galicia, in 1913. He was interned during the war and withdrew from the ministry in 1923, when the Manitoba conference enquired about his intentions. Arthur Rose replaced Woodsworth as superintendent of All People's in 1913 and was ordained in 1916. In 1921 he left All People's to attend medical college. On his graduation in 1924, he opened a Ukrainian hospital mission in Hafford, Saskatchewan.

The People's Forum

In 1910 Woodsworth rented the Grand Theatre on Sunday afternoons for people's forum meetings.[65] These gatherings were modelled after the "pleasant Sunday afternoons" that Woodsworth had observed in the Mansfield settlement house in London, England. Save for hymns and the occasional address about patriotism or Christianity in its broad sense, they had no religious content.[66] Instead, the forums presented guest speakers and discussions on scientific, economic, and social questions that held general interest, and there were social activities in the evenings. Examples of lecture topics were "the social segregation of vice," "popular astronomy," "the single tax," "direct legislation," "Shakespeare and his view of life," and the "new social revolution."[67] By mixing the different nationalities, the meetings eroded ethnic exclusivity.[68] They also furnished moral instruction for persons missed by the church's regular channels.[69] To judge by newspaper reports, the people's forum was a great success. Up to twelve hundred persons, mostly English-speaking, attended the afternoon sessions. An average of eight hundred persons, many of whom were "foreigners," attended social functions in the evenings.[70]

Settlement Work

Taken from British and American models, settlement houses were homes in immigrant districts for "average Canadians." The resident workers kept the homes attractive and devoted one evening each week to social work. In this way, the houses were islands of Anglo-Canadian influence. To an extent, Woodsworth's home served the purpose, but the first official settlement houses opened in 1912. North End House was for the mission's female staff, and Sutherland Court was for Wesley College students.[71]

Woodsworth's Resignation

In July 1913 Woodsworth resigned from All People's to become secretary of the newly formed Canadian Welfare League. The salvation of society, he now believed, required a community-wide response and specialist knowledge. Secular agencies were better suited to the task than churches, with their denominational divisions, doctrines, creeds, and preoccupation with needs of their own people. Apart from institutional work, such as that of All People's, the church's role was chiefly inspirational. Church members could serve on secular agencies that dealt with specialist issues, such as child welfare, and report back to their congregations on the social needs and ways in which church members could help. After six years in the church's "limited role," Woodsworth was ready for the front lines of Canada's social battles.[72]

   With Woodsworth's leaving, All People's lost a respected but controversial leader. In October 1913, members of the general board of missions regretted that Woodsworth "had been allowed to pass out of [church] work into the hands of a secular organization."[73] Mrs. W.E. Ross, the president of the WMS, wrote Woodsworth that

Lofty ideals, vision, and enthusiasm are not given to every man, and but few combine vision and the practical mind which enables them to bring their dreams to life ... Before your day, the Women's Missionary Society gave of its money to All Peoples. But the continually changing personnel was very trying and did not tend to increase confidence either in its effectiveness or its stability, but your advent brought a new day in which we have been glad to help in every way possible and stand ready to increase our grant when it becomes necessary.[74]

   A "Lover of Zion," in contrast, complained that Woodsworth had over-emphasized institutional work and scorned the work of saving souls.[75] Similarly the Reverend William Somerville had earlier

denounced the secular tone of the people's forum meetings. In a letter
to James Allen in 1911, he had asked, "what do you think of the way
the Reverend J.S. Woodsworth is spending his Sundays and the time
and money of the Methodist people ... I have no desire to undervalue
the work of Bro. Woodsworth for he has good organizing ability, nor
am I anxious to go heresy hunting ... But I say All People's Mission
has better work to do, and I hope you will see to it that mere amuse-
ment will not be held out as the chief work for a Sunday evening."[76]

George Moody, the Winnipeg barrister, and the Reverend Wellington Bridgman, a past president of the Manitoba conference (1907)
and a superannuated clergyman at Grace Church, judged that the
attention to "foreigners" at All People's was disastrous for Methodist
interests. As Bridgman complained,

We built two institutes in the North End in which we locked up the sum of
$25,000 and a Methodist preacher speaking of them the other day denomi-
nated them as two heaps of junk which were paying the church no appreciable
dividend. While we were putting Methodist money and missionary money in
"Institutes" the Presbyterians consistently stayed with their Immigration Chaplain in the Immigration Hall meeting incoming settlers and finding work for
the unemployed. As a result the only two strong churches in the North End
to-day are both owned by the Presbyterians and the foundation of their third
new church is erected. *Dr Mclean's Bethel Mission* has a Sunday school with an
average attendance of 340 per Sunday and that is more than the united
attendance of *the two institutes and Maple Street.*[77]

Arthur Rose, the bilingual Polish specialist mentioned earlier,
replaced Woodsworth as superintendent. In contrast to Woodsworth,
Rose valued personal salvation and down-played the "gospel of Canadian citizenship." Harry Atkinson joined the staff as a specialist in
foreign-boy's work in 1913. Otherwise, the mission's activities – institutional work, kindergartens, Sunday schools, and rescue work – were
stable through to 1925, when Methodists entered into the United
Church of Canada. The mission's nonsectarian, nonproselytizing
character also was long-standing.[78]

SUMMARY AND CONCLUSION

Clearly the All People's Mission was a complex affair. In general, it
aimed to turn immigrants into Protestant Anglo-Canadians with
upper-working-class and lower-middle-class living standards. The goals
of its staff varied, however. The "gospel of Canadian citizenship" was
important to Woodsworth but not to Arthur Rose or to non-Anglo-

Canadian personnel such as Miss Kochella, Frank Dojacek, Jaromir Kovar, B. Baligrodzki, and A. Sosnowski. Whereas J.S. Woodsworth embraced the radical social gospel, his staff valued personal, as well as social, salvation.

Woodsworth gained widespread respect from Methodists, but he was also controversial. Officials of the church's two missionary societies and Winnipeg's city mission board appreciated Woodsworth's leadership in institutional work, promotional activities, and organization skills. Other Methodists faulted him for scorning the evangelical side of the work. Some regarded any non-Anglo-Saxon mission work as a waste of Methodist resources.

The mission, in fact, turned few "foreigners" into Methodists. In 1914 the original Maple Street mission reported 131 members, but these were Old Country Methodists who had displaced the earlier non-Anglo-Saxon population. The institutes on Stella Avenue and Sutherland Avenue reported 38 members, but this number included staff and possibly Old Country protestants.

Indeed, making Methodists was a low priority at the mission for strategic reasons. "Foreigners" such as Poles had learned resistance to assimilationist agendas in the Old Country. At best, they could be brought gradually into protestantism. Thus the All People's staff tried to influence the values of "foreigners" without making them Methodists. One approach – the failed Polish project – was to reform an ethnic church through the use of financial support and ethnic-convert missionaries. A second approach was to convert the "foreigners" to protestant values. Staff members tried to win immigrant souls for Christ, particularly the souls of children in Sunday school and kindergarten classes. They also tried to steer the "foreigners" towards Methodist holiness by presenting staff as exemplars of the Christ-life.

All People's, with its institutes, settlement houses, and varied activities, was suited to the mixed ethnic population of the prairie metropolis. It was the prototype for All People's Missions in other Canadian cities, including Edmonton and Brandon, in the prairie region.[79] The majority of the prairie "foreigners," however, lived in rura bloc settlements of one ethnic group. Here, too, the Methodist church responded, for example, in Alberta's Star colony, Canada's largest Ukrainian bloc settlement.

9 The Ukrainian Missions in Alberta

During the quarter century after 1900, Methodists opened missions in Canada's largest Ukrainian settlement – Alberta's Star colony – and in nearby Edmonton. In 1912 the Methodist Ruthenian Workers in Alberta held their first annual convention and launched the *Canadian*, a Ukrainian-language newspaper. By 1914 the church had six missions and a staff of forty missionaries, missionaries' wives, doctors, nurses, cooks, domestics, and interpreters. After 1914 the church reorganized its Alberta missions and opened five Ukrainian missions in Saskatchewan and Manitoba (table 9.1).

By 1916 the Methodists had forty Ukrainian church members and two Ukrainian parsons. Most of the mission's staff, however, placed less priority on gaining church members than on saving souls, promoting moral uplift, and making Anglo-Canadians. In the process, they and the Ukrainian settlers touched each other's lives more deeply than the meagre statistics for church membership would suggest.

THE STAR COLONY

In 1892 Ukrainian peasant families began to take up homesteads in the Star colony, a 640-square-mile area that extended from thirty to seventy miles northeast of Edmonton (see map). The majority were Greek Orthodox families from Bukovynia. Most of the others were Greek Catholic families from Galicia, and the rest were Greek Orthodox families from Russia and Rumania.

Table 9.1
Methodist Ukrainian Missions in the Prairie Region, 1900–25

Mission	Society	Years	Special Facilities
Alberta			
Pakan	GBM	1900–21	Hospital (1906)
Wahstao	WMS, GBM	1904–25	School Home
Kolokreeka	WMS	1908–25	School Home
Edmonton	WMS, GBM	1908–25	Hostel, Institutional
Chipman	GBM, WMS	1910–25	
Lamont	GBM	1912–25	Hospital
Andrew	GBM	1915–21	
Smoky Lake	GBM	1921–25	Hospital, Community Centre
Radway	WMS	1921–25	School Home
Saskatchewan			
Insinger	GBM	1915–25	Community Centre, Nurse (1922)
Calder	GBM	1920–25	Community Centre
Yorkton	GBM	1920–25	School Home
Hafford	GBM	1921–25	Hospital, 1922–25
Manitoba			
Vita	GBM	1918–25	Hospital (1923)

Note: GBM = General Board of Missions; WMS = Women's Missionary Society.

The colony's largely Ukrainian Slav population reached 5,715 in 1901, 16,593 in 1911, and 33,053 in 1921.[1] Some of them migrated to Edmonton, whose Slav population reached 1,398 in 1911 and 3,959 in 1921. The numbers seemed larger to Methodists than the census figures showed. After travelling around the colony on three sides in 1919, the Reverend J.K. Smith estimated "at least 50,000 souls."[2] Methodist estimates for Ukrainians in Edmonton were 2,000 in 1911 and 5,000 in 1913.[3]

The Ukrainian settler aimed to reproduce the subsistence farming of the Old County, but with ample cheap land for his children and no landlord. Commercial farming was difficult in any case. The homesteads were thirty to one hundred miles from the nearest railway station, and around the town of Bellis the soil was "poor and stony" or "all sand."[4]

A settler family required five years or more to turn its homestead into a viable farm with cleared fields, livestock, and a traditional log house with plastered walls and thatched roof. The job required capital – $975 to $1,425. Some settlers had some funds from the sale of small farms in the Old Country, but in most cases, the male family head worked seasonally in railway construction, lumbering, or mining to raise additional monies.

The men lived "at fighting weight on the minimum of food and a maximum of toil."[5] So did their wives. In her husband's absence, the

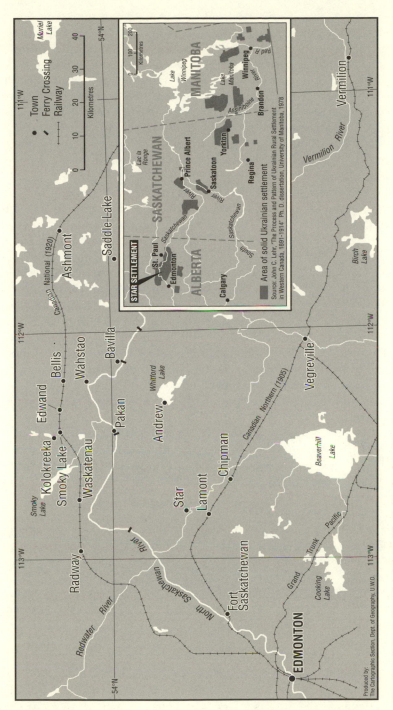

Map Legend

- **Town** ●
- **Ferry Crossing** ⌒
- **Railway** ┼

Inset map legend:

STAR SETTLEMENT

■ Area of solid Ukrainian settlement

Source: John C. Lehr, 'The Process and Pattern of Ukrainian Rural Settlement in Western Canada, 1891-1914' Ph. D. dissertation, University of Manitoba, 1978

Scale (inset): 0 100 200 Kilometres

Scale (main): 0 10 20 30 40 Kilometres

Main map labels

Muriel Lake, Saddle Lake, Ashmont, Bavilla, Wahstao, Bellis, Edwand, Kolokreeka, Smoky Lake, Waskatenau, Pakan, Whitford Lake, Andrew, Radway, Redwater River, North Saskatchewan River, Fort Saskatchewan, Star, Lamont, Chipman, Beaverhill Lake, Vegreville, Cooking Lake, Birch Lake, Vermilion River, Vermilion, EDMONTON

Canadian National (1920), Canadian Northern (1905), Grand Trunk Pacific

54°N, 54°N, 111°W, 112°W, 113°W

Inset map labels

MANITOBA, SASKATCHEWAN, ALBERTA, Lake Winnipeg, Lake Manitoba, Winnipeg, Brandon, Red R., Assiniboine, Yorkton, Prince Albert, Saskatoon, Regina, Lac la Ronge, River, Saskatchewan River, South Saskatchewan River, St. Paul, Edmonton, Calgary

Produced by:
The Cartographic Section, Dept. of Geography, U.W.O.

The Star Colony, Canada's largest Ukrainian Settlement, 1920

Ukrainian woman cleared bush, ploughed fields, planted, cultivated, and harvested crops, planted a garden, cared for poultry and hogs, and walked to the nearest village for potatoes and supplies.[6] The family faced ruin if either partner died or became chronically disabled.

The Star colony was remote from Edmonton for some years. People and supplies reached it on scows that descended the North Saskatchewan River. Alternatively, traffic moved overland along trails, for which Pakan, on the north bank of the river, was a junction point. In 1892 Pakan acquired a cable-ferry service and became the gateway for settlers heading north, on foot for Ukrainians and by horse or ox team in other cases.

The construction of rail lines and roads gradually reduced the colony's isolation. In 1905 the Canadian Northern Railway sliced through the southwestern portion at Vegreville, Chipman, and Lamont. In 1920 the railway cut through its northern fringe at Radway, Smoky Lake, and Bellis. In the process, the railway villages became important local centres, and Pakan, with its cable-ferry service, fell into the backwater.

Within the colony, economic development in the northern districts was slower than in the southern districts. The northern districts were settled later (after 1905 compared to after 1894), had poorer soils (classes 4 to 7 versus classes 1 to 3), and got rail connection to Edmonton later (1920 compared to 1905).[7] The Methodist missions opened before 1909 (Pakan, Wahstao, Kolokreeka) were in the northern districts – the least developed, most remote part of the colony. The missions founded after 1909 (Chipman and Lamont) were in rail centres in prosperous southwestern districts.

A WMS missionary, Ethelwyn Chace, recalled the isolation of the northern districts in 1907, when she taught school at Bavilla. For relief, she met weekly with two WMS missionaries from Wahstao at "streetcar corner," a point on the Saddle Lake trail where telegraph poles and their

single line of wire was the only link with the life we had previously lived. I having been a city school ma'am [at St Catharines] with perhaps a hundred contacts a day found this isolation very hard to bear. Oh, for some place to go. But there was no place, for the teacher. The only trip to the "outside" which you folks took was to Pakan for the mail once a week. How I used to envy you that … to hear my own language spoken by someone other than you two, and maybe be invited to have dinner at the Doctor's, see new faces and have a long drive.

Such isolation collapsed dramatically a decade later. As the CNR branch line approached Smoky Lake in 1919, Charles Lawford, the medical missionary at Pakan, bought land for a drug store in the

Smoky Lake town site. His plan was "to put in a druggist and have an office for myself there with phone communication between the druggist and here ... My home will be here but [I can visit] my office at Smoky Lake at stated hours, it being 9½ miles distant from here, which is nothing with auto."[8]

THE UKRAINIANS THROUGH METHODIST EYES

Galician Greek Catholics made up a majority of Ukrainians in the prairie region and a large minority in the Star colony. Lawford saw them as the high stakes in a struggle between Roman Catholic slavery and protestant liberty. Roman Catholicism was a national religion for French Canadians, and francophone bishops and priests dominated the Roman church's prairie dioceses. Thus, asked Lawford in 1909, "What are the evils today compared with those which will have to be met, and which we must inevitably groan under if the Church of Rome succeeds in uniting the Galician people to her church, and thus secures political supremacy by the united vote of the Galician and French people? What a stake the Church of Rome is playing for."[9]

As the majority of Ukrainians in the Star colony were Bukovynians, the Greek Orthodox religion and Russian Orthodox priests were Lawford's chief local opposition. In 1908 Lawford judged that the "Bukowinians" were ignorant of common gospel truths and "very lax in the things that the word of God is explicit about. The Sabbath is broken by dance parties in holiday time, Sunday afternoon once in awhile. Men start off for freight so near to the end of the week there is no hope of being home for Sunday, and hence they are found freighting on God's day of rest. Lying is prevalent, and ... The love of strong drink has been acquired by many in Austria."[10]

The Bukovynians lacked priests. In Lawford's area, the nearest Orthodox Church was at Wostock, twenty to forty miles distant from the settlers. By 1904 many of his neighbours had not been to church for four years.[11] Lawford disparaged the Orthodox priests in any case. His reasons, given in 1908, expressed his evangelical-protestant dissent from liturgical Christian traditions. The priests erred by giving church tradition equal authority with the Bible. Consequently the settlers accepted fables, believed in saints, and disobeyed God's explicit commands in the belief that the church sanctioned their behaviour. The priests "could do so much to uplift the people" if they would

preach the simple Gospel, instead of occupying so much time with the carrying out of elaborately-devised ceremonials and ritualistic observances ... But as a matter of fact, the service is so long that the people do not feel under obligation to remain, and so keep coming and going during the entire service. It is very lamentable to see so much time and thought occupied with nonessentials, and the truths of the Gospel that set forth the need of the inner spiritual life crowded out. What shall it profit that a system of religion shall succeed in establishing a people in religious forms if that system leads them not into loving union with Christ.[12]

In 1910 Lawford regretted "a tendency on the part of the priests to take intoxicating liquors with their parishioners when at weddings and other feasts." "The priest in the Greek church now in charge near here," noted Lawford,

seems from his own people's report to be a disgrace to any church. We are constantly hearing of drunken revels ... in which the priest is said to be the chief actor ... though the people may bow to his ecclesiastical authority, they cannot rely on the leadership of such a one for spiritual help. It is certainly a case of the blind leading the blind. Think of the absurdity of a man, in the name of religion, conducting a so-called religious service, the windup of which is the drinking of two gallons of whisky by the priests and the people. The priest became so intoxicated that he could scarcely remain on his feet and pleaded with his parishioners to help him home.[13]

Lawford's view of orthodox priests resonated with his colleagues in the Star colony. The priests' religion, opined Alice Sanford in 1913, "consists chiefly in performing religious rites. They do not yet know God as a personal friend."[14] As William Pike commented in 1915 "the young people are casual about confession, but the old people and children go. They are asked ridiculous questions like 'Did you drink milk in your tea this week?' If they were admonished about the telling of lies and stealing and other faults common among them, it would be doing some good. Instead they are taught that the trifling things enjoined by the church are the things of most importance, while the weightier matters are not taught. Little wonder that to lie and steal is almost second nature with them." The provision of church ceremonies on a fee-for-service basis was simply corrupt. The priests "come over here from Russia, remain five or six years, and make a fortune and retire. Their's is certainly a moneymaking concern, for they do absolutely nothing without being paid for it ... Baptisms, marriages, burials, and consecrations are done only for money. I know a case where the priest refused to bury an infant unless he got $25. I did it gratis. Even witnesses at a marriage and sponsors of a baptism must pay for the honour."[15]

Like Lawford, Pike deplored Ukrainian wedding feasts, which began two or three days before the wedding and continued after. At one such feast he surprised his hosts by declining whisky and drinking water for the toasts. Even so, the drinking, smoking, and dancing drove him out for the "pure ozone of the night." Reading between the lines, Pike disliked the Ukrainian practice of arranged marriage. In 1915 he noted how a young man would negotiate with a father for the hand of his daughter, who might be fourteen to fifteen years of age. In one case, an "old man" travelled fifty miles to Kolokreeka to woo a girl of seventeen; when she refused him, he offered his son.[16]

Edith Weekes, a WMS missionary at Wahstao, judged harshly the lot of Ukrainian women.[17] "Time and again," she wrote in 1907,

I have seen a man sit on the waggon while his wife led the oxen, or drop the potatoes into a hole which she had dug ready for them. A man marries a wife, frequently because he needs one to plaster the house for him, to milk the cows, to get in the hay while he goes to work on the railroad, buys himself comfortable cloths, boots, and mittens. Then he returns with the balance of his earnings to buy machinery, while she trudges the prairie, even with snow on the ground, barefooted, and wraps her hands and her baby in the sheep-skin coat which he has discarded.

When one looks upon this kind of thing it is difficult not to harden one's heart and band them all as inhuman, but we must not do so. They are but as their fathers were before them, and have no opportunity to learn ... that God made woman, not as the 'slave' of man, but as a 'helpmate.'

In 1919 T.C. Buchanan, the superintendent of missions for Alberta, accepted the need for a male missionary to "work alongside the missionaries of the WMS" due to "the low estimate put on women by these people."[18]

Time was to mellow Methodist judgments of the orthodox clergy, however. As May Laycock, a WMS missionary during the 1920s, remembered, the first priests were weak and uneducated, but not so the later ones. "The itinerant Mundare priest, Father Kolholsky," for example, "used to drop by Wahstao to discuss the sacraments. He urged the people to use Methodist facilities such as the CGIT and youth activities because his field was too big to manage their Christian education. His children came to our youth organizations."[19]

To Lawford during the early years, however, the priests exercised a bondage "worse than any African slavery." A general problem was that 95 percent of the Ukrainians were illiterate, could not read the Bible, and hence looked to their priests for religious guidance.[20] At the same time, Lawford saw a "great danger ... that these people, in their efforts for freedom, will drift to Socialism, for Socialistic literature is coming into every settlement."[21]

THE PAKAN MEDICAL MISSION, 1900–14

The Reverend Charles H. Lawford, MD (1863–1952) founded the Methodist Church's Ukrainian mission field. Lawford was born in England, raised in Toronto, and moved with his family to Manitoba in 1879. In 1889 he obtained his school teacher's certificate and entered the ministry. He was ordained in 1892, completed his theological studies at Wesley College in 1896, and graduated in medicine from Wesley College in 1900. The outbreak of the Boxer Rebellion wrecked his plans to become a medical missionary in China, so he volunteered for Ukrainian mission work in the Northwest Territories.[22] On paper his qualifications were impressive. As May Laycock remembered, however, he had been rushed through theology and medicine on the assumption that he was to serve a primitive people. In time, this caught up with him.[23]

Pakan held practical advantages for Lawford's mission. With its cable ferry service across the North Saskatchewan River, it was a natural gateway to Ukrainian settlements on the north side. Pakan also had rich significance for Methodists: it was formerly Victoria, the Methodist mission settlement founded by George McDougall, who had perished in a snowstorm in 1876. Following the defeat of the Northwest Rebellion in 1885, the government had renamed the settlement Pakan, after a Methodist band chief of the Cree who had remained loyal to the government.[24]

On arriving at Pakan in 1900, Lawford moved into the old log mission house that had "just enough room for a kitchen and bedroom on the ground floor, and a bedroom in the loft, reached by ladder." Almost immediately, he left for Winnipeg to have his foot amputated, an operation made necessary when "a fall on my ankle, previously strained, caused arthritis and abscess formation."[25] He returned in 1901 with an artificial leg and with his sister Kate as housekeeper. In July 1902 Lawford visited Toronto to marry Alice Smith, a nurse who had "taken a course of Bible study at Moody's" and who, like her husband, had hoped to serve in China. To make way for Alice, Kate Lawford moved to Edmonton.

Lawford never became fluent in the Ukrainian language, so he held Sunday services with an interpreter, hoping to attract a few Ukrainians when they had no church of their own. He handed out religious tracts to the few settlers who could read. The tracts probably were copies of a *diaglot*, an English Ukrainian version of the New Testament that the Bible society sold.[26]

The tracts had more impact than met the eye. Those "who could read," recalled William Pike, "were proud of that ability and shared it with those not so fortunate. Where there was one reader, there were usually ten listeners. The illiterate ones welcomed anyone who could read to them [and] missionaries took advantage of that."[27] Similarly, men near Wahstao eagerly purchased Bibles. Men who could read then read to the others. In time even the local Greek orthodox priest thanked the WMS women for the literature.[28]

Meanwhile, Lawford's literacy in English and knowledge of Canada made him a valued local expert on matters such as assembling farm machinery, paying bills, and obtaining information concerning land laws and the organization of school districts. In addition, he gave his name "as security to the merchants to get flour, &c. for women whose husbands were away earning money on the railway," thereby winning "the respect, confidence, and deep esteem of these foreigners, which has been no small factor in reaching them ... with God's Word."[29]

In retrospect, the attraction of Lawford's medical services for Ukrainians seems problematic. Although the settlers were twenty miles from another doctor and eighty-five miles from the nearest hospital, microbiological medicine, with its chemical therapies for infectious disease, was unavailable to doctors before the First World War. As Methodists found at their Vita, Manitoba, mission during the 1920s, moreover, the Ukrainians favoured home cures, accepted sickness as divine visitation, and used doctors as a last resort.[30]

Even so, Lawford wrote in 1904 that his medical work was "the one thing used of God to prevent us from being defeated in our efforts to gain an entrance to the people."[31] Lawford's coverage area for house calls extended twenty-five miles in any direction. All this, he later recalled, "had to be travelled by team ... What we do with a car to-day in one hour would take all day driving with horses then." He acquired an automobile in 1913.[32]

Lawford's journal entry for 27 February 1905, illustrates the nature of his work:

Case 1 Three Austrian farmers, from about three miles, asking me to write Edmonton Land Office for permits for logs to cut into lumber for their homes.
Case 2 Austrian, from about eight miles, for medicine for his wife, also to have letter written re land he wishes for his farm.
Case 3 Young man (Métis) with suppurative middle ear disease.
Case 4 Two Austrians, one to get medicine, the other to get letter written. Both from this neighbourhood.
Case 5 Austrian, from twelve miles distant, tooth extracted, treated one prior to filling.
    (Dinner)

P.M.

Case 6 Austrian to see about money due him for work for the Canadian Pacific Railway, for which I had previously written. From about thirteen miles.

Case 7 Canadian settler, from about twenty miles distant, to have tooth extracted.

Case 8 Austrian settler, from six miles south, to get instructions how to proceed to conduct business in forming school district.

Case 9 Two Austrians, from twenty miles east, for me to write re homesteads.

Case 10 A trustee of the Greek church ten miles east for me to write re logs they wish the government to give them for their church.

(Supper)

Case 11 Austrian, accident on hill, team ran away, came for one of my horses to overtake his.

Case 12 A trustee of another Greek church, to have me write a list of men and the number of logs they were contributing to their church, and write re the grant of land they desire.

About 11 p.m. Good-night.[33]

Alice Lawford served the mission as nurse, teacher, and house-keeper. As her husband acknowledged, "those first six years imposed a very heavy burden ... not only on me but on Mrs. Lawford." On one occasion, following surgery for which Alice gave the anaesthetic, a farmer's son with empyema convalesced for a month in the Lawfords' home. On another occasion, with lunch on the table, a female patient arrived "with an infected mastoid and spreading infection that threat-ened abscess of the lateral lobe of the brain. While Mrs Lawford removed the dinner I prepared the instruments and then, with the patient on the dining room table, Mrs Lawford gave the anaesthetic. I opened the antrum and finished the operation and with some blankets laid her on the dining room floor where she would be under observation. The dinner was again set and we had our meal."[34]

In 1904 the general board issued funds to build Lawford a new res-idence and a hospital. "Accompanied by the doctor, carpenters and crew," scows with the lumber and supplies floated downriver from Edm-onton. In 1906 the carpenters finished the seven-room house with office. In 1907 they completed the George McDougall Memorial Hos-pital, a three-story building with fifteen beds, kitchen, maid's room, and nurses' quarters.[35] There the Lawfords, two nurses, and a cook faced a life that impressed a medical assistant as "utterly devoid of home life of any nature." With the nurses burdened with washing and scrubbing, as well as professional duties, Lawford had difficulty holding staff.[36]

Lawford was certain that the Ukrainians would appreciate the Meth-odist facility. Isolated and with little savings, they could not have financed a hospital on their own. Dr H.R. Smith, formerly of Star and now on the hospital's two-man advisory board in Edmonton, was satisfied to end a Roman Catholic "monopoly of the hospital business" that enabled Rome to "win a great many protestant children and young adults to their faith."[37]

By 1910 the hospital drew patients "from Manville, Saddle Lake, Vegreville, Scarrow, Lamont and from as far north as they are settled. Thus through our hospital we reach about three times the number of people we could by our Sabbath services alone."[38] One drawback concerned Lawford's fees. Although he charged the minimum that the Alberta Medical Association's fee structure permitted, and less where need existed, Dr Smith in Edmonton worried that

the medical work as at present charged for is doing the mission work harm. It is impossible to show the people the justice of when they shall call the Doctor to their home and do not ask him to return and he sees fit to make several visits more and charges them for each of these visits ... They consider they have been robbed and especially so in cases where they cannot see the benefit of the additional visit ... it does not help the case any to point out this is the custom of the country or that the law permits such. To them it is stealing and the worse because it is done by the church.[39]

Lawford strove constantly to give his hospital a Christian atmosphere. "Our hospital work," he explained,

is not alone a work of saving life and lessening suffering and deformity. Our constant aim is to provide for the souls of these people. To this end we furnish all patients who can read with a copy of the Scripture in their own language; this the foreigners never fail to use.

My assistant, Metro Ponich, has had many opportunities of reading the Scripture to those who cannot read for themselves, and of speaking with much acceptance the truths which point out man's need and God's salvation. On Sabbath evenings a short service is held in the hospital when the conditions of the patients and other circumstances will permit.

The personal factor is perhaps the greatest factor for good in our hospital work. Patients come in, say, for a week [and] morning and evening I visit them. Christian nurses are in constant touch with them and when they return to their homes, they carry with them the feelings of friendship and regard which go far toward opening the way for future work.[40]

In 1912 Lawford sacked Dr Christopher F. Connolly, ostensibly because the young medical assistant had admitted to playing cards and smoking in public. "Months of observation," had convinced Lawford that his young assistant "was not placing God first in his life."[41]

From 1908 to 1912, Lawford worked sixteen to eighteen hours a day, seven days a week.[42] As hospital superintendent, he managed the staff of four, kept the accounts, ordered supplies, and answered a voluminous correspondence. As physician, he saw patients in the hospital, made house calls over a 250-square-mile area, and was coroner and health officer for the district. As missionary, he held two Thursday prayer meetings and two Sunday services.

Through his varied activities, Lawford aimed to convert Ukrainians to protestantism and turn his converts into Methodists. At first he put off asking them to become Methodists. "To expect them to accept an entirely different religious system" was "expecting too much. Nothing short of a widespread revival of religion would lead them to be willing to join such a system as ours and even then the most would hesitate to discard ... what for generations they have regarded as the means of Grace ordained by God."[43]

In 1908 competition turned Lawford to an aggressive strategy. In August a Russian Orthodox church appeared on his side of the North Saskatchewan River. He also had learned that Roman Catholic missionaries were transferring to the Greek rite in a bid for Galician support.[44] With these developments his mission had reached "the point where questions bearing on the difference in our systems of religion have to be met ... now it seems to be our duty to declare the whole counsel of God, and thus set forth as clearly as possible the Gospel teaching, even where it opposes custom and doctrine.[45] Thus, he refused one settlement's invitation to become its priest because the settlers required that he pray to the Virgin Mary and the saints.

At the same time, Lawford accommodated Old World traditions that were compatible with the essentials of his faith. In one case, for example, after administering the sacrament and confession to a dying man, he allowed the family to burn a candle by the body, so that the departed would have a light to see by in the life to come. To Lawford this custom was pure superstition but a harmless one. Eventually, he hoped, such customs would wither away. Thus, in 1912 he took pleasure in the baptisms of three children, the first he had done "in the regular way."[46]

His aggressive tactics won him Canada's first Ukrainian Methodist congregation. In 1909 two Ukrainians joined the church as local preachers, and headed for the ministry. One was Demetrius (Metro) Ponich, a twenty-one-year-old Galician who was Lawford's "chore boy and interpreter." The other was Taranty Hannochko, a Russian Ukrainian who had settled "among the Austrians" at Bellis with his wife and young family in 1901.[47] By his own account, Hannochko had been a "convinced Christian" when he settled at Bellis. He had helped several Austrians to find Christ before deciding to become a preacher and before meeting Lawford.

Hannochko and one or two other early supporters of the Methodists possibly were Old County Baptists. In her address to the Alberta branch of the WMS in 1913, Alice Sanford, then of Kolokreeka, noted a "small number of Baptist" Ukrainians in the Star colony. According to a 1967 community centennial history, WMS missionaries held Sunday school in a Russian Baptist settlement to the north of Wahstao in 1906. In 1916 Baptists built a church at Bellis, where Hannochko and his family had settled in 1901. In the same year the Alberta conference gave Hannochko "special ordination" and stationed him on the Wahstao circuit, which included Bellis as a preaching place.[48]

Whether or not Baptists were an influence, thirteen Ukrainians became Methodists in 1910 and five joined in 1911. By 1912 Lawford's congregation had twenty church members and eight adherents.[49] In 1910 Nicoli Gologhan had fitted up half his house for Methodist worship at his own expense, and neighbours contributed a stove, lamps, and coal oil. The result was a comfortable meeting place that attracted thirty to thirty-five persons each Sunday.[50] In 1911 John Olexiuk, a farmer near Wahstao, and Nicoli Veranka, who farmed near the Gologhan home, became local preachers. In addition, Olexiuk donated four acres of land for a Methodist church and cemetery, and neighbours supplied the materials and labour. The result was a log building known as Olexiuk's church – the first Ukrainian Methodist church in Canada.[51]

The Ukrainians who attended Lawford's services risked the ostracism of their countrymen. After administering the sacrament to twenty-five Ukrainians in 1909, Lawford worried that "some may shrink back under the strength of the opposition that may arise as soon as this is generally known."[52] In 1910 he led prayers for six new converts who, "though they know the joy of sins forgiven ... are beset on every hand by persecution from those still in darkness."[53] During 1910, claimed Lawford, Roman and Greek priests tried to stop mothers and children from receiving the services of the WMS ladies and "repeatedly ... have broken up the children's classes."[54] Finally, Ponich's decision to become a Methodist "deeply hurt" his parents "who mourned it and felt that he had taken a step that shut him out of heaven." Ponich himself remembered the "Russian Old Monk priest in Pakan church" who said to the congregation, in the presence of Ponich's parents, that "If I had a son that would do what Metro Ponich did, I would shoot him."[55]

THE WMS SCHOOL-HOME MISSIONS, 1904–14

The WMS opened school-home missions at Wahstao in 1904 and Kolokreeka in 1909. Although these missions were as important as Lawford's work, the WMS presented them as supplements to the work of the "general-board" men. Whereas Lawford dealt primarily with the

Ukrainian men, "the ladies found it easier to reach and evangelize the women and children."

To fulfil "their chief aim, individual regeneration and salvation," the lady missionaries worked through "school teaching and religious education" and met "the need for social service." The WMS generally stationed them "in groups of twos and threes ... [with] no choice in companionship." It trusted "each worker [to] apply her talents to the best advantage either as teacher, housekeeper, social service worker or evangelist."[56] A school-home mission's staff consisted of a supervisor, a teacher, an outside worker, and sometimes a trained nurse. Their activities "were never rigidly divided; rather they were mutually planned," and all shared in them.[57] They included school teaching for day schoolers and boarders, Sunday school, home visitations, social services such as the distribution of clothing and medical assistance to needy families, receptions, and temperance rallies.

The Wahstao Mission

"Wahstao," meaning "something shining" or "something that reflects light," was the Cree name for a hill that sloped down to the North Saskatchewan River and was visible for miles in every direction.[58] In July 1904 Retta Edmonds and Jessie Munro moved there from Ontario. In the company of Dr Lawford and T.C. Buchanan they arrived by way of the "old Saddle Lake trail," which followed along the north bank of the river and was filled with "ruts, stumps ... and mosquitoes all the way."[59] For three months they used Lawford's tent for living quarters and a Sunday school while one William Leonard erected a two-thousand-dollar building that served as home, chapel, school, and dispensary. When a cold wave struck on 7 October, they moved in "before the plaster was set" and "with shavings in the porridge."[60]

Edmunds and Munro easily contacted nearby families. First, they secured an interpreter – Ustenna ("Stenna") Zacharuk, a "shy little girl from the adjoining farm" who had a "smattering of English" and ventured in to sit on the side of the cot and learn 'Jesus Loves Me.'" Then they visited homesick farm wives. "Sometimes, the only contact was a smile and a handshake," wrote Ethelwyn Chace, who recalled the mission's early days in a memoir written during the 1940s.[61] As the *panyas* ("ladies") continued their visits,

the women welcomed them warmly and an hour's call was none too long. Most of the men were away working in the mines or on the new railways in order to amass a little capital to equip their farms and the women were lonely. In the old country the houses were near together in village or town and the farmed land some distance away. But here, in this wild country, the houses were a half mile apart and with small children to care for, it was easier to stay at home than go visiting. Then the intense cold of the winter and the deep snow! Even home had few comforts. One woman was left at home during a long winter, her supplies being one bag of flour and another of potatoes. Fortunately, she also had a milch cow, which benefit she shared with her neighbor. No wonder they welcomed friendly visitors. A friend told me not long ago, "You ladies have no idea how glad our mother was to see you drive in at our gate. She often spoke of it."

"Their lives were so lonely," observed Chace, "and I'm sure homesickness for the land of their fathers must have often nearly overcome them. And their inner resources seemed so meagre when reading books was beyond them."

With the mothers receiving visits, the *panyas* opened a day school, children wandered in, and attendance improved. Men and older boys anxious to learn English turned up in the evenings "and seemed to think it worthwhile." In time young men spent "the winter in the neighbourhood, just for the chance of attending our night school ... The children came on Sunday mornings too and learned hymns and Bible verses in English. They certainly enjoyed singing even before they had taken in the meaning of the hymns." "With some of the grown-ups we meet now-a-days," mused Chace, "those Sunday mornings are their happiest memories."

"The work [of Edmunds and Munro] that winter," continued Chace, "was not easy. Driving along hilly trails, around sloughs, over frozen creeks and through scrub, wading through deep snow to tie up the horse, emerging from heated interiors to bitter cold outside – all brought hazards to health and nerves. Trying to make sense, too, out a foreign language was a strain, as every missionary knows. During the first year it became evident that neither lady was rugged enough to stand the strenuous life very long." Munro withdrew from Wahstao for health reasons in 1905, as did Edmunds in 1906.[62]

The work passed to replacements from Ontario – Edith Weekes (1905), Caroline Cartwright (1906), Ethelwyn Chace herself (1907), and Ella McLean (1908). Cartwright, a native of Smithville, had served two years as deaconess in Napanee. The others were graduates of Victoria College. Weekes and Chace had been rejected as physically unfit for the China mission field.[63] "Chacie" was a teacher from St Catharines. When Robert Fletcher, Alberta's "supervisor of schools among foreigners," opened the colony's first public school, at Bavilla in 1907, he asked her to teach the first term. McLean replaced Chace for the summer term, and then she too joined the Wahstao staff.[64]

Over the years marriage trimmed the WMS ranks and called forth replacements. In 1909 Cartwright married Arthur Hencher, a homesteader from seven miles away, with Lawford officiating. In 1910 Weekes married William Leonard, the builder of the Wahstao and Kolokreeka school-homes who was to become a China missionary in 1913. T.C. Buchanan officiated, and for "the main dish for the wedding repast," William Pike "shot enough prairie chickens that each guest had half a bird to eat." In 1913 Ella McLean married Percy Sutton, another Ukrainian missionary. After Mclean's death in 1914, Sutton married her replacement at Kolokreeka, Phoebe Code from Trowbridge, Ontario.

The Kolokreeka Mission

As "outside workers," Weekes and Cartwright did house visits, using Stenna Zacharuk as interpreter. In 1905 Weekes "harnessed Maud, the horse, and drove a dozen miles west" to start a Sunday school in the home of Nicoli Gologhan, and in 1907 Cartwright began a Sunday school further north, at the home of John Nikolichuk. Possibly Lawford made the contact, since the ladies needed directions to find the place, "not knowing where he lived." In 1908 Weekes and Chace selected land on White Earth Creek for a second school home. The ladies named the mission Kolokreeka: an improvised Ukrainian-English word for "beside the creek." In 1909 Weekes and Mclean staffed the mission, living in a tent while William Leonard erected an unpretentious building with "a basement, kitchen, dining-sitting room, pantry, three small bedrooms, [and] two wee dormitories with room for eight in each."

The Work of the Missions

The Bavilla school lacked a teacher when McLean left. With no public school in the area, the Wahstao day school was "soon filled to capacity." In 1907 Weekes conceded that the children were "irregular in attendance" due to indifference, work at home, severe weather, bad roads, and insufficient clothing. Even so, they learned English and internalized "the principles of truth and gentleness and honor."[65] In 1912 the WMS enlarged the Kolokreeka building to accommodate thirty children. In 1914 the home had thirty-one boarders, thirty day schoolers – and "growing pains." In 1916 the WMS gave the Wahstao mission a new and larger building.[66]

"To make the English language intelligible to the Ukrainian children," noted Chace, "required some unique tactics. A series of little stuffed animals which some knowing friend had tucked among my luggage proved invaluable. Pictures of all kinds illustrated reading lessons. 'Where is the lesson to-day?' a little girl once asked. She turned the pages of her reader till she came to a picture of a fox. In her language a fox is a 'less.' The new children found it all very interesting and [were] apt pupils. But spelling! oh my! So few of these English words were spelled as they sounded."

Sunday schools were a second school-home activity. The ladies held them at various locations and taught the children to sing from the Canadian Hymnal. Edith Weekes "was very musical and when the organ, sent from Toronto and waylaid a year, arrived, she made good use of it, teaching the children to sing hymns and also getting them to sing their beautiful Ukrainian folk songs." Weekes herself "found it truly inspiring to hear from a childish throat the strains of 'Come to the Saviour,' or 'What a Friend We Have in Jesus.' Perhaps the Gospel truths in hymns and verses are not all comprehended. But they are stored in the memory, and will some day be a source of strength."[67]

The mission staffs also held receptions, distributed clothing to needy families, and gave medical assistance to reach the Ukrainian mothers. In 1909 the Wahstao ladies organized a temperance rally, at which twenty-one Ukrainians took the pledge.[68] In 1909 Stenna Zacharuk became the first Ukrainian at either mission to "receive Christ as her personal Saviour." After this, noted Chace, she was "more helpful than ever." When Stenna eventually "left us for greener pastures and wider experience, she sent her young sister to take her place."[69]

Language

"The primary effort of those early missionaries, both women and men," recalled William Pike, "was to acquire the Ukrainian language – they just *had* to have it to do effective work." At Wahstao, the ladies worried that Stenna, their interpreter, "might soon be leaving. Another interpreter would be hard to find, and in any case heart to heart contacts are so much easier to establish in a common language."[70]

How to learn Ukrainian was a puzzle. Although a few of the Ukrainian men could read the language, they "knew nothing of its structure [and] so could not help us." When the ladies ordered an English-Ukrainian grammar from Europe, they received back a German-Ukrainian dictionary. Not for nothing, however, was the "scholarly Edith Weekes" the gold medallist in modern languages at Victoria College. Weekes "went into concentrated study" and "in no time at all" came up with a WMS "grammar for beginners." Even so, the language study was hard going. "It meant mastering the script as well as print," recalled Chace, and they really seemed at first to have nothing in common. We were glad to find that Ukrainian was strictly phonetic and so quite easy to read; but alas for the inflections! Fourteen forms for every noun, twenty-eight for every adjective! As for the verbs, regular and irregular, perfect and imperfect, they followed no rules ever heard of before. Prepositions might demand to be followed by any one of five or six cases and verb prefixes seemed each to be a law unto itself. But Ukrainian, with all its difficulties, proved to be a fascinating study, and we were always encouraged by the fact that the five-year old children could speak it glibly. Why not we – in time?

Chace's first attempt to give a Bible reading in Ukrainian, in 1908, was a disaster. On the occasion,

Eight or ten women gathered at a farm house at about 10 a.m. to patch a quilt, each for herself, the mission supplying the patches ... We sewed till between three and four, then the work was put away and the tired women settled themselves patiently for the worship service. Singing and reading passed off very well, then an interruption occurred. From a dark corner, made darker with a heavy grey blanket, a hen walked out. She was quite inoffensive, just tired of close confinement. But she evidently had not been alone under the blanket, and the ray of light that she had let in deceived her male companions into thinking that the dawn had come. You know what roosters do at dawn. Well they did it. There may have been seven of them or seventeen; it sounded more like seventy. Their raucous crowing filled all the air. Every Ukrainian word that I had memorized so carefully fled from me, and I broke into violent perspiration as I looked in vain to the women for some interest and inspiration. They looked as if they cared not a whit whether they heard me or the roosters and I had to hurriedly close the service in deepest embarrassment.

Despite the debacle, Chase had gained good language skills through school and Sunday school teaching. Thus at her second meeting "the day was less cold and the poultry were out where they belonged. My message met with good attention and I drove home happy." Similarly Edith Weekes and Ella McLean reportedly were "both advanced in language" when the Reverend J.K. Smith visited them at Kolokreeka in 1909.[71]

The Panyas as Family

The Ukrainian settlements were thickets of families and neighbours from Old Country villages. In time the *panyas* became part of the transplanted networks. In 1908 Caroline Cartwright took seven-year-old Catherine Fergerchuk on her vacation "back east." Cartwright's daughter, Mary Hencher, was to marry a Wahstao boy, Bill Repka. In 1918 Chace acquired her first "grand-child" when "Mary Bilar-Repka's little two-year old started calling me *Baba.*" Years later, like Lawford, Chace had a vast knowledge of local families – their marriages, the names of their children, and where they had scattered across the United States and Canada.

The Evangelical Goal

"How we longed to give those women the comfort and hope ... from the wonderful Gospel of Jesus!,"recalled Ethelwyn Chace. As she noted in her address to the Alberta branch of the WMS in 1914, however, she and her colleagues had "no wonderful recipe for making Christians ... The people are satisfied with their religion and not anxious to adopt ours. Also they consider themselves much more religious than the missionaries because they observe so many Holy Days."[72]

In *Sensitive Independence*, Rosemary Gagan argues that the *panyas* failed to win converts and gradually abandoned "direct unadulterated evangelism." Conversely, "the women were at their best when they assumed the roles of social service workers, not the guardians of the public morality." Thus in 1919, when T.C. Buchanan visited Wahstao, the staff were "reluctant to offer any hard statistical evidence of their 'success in leading young people ... to Jesus' because there had been so few converts. They were usually satisfied if they could help immigrants adapt to Canadian ways and if they were able to give the children and young people the advantages of a Canadian education."[73]

Gagan, however, misreads Buchanan's letter.[74] "What I heard and saw," wrote the superintendent, "established me more firmly in the belief that the policy we have been pursuing is the proper policy, namely, the evangelization of this people looking ultimately to their conversion. Other agencies have been employed ... but the goal kept constantly in view has been the bringing of this people ... to believe in Christ as a personal Saviour, followed of course by Christian living."

What is more important, Buchanan allowed for conversion without church membership. The converts, "being young people ... were not asked to leave the church of their parents and join the Methodist church ... We as a church are not in this work to make Methodists of our converts."[75] Buchanan's statement squares with evidence in the *Wahstao Diary* for the years 1911–27: "At intervals the boys and girls were given an opportunity to witness to their faith in Christ, but there was no church congregation for them to join, and sometimes no pastor to whose care to recommend them. No sustained institution was ever built up."[76]

Thus unlike Lawford, the *panyas* were out for converts, not church members. Similarly, it was in response to Buchanan's query about converts that the Wahstao staff were "rather slow to give statistics and very conservative in their reckoning; however, they counted fifty persons, all young people, who[m] they believed had accepted Christ and were leading exemplary Christian lives."

OTHER MISSIONS AND MISSIONARIES

Chipman and Lamont

In 1905 a Canadian Northern Railway branch line sliced through the fertile southern part of the Star colony. Chipman and Lamont, eight miles apart on the line, had mixed Anglo-Ukrainian populations and Ukrainians in the rural districts nearby.

The Reverend J. Kenneth Smith opened the Chipman mission in 1910. "J.K.," a Victoria College graduate from Brampton, Ontario, had taught in the Ukrainian school at the village of Star before coming to Chipman on a "roving commission." He travelled constantly through the colony, preaching "wherever he could gather a group." At each stop, he sold Ukrainian New Testaments at cost or gave them away.

In 1911 C.W. Watson Ross came to Chipman as a probationer. He had learned Ukrainian as a child in Rossburn, Manitoba, where Lawford's parents had lived. (His father was Hugh Ross, after whom Rossburn was named.) In contrast to Smith's roving commission, Ross had five preaching appointments at which Anglo-Canadians and Ukrainians intermingled. In 1912 the WMS transferred Ethelwyn Chace from Wahstao to Chipman. She lived with Ross's family, visited women in their homes and held Sunday school. In December 1914 Smith and Ross held "continuous services" throughout the district, and at Chipman nineteen persons "came forward, began somewhat to pray, [and] some declared verbally their acceptance of Christ."[77]

In 1912 Smith moved to Lamont, where the Missionary Society planned to establish a twenty-bed hospital on a shared-cost basis with the local residents. The hospital opened in 1913 at a cost of $13,500, of which $6,000 came from local subscriptions, $2,500 came from the Missionary Society, and $5,000 was debt. The hospital's running costs were $8,000, of which $5,000 came from the Missionary Society and $500 came from the WMS. Other revenues came from patients' fees ($5,100), the government of Alberta ($1,200), and "friends of the hospital" ($200). The doctors charged fees to the patients. They took nothing from the hospital fees or the Missionary Society.

The Lamont hospital was deep in Methodist connections. Its super-intendent, Dr A.E. Archer, was a Methodist preacher's son who had taken over Smith's practice at Star in 1906. His partner in medical practice at Lamont, Dr Will T. Rush, had been a college roommate of the Reverend F.C. Stephenson, founder of the Young People's Forward Movement for Missions. Archer's wife, a trained nurse and anaesthetist, "gave freely of her time and energy in assisting the staff." The superintendent of nurses, Miss Shuttleworth, had served the WMS in Japan.

Although doctors Archer and Rush were not medical missionaries, they were "strongly missionary in outlook." As the *Christian Guardian* described their work in 1914,

The helpfulness here is not only physical. There is a rare Christian atmo-sphere. Every individual who is privileged to enter – may I say privileged to be sick enough to enter – is for the time being adopted into this sociable Christian family. A sincere personal interest is taken in the welfare of each one, and he begins to feel better from the moment he enters. The source of this influence is three-fold. The doctors, A.E. Archer and W.T. Rush, have the genuine missionary spirit, and it would be difficult to overestimate their Christian influence, whether within or without the hospital. The doctors are well supported in this respect by the nursing staff, consisting of Mrs S.C. Slaughter as head nurse and six nurses in training. Then there is J.K. – almost everybody in this part of the country knows J.K. Smith, missionary to the Austrian people and located at Lamont. Mr Smith is an expert in the use of the Ruthenian language.[78]

Thus the staff taught Christianity by living it. Their work also promoted Anglo-Canadian health standards, removed prejudice, and opened doors for missionaries. In 1914, for example, Ethelwyn Chace became "quite intimate" with a Ruthenian priest whose wife was receiving hospital care. "Such opportunities," claimed Rush, "come from the hospital."[79]

The Edmonton Missions

In 1908 ladies of McDougall Methodist Church discovered young girls from the colony who were penniless, stranded, and looking for work. They responded by renting a room for a shelter in a building where Mrs Margaret Sherlock Ash, a former WMS missionary, had a suite. Later in the year, Retta Edmonds, a "restored and refreshed" Jessie Munro, and their Ukrainian housekeeper, Mary Bilar, arrived from

Wahstao to open a second centre. Munro lasted a year, when, again, she withdrew for health reasons.

In 1911 the two centres had twenty temporary and four permanent boarders and provided Sunday school, night classes in English, a sewing class, and medical care. In 1912 the WMS opened a Ruthenian Home to consolidate the work. Over the next five years, the home provided "hundreds" of girls with temporary shelter, respectable jobs, and a place to rest during their free hours.[80]

The aggressive WMS staff were hard to ignore. "Last Sunday afternoon," wrote Miss Ida Clarke, "I went to a hotel where three or four girls work and waited in the kitchen until they got through, and 'compelled' two to come with me to Sunday school." Three more hotel employees yielded to her persuasions after her sixth visit.[81] In cooperation with the police, the ladies also did rescue work for girls who had fallen outside the law.[82]

In 1909 Lawford, J.K. Smith, and Taranty Hannochko recruited William Pike for the Ukrainian work on the occasion of his ordination at the Alberta conference sessions in Red Deer. Pike was a graduate of Victoria College from Harbour Grace, Newfoundland. There his parents had forbidden him to look at the Roman Catholic church when visiting relatives on "the other side." Years passed before he entered a Roman church.[83]

The general board gave Pike six months at Pakan for language study and then sent him to Edmonton in December 1910. With Metro Ponich, now a student at Alberta College, as his interpreter and assistant, Pike held Sunday services in two Ukrainian homes in different parts of the city.[84] He also helped WMS workers to run Sunday schools and mid-week groups.

In 1912 the general board rented a building in which Pike and WMS missionaries provided a reading room, mid-week groups, Sunday schools, Sunday services, and instruction in Ukrainian to immigrants who wished to become literate in their own language. "Some of us," commented Pike, "worried that classes in Ukrainian might be un-Canadian." However, "the larger question of the kingdom led us to think that, if the teaching of their own language to the people helped us to win them for Christ, we were justified in teaching it."[85]

Methodists also used the building to publish the *Canadian*, a bimonthly Ukrainian paper inspired by Lawford, who expected it to do the work of forty ministers. The editor, Michael Bellegay, "a graduate of the University of Lemburg, a cultured scholar, [and] a gentleman," knew Greek, Latin, and German, as well as English. By 1916 his paper was a four-page weekly with news, religious editorials, Sunday readings, an annual subscription cost of $1.00, and a circulation of 600.[86] Its annual cost to the missionary society was $2,800, including Bellegay's salary of $1,140 and $840 for his brother for work in the pressroom.

Pike wrote his sermons in English, translated them into Ukrainian, had Bellegay correct the translation, and then memorized them – "a very thorough method of study." Even so, his work left little time for study, and after four years he was still "sadly handicapped by not being master of the language."[87] To remedy his deficiency, he returned to the colony, at his own request, for the years 1915–18. There he opened a mission in Andrew and then served in Chipman, and J.K. Smith left Chipman to replace Pike in Edmonton.

Although Pike emphasized soul-saving during his first years in Edmonton (1910–15), his evangelicalism took a social direction during his years in the colony (1915–18). On his return to Edmonton in 1919, this son of Newfoundland was a self-proclaimed "Canadianizer" who sought "to interpret to the New Canadian the highest and noblest type of Canadian citizenship that I know. I believe that type of citizen has its prototype in Jesus, and so I try to live the Christ life among them [to] lead them to my Christ ... There would be little of the foreign problem in Canada if more of the supposedly Christian people were more like the Master. Christ is the solution of this and all other problems ... We have to be more Christlike to the 'stranger within our gates.'" Pike believed that the Ukrainians could feel Christ in his work, but he "never actually told them."[88] In 1922 he reported that his mission reached 425 people but had no church members or adherents.[89]

The Homestead Missionaries

In 1912 two young Englishmen, Percy G. Sutton and W.J. Hampton, graduated in theology from Wesley College, were ordained, married, and became Ukrainian missionaries in the Kolokreeka area. Sutton's wife was Ella McLean, formerly a WMS missionary at Kolokreeka. After her death in 1914, he married Phoebe Code, another Kolokreeka missionary.

The general board let these men take up homesteads "so that, if possible, through agricultural kinship they might reach the Ukrainian farmers." In Pike's view, the experiment "failed in both cases ... Sutton was a zealous student of the language, Hampton not at all ... Neither of them ever preached in Ukrainian, but both ministered to Anglo-Saxon congregations adjacent to the colony." Sutton was less skilled at farming than his neighbours.[90] Hampton never got untracked. He lived among English settlers for two years, ostensibly because he could not find a place in a Ukrainian-settled area. In January 1913 he took over Dr Connolly's homestead north of Wahstao, but lost its house and contents in a fire. In 1916 he enlisted, never to return. Sutton lasted as a "bilingual missionary" until 1922.[91]

The Ukrainian-Convert Missionaries

Taranty Hannochko and Metro Ponich were the only Ukrainians to become ordained Methodist ministers. In 1912 Hannochko opened a Ukrainian mission in Calgary as a married local preacher.[92] With the outbreak of war in 1914, many of Calgary's Ukrainians lost their jobs and left the city. In 1915, therefore, the church sent Hannochko to Wahstao. With him came four bachelor converts who formed a company, The Farmers' Christian Society, and took up adjoining homesteads near Pakan. After living together for a month in their common household, they sent one of their number, Kepha Boleychuk, "out to hunt" for a wife. At Kolokreeka he found Paketza, a seventeen-year-old, and with the WMS matron serving as intermediary, he won her consent.[93]

In 1916 Hannochko received special ordination. Clearly he was no Canadianizer – his English was on par with Lawford's Ukrainian. Like Lawford, he was out for converts and encouraged his converts to become Methodists. In 1915 one convert chose to "remain in my own religion," but added: "I have six children. I let them do what they want."[94]

Metro Ponich, Lawford's "chore boy and interpreter," became a Methodist in 1909 and passed five years in Edmonton at Alberta College, three of them as a probationer. In 1915 he was ordained and married Madeline Fischuk, and in 1916 the conference stationed him at Andrew.

Ponich was also out for converts but not necessarily church members. In 1972, he remembered the Methodist missionaries, especially the women, as "heroes [who] opened the way for other protestant churches ... and the Bible to the people. [They] caused people to demand better priests. In [the] early days [the] Bible was for the priest in church. Now anybody may have one, read it and comment on it too. We removed many stones out of the way to free thinking and liberation of thought." Also like Hannochko, Ponich was no Canadianizer. As he noted,

Assimilation was a threatening word to Ukrainians and was much in evidence amongst missionaries ... I always said make a good Christian and he will be a good Canadian. I meant by this not to tell them they should use English language and ways of social life.

One missionary said to a Ukrainian young mother that she should talk to her pre-school age children in English because this was an English country. I believed that Canadianization should be left to public schools and that it will come naturally.[95]

In Ponich's view, the Anglo-Canadian missionaries' policy of assimilation discouraged Ukrainians from offering themselves for the work. What is more important, Anglo-Canadian Methodists considered that ethnic Ukrainian clergy were unreliable for the task of Canadianization. Thus in 1915 T.C. Buchanan wrote "re. [the] Austrian who wants to enter our work," that "we are not contemplating any additions to our Austrian staff for some time. Currently Demetrius Ponich is at Alberta College and will soon finish his probation. He is the only additional worker we have in mind."[96]

In 1917 twenty-three Ukrainian Methodist missionaries opposed plans to amalgamate their Edmonton paper, the *Canadian*, with *Ranok*, the Presbyterian paper in Winnipeg. As managed by former priests of the Independent Greek Church, *Ranok* lacked the "Canadian soul and evangelical outlook" of the Methodist paper.[97] As Ethelwyn Chace elaborated,

I do not know any part of the Presbyterian church where we are as much at variance as the Ruthenian field. Union seems to present few difficulties on English-speaking missions; our aims on the foreign field are identical; publishing concerns seem to be carried on along similar lines; but when it comes to Ruthenian missions we differ, and differ radically. Those of us in the field who have wished most for co-operation have found it impossible ... The Presbyterian paper does not embody the spirit of the Presbyterian church. If they have failed to produce a paper that rightly represents them, why put our organ under the same influence?[98]

THE END OF AN ERA

In 1920 a CNR branch line cut through the country north of Pakan. This development created railway villages at Radway, Smoky Lake, and Bellis, and left Pakan and Wahstao in the backwater. Methodists responded by opening mission work in Smoky Lake and Radway in 1921. In 1922 the George McDougall Memorial Hospital and the nurses' home at Pakan were "jacked up on wheels" and moved 9½ miles to Smoky Lake.[99] All but one Pakan church member transferred to the Smoky Lake circuit.[100] Lawford resigned, ostensibly because he found the work too strenuous. He operated a drugstore in Smoky Lake until 1944, when he retired to Edmonton and became a Baptist.

In fact, Lawford was ousted and did not go quietly. In a bid to hold on to the hospital building, he tried to turn it into a school home or orphanage.[101] As May Laycock observed, the church had rushed him through theology and medical school on the assumption that he was serving a primitive people. He never took a refresher course in medicine and never left the Pakan mission. By 1920 his aggressive prose-lytizing was out of fashion. "All of us," recalled William Pike, "found him narrow in outlook."[102] His medical skills also were wanting. In 1914 he had narrowly avoided a malpractice suit, and in 1920 the Missionary Society barred him from performing major surgery. "I am sorry to say," wrote a Pakan resident in 1920, "that Dr Lawford has not had the confidence of the district for a long time."[103]

In 1920 the Methodist and Presbyterian churches entered into cooperative arrangements, in anticipation of church union. The Presbyterians took over the Andrew mission. The *Canadian* merged with the Presbyterian paper *Ranok* ("Morning") to form the *Canadian Ranok,* published in Winnipeg.[104] Michael Bellegay lost his job as editor and left for Chicago to sell real estate. In Edmonton the churches merged their four mission centres into one jointly sponsored All People's Mission and named Pike as superintendent.[105]

The Lamont hospital expanded to a fifty-five bed facility in 1917, at a cost of $14,000, half paid by the local population. In 1920 the Missionary Society paid $40,000 to expand the hospital capacity to sixty-five beds, give it "thoroughly up-to-date equipment" including an x-ray laboratory, and provide a nurses' residence. In 1922 the American College of Surgeons certified it as a standard hospital, the only Canadian hospital listed that was not situated in a city.[106]

As the hospital's medical facilities improved, it became less like a mission. In 1919 the Reverend Thomas D. Jones complained that doctors Archer and Rush had ignored the hospital's local subcommittee when engaging a new matron (the subcommittee consisted of the two doctors and two pastors – Jones and C.W.W. Ross). Indeed, they had not thought to ask a prospective candidate about her religious affiliation ("she might have been a Roman Catholic"). As Jones continued,

The lady they finally engaged is a Baptist, able for the task of managing the hospital, a loveable type, but altogether separated from our vision of missionary work. Her predecessor, Miss C.M. Musselman, became a dear friend of ours. She was a Presbyterian & confessed that she intended running the hospital as a hospital. The missionary side was not in her calculations. Had Brother Ross and I been considered, we would most certainly have held out for a Methodist appointee with missionary vision. I insist that to get the best results, the Matron

must be seized with the missionary side of the work. Again the importance of
this is increased when it is remembered that the Matron engaged the Probationers & other workers. We have had several who have not made any secret
of their coldness re. matters of religion, and in an otherwise splendid group,
few members of the staff to-day have any vision of missionary service. I see this
ahead – that the Hospital will become (apart from the visiting by bro. Ross)
just a plain Hospital with its simple mission of healing sick bodies.[107]

SUMMARY AND CONCLUSION

The general board and WMS missionaries worked together, the former
catering to the Ukrainian men, the latter working with women and
children. The missionaries converted many, but had only forty church
members in 1914. With the exception of Lawford and Hannochko,
the missionaries gave low priority to "making Methodists."

As a group, the missionaries worked in four directions: saving souls
(or winning converts), working at moral uplift, making Anglo-Canadians,
and making Methodists. The goals were complementary for Lawford.
Others considered that the goals worked at cross-purposes and excluded
certain of them. The WMS school-home missionaries declined to try to
make Methodists lest they ruin their work of converting children. Pike
declined to make Methodists lest he alienate Ukrainians from Anglo-
Canadian protestant influences. In contrast, Metro Ponich rejected
Anglo-Canadianization lest he impede the work of winning converts.

Effectively the missionaries were a heterogenous group whose stated
goals were in tension with each other and in flux. The use of Ukrainian-
convert missionaries was problematic for Anglo-Methodists. The convert's Ukrainian language skills were an advantage for saving souls, but
his ethnic culture made him unreliable for imparting Anglo-Methodist
Canadian values. Two or three convert missionaries were fine. A larger
number, as Presbyterian experience demonstrated, caused problems.

If Canadianization and proselytizing were issues that divided the missionaries, then soul-saving, holiness, and moral reform were glue that
gave them unity. Certainly, whisky, dancing, and cigarettes had no place
in Methodist hospitals and missions. Temperance rallies and commu-
nity-centre missions were among the strategies used by Methodists to
counter them in local communities. If one considered the "moral
uplift" of the nation, mused Lawford in his retirement years, then the
missions had involved lives and money well spent. People from the
colony had "scattered far and wide ... They have gone with the ideals
imparted to them."[108] As Pike remarked, "Many streams of Canadian
life have flown into the Canadianization of the New Canadians, some

of them bad, most of them good and constructive. I venture to assert that the church ... contributed more to their cultural and spiritual potential than anything else."

Soul-saving evangelicalism persisted at the centre of missionary life. At their fifth annual conference in 1916, for example, the Methodist Ukrainian missionaries debated whether their work should "emphasize good citizenship or personal religion. In other words, should reform begin at the outside or the inside? When these queries have emerged from time to time," remarked T.C. Buchanan, the "unanimous verdict has been [that] our first duty is to evangelize. This year ... the matter of social service versus direct religious appeal was never broached seriously. The question before us was, how best to promote the cause of evangelism and win the people to a living faith in Jesus Christ."[109]

William Pike possibly was a silent dissenter. Living the Christ life rather than accepting Jesus as the Saviour was his top priority. He assumed that the Ukrainians could feel Christ in his work. But he never actually told them so.

Conclusion

White settlers flooded into Canada's prairie West during the years of the Laurier settlement boom, from 1896 to 1914. They came from central Canada, Britain, the United States, central Europe, and the Atlantic provinces. The regional population grew from 250,000 in 1891 to 1.7 million in 1916, and contemporaries expected millions more.

In hindsight, their expectations went unrealized. The First World War halted the flow of immigrants, and although immigration resumed during the 1920s, it was at less than the prewar pace and ended with the depression of the 1930s. Thus, the prewar years were the region's golden era for settlement. The 1920s were a decade of filling out and consolidating the prewar peopling of the plains.

This book has examined the Methodist response to the settlement boom. It discusses the religious tradition that the church transported to the prairie region, the church's supply of money and clergy for church expansion, and the church's response to non-Anglo-Saxon immigrants. It is not a regional case study for the scholarly debate about religiosity in Canadian society, but it does advance the debate as a byproduct of its central problem. Its church history brings fresh detail to scholarship about the prairie region during the period of study. It elaborates national stories about nation building, the marginalization of native peoples, and the massive alteration of the environment.

The settlement boom gave Methodists a chance for institutional growth, strengthening protestantism in Canada and making Canada a major player in the global outreach of protestant missions. The boom also gave them a chance to fail. The expansion of home missions made heavy demands on Methodist supplies of money and clergy. The prairie population was a difficult constituency, with both rural and urban problems and large numbers of non-Anglo-Saxon immigrants, bachelors, and immigrant co-religionists. Methodist pastors engaged in bitter competition with Roman Catholic and Greek Orthodox clergy and in not-so-friendly rivalry with Presbyterians and Anglicans.

The Methodist Church managed prairie church expansion with a centralized polity and heavy influence from the central Canadian conferences. As the prairie conferences developed, the church's centre of gravity shifted westward and some prairie Methodists chaffed under the administration of missions from Toronto. To hold the loyalty of the Western men, the church shifted some of the administrative control to the prairie region.

As discussed in chapter 2, the Methodist Church was a cross-class institution, with heavy representation of families headed by established farmers and upper-working-class and lower-middle-class men. All groups contributed to the mix of values that constituted the Methodist religious tradition and Methodist understandings of respectability. In this context, families were likely to seek the respect of their social peers more than of distant social betters.

Gender and life course, as well as class, shaped Methodist notions of respectability. Women made up a majority of the members, and evangelical doctrine matched values of domestic feminine culture. Their contributions to church decoration developed naturally from work they did in their homes. The feminine content of Methodist respectability clashed with masculine values for bachelors but not with masculine values for married men. Thus bachelors seldom became church members, while married men commonly did.

As in the larger society, men filled the church's leadership positions. Images of muscular Christianity and an all-male pastorate helped to shore up their masculine insecurities in an institution heavily influenced by women. This reinforcement of pastoral masculinity was essential for the recruitment of bachelor probationers.

Methodists were less attached to church life than one might suppose. In Ontario a minority of Methodists attended morning services on a given Sunday. In three small towns, less than half the Methodist families included a church member. Bachelors stayed aloof from the church in droves.

Although a Methodist presence in the prairie region dated from 1840, it had little influence on the church's regional culture after 1896. The early years were largely about native missions, which were a declining priority during the settlement boom. What is more important, the influx of Methodists during the settlement boom swamped the regional influences from earlier years.

The world Methodist tradition and the Canadian tradition were evolving and variegated, with elements that were both complementary and in tension. The Methodist tradition continued a long-term emphasis on personal salvation for an afterlife and personal sanctification, but it placed growing emphasis on social salvation and Christian nurture for children. It carried forward a tension between denominationalism and religious movement. The emergence of cross-denominational issues, physical demands on protestant resources, and negotiations over church union with the Presbyterians strengthened the religious-movement side of the prairie Methodist tradition. In general, Methodists reworked elements of their tradition to meet new circumstances, with outcomes that varied by social class, gender, and life course. Methodists promoted trends or resisted them, working within the church or leaving it for Methodist splinter groups such as holiness-movement churches and the Salvation Army.

The Missionary Society and the Women's Missionary Society raised the money for prairie missions, discounting, of course, the involuntary contributions of the missionaries, who received less than the church's minimum salary. The Missionary Society divided its money between home and foreign missions. Its home field included ordinary English-speaking missions and missions to non-Anglo-Saxons but not Indian and Oriental missions. The WMS gave to overseas missions and non-Anglo-Saxon missions in Canada.

The Missionary Society cooperated with educational movements to stimulate giving to its regular funds. The real-dollar amount of giving followed a rising trend, though it was not enough to keep pace with real-dollar expenditures. The society used wealthy laymen to raise special funds, the most important being its million-dollar Mission Plant and Extension Fund.

Otherwise it relied on small contributions from the masses, rather than large gifts from magnates. Some magnates gave little, because they disputed the society's spending priorities (e.g., there was too much emphasis on non-Anglo-Saxon missions or not enough) or its administrative practices (they were too centralized or not centralized enough). What is more important, the church had too few wealthy members to make much of a difference.

Prairie church expansion required money from central Canada, where two-thirds of the church's members lived. The real-dollar amounts required for English-speaking missions increased slowly to 1906 and then sharply, primarily to meet needs in Alberta and

Saskatchewan. The real-dollar amounts spent on non-Anglo-Saxon missions grew explosively. In part, the Missionary Society responded by cutting grants to Indian missions after 1910. It also challenged missions to become self-supporting, tried to create self-supporting city mission boards, and entered into cooperation agreements with the Presbyterians. Its five mission superintendents for the prairies were key officials for directing expansion and finding economies.

The Methodists had fewer missions in the prairie region than Anglicans and Presbyterians. They spent more on salary grants to missions than Anglicans and about the same as the Presbyterians. Compared to the other two churches, they invested less in Saskatchewan and more in Alberta.

The Methodist Church used student summer supplies, lay supplies, probationers, and ordained men to staff stations. The all-male clergy had to meet stiff educational requirements. In most cases, the church barred them from homesteading to supplement their meagre incomes. For financial reasons – a lower minimum salary – most recruits for the prairie pastorate were unmarried probationers.

By 1905 the rapidly developing prairie conferences experienced massive shortages of men, especially in Alberta and Saskatchewan. Conferences in central and eastern Canada were unable to meet the demand in western Canada, partly because of competition for men from the church's overseas missions and partly because of conditions following the Methodist Church union of 1884. American Methodist clergy were largely unavailable for the Canadian West. Thus Britain, and especially England, became the church's second major supplier of men for prairie service. Officials in the missionary society were grateful for their British recruits, but they favoured Canadian men, who were familiar with Canadian Methodist traditions.

A high quit rate for prairie clergy exacerbated the shortages of men. Low, uncertain salaries were one source of the problem. Other causes were the large number of inexperienced probationers in the region and the difficulty in supervising them with ordained men. The career of Stephen Byles exemplifies the difficulties that confronted "green Englishmen."

Of 663 prairie clergy for whom the writer has information, 57 percent were Canadian-born and 41 percent were born in Britain. The proportion of British-born men was below average in Manitoba and above average in Saskatchewan and Alberta. The influence of British clergy on Canadian Methodist traditions was less than their numbers would suggest. Canadian men held most of the senior positions, and the Britons acquired Canadian ways.

Both the Methodist census population and church membership in the prairie conferences rose notably during the years 1896–1914 but lagged behind population growth. In census population the Methodists placed a "sickly third" behind the Anglicans and Presbyterians. In church membership they ranked second, slightly behind the Presbyterians.

Compared to Ontario, prairie church members made up a lower percentage of the Methodist census population. The regional difference was small, however, and low religiosity in the prairie region is not the explanation. Prairie Methodists had a lower population density and therefore less access to Methodist church services. Moreover, a larger proportion of prairie Methodists were bachelors and immigrant co-religionists, who were difficult targets for church membership in either region.

Methodists and Presbyterians were comparable for nurturing children into church membership and church expansion programs. Presbyterians had more Sunday schools but fewer Sabbath scholars. They also had more circuits, but the difference came from student missions, which commonly closed for the winter months. Both churches fared better than the Anglicans in the development of Sunday schools and church expansion.

Immigration added more Anglicans and Presbyterians than Methodists to denominational census populations. It had a small influence on Anglo-Canadian church memberships, however, because the immigrant co-religionists tended not to join the Canadian churches. Similarly, denominational census populations included many immigrant co-religionists who were inactive in Canadian church life. Thus, contemporaries erred in using these census populations as the measure of their competitive success.

The revised church membership statistics, rather than the census statistics, provide the better measure. All things considered, the Methodist and Presbyterian achievements in church membership were impressive given the difficulties that the churches faced – low population densities, great numbers of bachelors, weak support from immigrant co-religionists, and large non-Anglo-Saxon immigration.

Methodists regarded non-Anglo-Saxons as non-preferred immigrants. Thus, they opposed immigration from the European continent or discouraged government from promoting it or favoured government medical inspections to screen out the unfit.

Methodists looked chiefly to the public schools to turn the non-Anglo-Saxon immigrants into Anglo-Canadians, but to their dismay, the provincial governments on the prairies failed to develop their schools to Methodist specifications. Roman Catholic archbishop Langevin's opposition to compulsory public schooling legislation, a shortage of Anglo-Canadian teachers, the emergence of ethnic bilingual teachers and ethnic nationalism, and peasant resistance from Slav immigrant groups influenced the outcome. Even so, countervailing influences were integrating the ethnic communities with the larger society and undermining resistance to the Methodist design.

The Methodist and Presbyterian Churches opened missions among non-Anglo-Saxon immigrants to continue the work of assimilation where the public school left off. Ukrainians were the chief ethnic target of the protestant missions. These peasant people had arrived in the prairie region without their priests, their local leaders in the Old Country. Nevertheless, competition from several churches, the emergence of educated laymen as ethnic leaders, the beginnings of ethnic nationalism, and peasant distrust of outsiders made protestant mission work difficult.

From the Methodist standpoint, Ukrainian religious life on the prairies gave rise to three key developments during the years 1896–1914. One was the failure of the francophone Roman Catholic mission and its transformation into a pseudo–Greek Catholic diocese in 1912. The second was the rise and fall of the Independent Greek Church, a failed protestant experiment for its Ukrainian leaders and their Presbyterian sponsors. The third was the slow diffusion of the Russian Orthodox mission among Bukovynians and some disgruntled Galician Greek Catholics. Bukovynians, in turn, were in the majority in Alberta's Star colony, where the Methodists located missions.

The All People's Mission clearly was a complex affair. Its common purpose was to turn non-Anglo-Saxons into protestant Anglo-Canadians with upper-working-class and lower-middle-class living standards. Otherwise, the goals of its large staff varied. The "gospel of Canadian citizenship" was important to J.S. Woodsworth but not to Arthur Rose and non-Anglo-Saxon staff members, such as Miss Kochella, Frank Dojacek, Jaromir Kovar, B. Baligrodzki, and A. Sosnowski. Woodsworth embraced the radical social gospel, but many on his staff emphasized personal salvation for an afterlife.

Woodsworth received widespread respect from Methodists, but he was a controversial figure. Officials of the church's two missionary societies and Winnipeg's city mission board appreciated Woodsworth's organizational skills and his leadership in institutional work and promotional activities. Other Methodists faulted him, however, for neglecting the personal salvation side of the work. Some Methodists even viewed non-Anglo-Saxon missions as a waste of resources.

The mission did in fact turn few non-Anglo-Saxons into Methodists. In 1914 the original Maple Street mission reported 131 members, but they were Old Country Methodists who had displaced the earlier non-Anglo-Saxon population. The institutes on Stella Avenue and Sutherland Avenue reported 38 members, but this number included staff and possibly Old Country Protestants.

Indeed, "making Methodists" was a low priority at the mission for strategic reasons. "Foreigners" such as Poles had learned to resist assimilative agendas in the Old Country. At best they could be brought gradually into protestantism. Thus, the All People's staff tried to convert the immigrants to protestant values without going so far as trying to make them Methodists. They used various stratagems. One – the failed Polish project – was to reform an ethnic church through the use of financial support and ethnic convert missionaries. Another was to use Sunday school and kindergarten classes to win the souls of immigrant children. A third was to steer the immigrants toward Methodist holiness by presenting themselves as exemplars of the Christ-life.

All People's, with its institutes, settlement houses, and variegated activities, suited the mixed ethnic population of the prairie metropolis. It was the prototype for All People's Missions in other Canadian cities, including Edmonton and Brandon in the prairie region.

The majority of the non-Anglo-Saxons on the prairies, however, lived in rural bloc settlements of one ethnic group. The Ukrainians were the key ethnic group in the Methodist Church's concern about non-Anglo-Saxon immigrants. It responded by opening several missions in the Star colony, Canada's largest Ukrainian settlement, and in Edmonton. The general board and WMS missionaries worked together, the former catering to the men, the latter working with women and children. The missionaries won many converts but had only forty church members in 1914. With the exception of Charles Lawford, "making Methodists" was a minor or long-term objective for them.

As a group, the missionaries had four general goals: saving souls (or winning converts), fostering moral uplift, making Anglo-Canadians, and making Methodists. As explained in the previous chapter, the goals overlapped and were complementary for Lawford. Others considered that the goals worked at cross-purposes, and they excluded some of them. The WMS school-home missionaries, for example, declined to make Methodists lest they ruin their work of converting children. W.H. Pike declined to make Methodists lest he alienate Ukrainians from Anglo-Canadian protestant influences. In contrast, Metro Ponich rejected Anglo-Canadianization lest he impede the work of winning converts.

Thus, the missionaries were a heterogenous group whose stated goals were negotiated in tension with each other and in flux. Methodists also negotiated the place of Ukrainian converts in mission work. From an Anglo-Methodist perspective, convert missionaries had advantages for saving souls but were unsound for the task of giving the Ukrainians Anglo-Canadian values. Two or three convert missionaries were fine, but a large number, as Presbyterian experience demonstrated, caused problems.

Despite their differences, the missionaries largely united on the work of soul-saving, holiness, and moral reform. These tasks, in turn, helped to bridge Methodist differences with Presbyterians and other evangelical protestant confessions.

Notes

INTRODUCTION

1 See also Hallett and Davis, *Firing the Heather.*
2 Classic references include Riddell's *Methodism in the Middle West* (1946); Brooks's 1972 doctoral dissertation, "Methodism in the Middle West"; Mann's *Sect, Cult and Church* (1955); and Burnet's *Next-Year Country* (1951).
3 Marks's *Revivals and Roller Rinks* and Voisey's *Vulcan* are notable exceptions, but these are primarily works of social, rather than church, history.
4 Airhart's review of Marshall's *Secularizing the Faith* and Marshall's review of Airhart's *Serving the Present Age.*
5 For a published summary of the argument of the thesis, see Emery, "Ontario Denied."
6 Hallett and Davis, *Firing the Heather,* 188–9, 194–5; Warne, *Literature as Pulpit*; Hancock, *No Small Legacy.*
7 Laudan, *Progress and Its Problems.* The core assumptions are ontological and methodological. They are about *thing-ness* (what is real) and *how-ness* (methodology). Early Methodist tradition, for example, treated a conversion experience as real and the emotional camp meeting as appropriate methodology.

CHAPTER ONE

1 *Christian Guardian,* 17 November 1909, cover-page quotation from Rowell's address entitled "Canada's Opportunity at Home and Abroad." See *Canada's Missionary Congress,* 39, 42.

2 Potyondi, "Loss and Substitution"; Worster, *Under Western Skies*, 34–52.

3 Brooks, "Methodism in the Middle West," chap. 1; Semple, *The Lord's Dominion*, 174–6; Riddell, *Methodism in the Middle West*, 14–16.

4 Grant, *Moon of Wintertime*; Miller, *Shingwauk's Vision*.

5 Riddell, *Methodism in the Middle West*, 68.

6 Voisey, *Vulcan*, 37–8, 77.

7 Martynowych, *Ukrainians in Canada*; Lehr, "Peopling the Prairies with Ukrainians."

8 Martynowych, *Ukrainians in Canada*.

9 Rowell's address to the Methodist general conference in Winnipeg, *Christian Guardian*, 17 September 1902. "Intense enthusiasm prevailed at the close of Mr Rowell's masterly, statesmanlike address. It was one of those addresses that cannot be put on paper and give the reader any adequate conception of the eloquence and fervour that characterized it."

10 For Riddell, see *Christian Guardian*, 26 July 1905. For Rowell, see *Canada's Missionary Congress*, 41.

11 Calculated from data in *Census of Canada*, 1911.

12 Canada, House of Commons, *Debates*, 1906, 5603, T.S. Sproule's speech in support of the Lord's Day bill. For other expressions of this idea, see Minutes, Toronto conference, 1896, pastoral address; Allen Papers, Rev. Oliver Darwin, Saskatchewan conference, to James Woodsworth, Winnipeg, 30 June 1906; *Christian Guardian*, 7 December 1898; article by Rev. R.O. Armstrong, Winnipeg, 31 March 1911; article by Professor C.E. Race, Alberta College, Edmonton, 18 August 1909.

13 *Annual Report*, Missionary Society, 1907–8, 55–6. See also *Christian Guardian*, 24 January 1899; Rev. James Woodsworth, superintendent of missions for the Manitoba and Northwest conference, to editor, 28 March 1902; article by Rev. Hiram Hull, Rat Portage, Manitoba conference, 5 August 1902; editorial, 26 October 1904; article by Rev. J.E. Hughson, *Missionary Bulletin*, 1908, 397–411.

14 "Address by Hon. Clifford Sifton," *Christian Guardian*, 16 November 1902; Rev. Wellington Bridgeman, Manitoba conference, to editor, 8 February 1911; Manning Papers, Rev. John Maclean, Morden, Manitoba, to Rev. C.E. Manning, Toronto, 8 February 1911.

15 Manitoba and Northwest conference news, *Christian Guardian*, 16 November 1898; see also 1 February 1899. Argue had migrated west from Ontario in 1881.

16 Sutherland Papers, F.J. Fydell, probationer, Austin, Manitoba, to Sutherland, 7 August 1907; *Christian Guardian*, 6 December 1904 (Lenora); see also 25 September 1907 (Oak Lake); Allen Papers, Allen to Rev. John Maclean, Morden, Manitoba, 10 March 1909; Report of James Woodsworth, superintendent of missions, Manitoba conference, 1912.

17 Ayers makes this argument for the Old South region of the United States during the years 1877–1906. See Ayers, *Southern Crossing.*

18 *Christian Guardian*, 27 May 1896; see also Alberta conference news, 18 December 1907.

19 "Survey of Church Conditions in the Dominion of Canada Made by a Joint committee of the Methodist, Congregational, and Presbyterian Churches," *Acts and Proceedings*, General Assembly, Presbyterian Church, 1914, 365.

20 *Christian Guardian*, 28 March 1906.

21 Marks, *Revivals and Roller Rinks*, 30–7.

22 Calculated from data in *Census of the Prairie Provinces, 1916*, xxvi, table 14.

23 In 1921 the number of bachelors for each single female ranged from 3.6 to 8.9 in in Alberta's rural districts, but only from 1.8 to 2.2 in Ontario's rural districts. These findings are for five-year age groups between 20–24 and 40–44. See Voisey, *Vulcan*, 18–20.

24 Supplement, with stenographic report of the proceedings of the general board of missions, 1909, *Christian Guardian*, 2 February 1910.

25 Ibid., 11 March 1908.

26 Ibid., 13 January 1909.

27 *Missionary Outlook*, February 1909.

28 Woodsworth, *Strangers within Our Gates*, 222.

29 *Christian Guardian*, 30 April 1902, 21 May 1902.

30 Ibid., 8 April 1908; see also *Annual Report*, Missionary Society, 1912–13, viii–x.

31 *Christian Guardian*, 23 February 1910.

32 Ibid., 10 November 1909. For other expressions of fear of Roman Catholics, see Minutes, London conference, 1896, pastoral address; *Missionary Outlook*, October 1911; Allen Papers, C.H. Lawford, Pakan, Alberta, to Allen, 4 March 1908; George N. Jackson, secretary of the Winnipeg City Mission Board, to Allen, 26 March 1909; C.H. Lawford to Allen, 9 November 1911.

33 See Allen Papers, Proceedings of the Commission on Foreign Missions in Western Canada, Winnipeg, 28 August 1909; copy of speech given at Wiarton, Ontario, by Irving Grok, Shallow Lake, Ontario, 29 September 1904; Woodsworth, *Strangers within Our Gates.*

34 *Christian Guardian*, 14 January 1903.

35 Allen Papers, Proceedings of the Commission on Foreign Missions in Western Canada, Winnipeg, 28 August 1909.

36 Ibid.

37 Woodsworth, *My Neighbor*, chap. 1.

38 Article by Rev. Ernest Thomas, Lachute, PQ, *Christian Guardian*, 22 February 1905; see also article by A. McKibbin, 1 November 1911.

39 Ferrier, "Indian Education in the North-West."

40 Ibid. For J.S. Woodsworth's similar view, see Mills, *Fool for Christ*.

41 Canada, House of Commons, *Debates*, 1904, 6948, 6856; cited in Miller, *Shingwauk's Vision*, 135.

42 Riddell, *Methodism in the Middle West*, 224, 243, 296.

43 *Christian Guardian*, 9 October 1907.

44 Allen Papers, Rev. B.W.J. Clements, Wessington, Alberta, to Allen, 13 February 1907; see also Rev. A.R. Aldridge, Vermillion District, Alberta, to Allen, 17 September 1907; Rev. W.P.M. Haffie, Shaunauvon, Alberta, to Allen, 20 August 1914.

45 Letter from Rev. F.W.H. Armstrong, Lesser Slave Lake, Alberta, *Missionary Bulletin*, 1910, 619; Allen Papers, Rev. T.C. Buchanan, Parkland, Alberta, to Allen, 15 November 1906; Rev. Thomas W. Bateman, Wainwright, Alberta, to Allen, 12 August 1908.

46 *Christian Guardian*, 31 August 1904.

47 Ibid., 13 February 1907.

48 Carman Papers, G.W. Brown, Regina, to Carman, 10 July 1912; Allen Papers, J.T. Brown, Regina, to N.W. Rowell, Toronto, 10 July 1912; report of Rev. Oliver Darwin, superintendent of missions for the Saskatchewan conference, 9 August 1912; *Christian Guardian*, 9 October 1912. To help Regina Methodists cope with their $30,000 net loss, the general conference issued a $15,000 two-year loan. See Allen Papers, Rev. Oliver Darwin to Allen, 13 July 1912; extract from the minutes of a meeting of the local sub-committee of the general board of missions, 24 July 1912.

49 Allen Papers, Rev. Frank Coop, Wilcox, Saskatchewan, to James Woodsworth, Winnipeg, 21 November 1907; Rev. Charles H. Hopkins, northern Alberta, to T.C. Buchanan, 28 July 1910; see also Manning Papers, Rev. E.I. Pratt, Turner, Saskatchewan, to C.E. Manning, Toronto, 8 July 1908; letter from Rev. W.T. Young, Millet, Alberta, *Missionary Bulletin*, 1908, 1009; letter from Rev. Henry Munton, Tofield, Alberta, 1909, 119; 1910, letter from Rev. Russell Dynes, Gull Lake, Saskatchewan, 479–80; letter from Rev. George F. Deynes, Golenville mission, Calgary, 1910, 611; letter from Rev. and Mrs. A.D. Richard, Camrose, Alberta, 1910, 920; letter from Rev. E.F. Morrow, Senlac, Saskatchewan, 1913, 470; Manitoba and Northwest conference news, *Christian Guardian*, 4 January 1899; description of conditions at Shellbrooke, Prince Albert District, 6 November 1907; "One Who is Desirous for the Good of the Church of Christ," to editor, 2 February 1910.

50 Allen Papers, Ethel Anderson Armstrong, Dunvegan, Alberta, to "fellow workers," 24 March 1913; see also T.F. Serafout, Calgary, to Rev. G.W. Kerby, Toronto, 10 August 1907; description of the funding of White Whale Lake mission, *Christian Guardian*, 1 April 1908.

51 Letter from Rev. W.T. Young, Millet, Alberta, *Missionary Bulletin*, 1908,
   1009. See also Sutherland Papers, Rev. T.R. McNair, Davidson,
   Saskatchewan, to J.N. Shannon, Toronto, 3 November 1905; Allen
   Papers, Rev. Thomas W. Bateman, Wainwright, Alberta, to Allen,
   12 August 1908; description of pastor's shack at Exshaw, Alberta, by
   Rev. G.A. Hipkin, pastor, *Christian Guardian*, 6 November 1907.

52 Allen Papers, Allen to John W. Roberts, Lancashire, England, 21 September 1908.

53 Article by Rev. J.E. Hughson, *Missionary Bulletin*, 1908.

54 Allen Papers, Rev. Oliver Darwin to Allen, 5 and 22 March 1909. For
   other examples of physical mishaps suffered by prairie clergy, see
   description of the misadventure of Rev. A.E. Galway and R.V. Clement,
   Christian Guardian, 5 December 1900; experience of Rev. A. Henderson,
   22 July 1903; experience of Rev. Thomas Lawson, 29 July 1903; account
   of the death of the son of Rev. Frank Finn, 6 April 1904; description
   of the tour of the west by Rev. Nathanael Burwash and his son,
   24 August 1904; account of the accident of Rev. E. Telpher, Pembina,
   28 February 1906.

55 Address given by N.W. Rowell to the Manitoba and Northwest conference, Epworth League convention, *Christian Guardian*, 2 September
   1902.

56 Interview with Buchanan, ibid., 25 March 1903.

57 Observation of Rev. William Meikle, an evangelist who had been conducting union (interdenominational) revival services in Manitoba for the
   previous fourteen months, ibid., 13 May 1896; article by Professor
   W.F. Osborne, Wesley College, 4 March 1903; Rev. Alexander Sutherland to editor, 9 December 1903; comment by Rev. H.G. Cairns, Arcola,
   Manitoba, 23 March 1904; article by John W. Eedy, Alberta conference,
   1 May 1907.

58 Article by Rev. J.E. Hughson, *Missionary Bulletin*, 1908, 403. See also
   Minutes, Alberta conference, 1910, report of the committee on state
   of the work, 68–71; Allen Papers, J.N. Shannon, Mission Rooms, to
   Rev. Oliver Darwin, 17 June 1907; W.J. Robertson, St Catherines,
   Ontario, to editor, *Christian Guardian*, 19 October 1898; W.H.R. to
   editor, 1 March 1905; Rev. H.G. Cairns, Saskatchewan conference,
   to editor, 23 April 1913.

59 Letter from Rev. R.R. Morrison, Outlook, Saskatchewan, *Missionary Bulletin*, 1910, 488.

60 Allen Papers, Rev. Arthur Barner, Alix, Alberta, to Allen, 27 January
   1907; Rev. T.J. Johnston, Clover Bar, Alberta, to Allen, 15 September
   1908; article by H.H. Fudger, treasurer of the Missionary Society, *Missionary Outlook*, June 1906; article by T.A.P., October 1912.

CHAPTER TWO

1 As standard boilerplate information for the Saskatchewan conference shows, *station* was an alternative term for *circuit*, not an *appointment* on a circuit, as one of the expert readers of this work mistakenly believes. In 1915, for example, the conference table "Names of Circuits and Pastors in Charge" reports Richardson as a circuit with three preaching appointments in the charge of A.W. Ingram. The conference's annual list, "Stations of Ministers and Probationers," gives Richardson as a station in the charge of A.W. Ingram. See *Methodist Year Book*, 1915, 361, 383.

2 Semple, *The Lord's Dominion*, 209; Christie and Gauvreau, *A Full-Orbed Christianity*, 35.

3 Van Die, *An Evangelical Mind*, 190.

4 Allen Papers, Allen to J.H. Ashdown, Winnipeg, 14 September 1909; article by Rev. F.B. Stacey, *Christian Guardian*, 21 July 1909.

5 Allen Papers, Proceedings of the Commission on Foreign Missions in Western Canada, Winnipeg, 28 August 1909, statement by Rev. James Allen, chairman.

6 Article by W.G. Hunt, Calgary, *Christian Guardian*, 11 March 1908; article by A.R. Ford, 8 December 1907; Carman Papers, G.W. Brown, Regina, to Rev. Albert Carman, 31 December 1909. Brown was named lieutenant-governor of Saskatchewan in 1910.

7 *Christian Guardian*, 8 December 1907.

8 Allen Papers, Allen to Darwin, 27 December 1907.

9 Inferred from information in the minutes of ninety-one prairie quarterly boards.

10 Allen Papers, Rev. T.C. Buchanan to Allen, 17 January 1907; Rev. Arthur Barner, Alix, Alberta, to Allen, 29 January 1907; Allen to Rev. Wellington Bridgeman, Manitoba conference, 28 December 1906; Allen to W.J. Conoly, Namao, Alberta, 7 December 1906; Allen to Rev. T.C. Buchanan, 25 January 1907; Allen to Rev. G.W. Kerby, Calgary, 6 February 1907; Allen to Rev. R.E. Finley, Daysland, Alberta, 6 February 1907.

11 Alberta conference news, *Christian Guardian*, 12 September 1906; article by Arthur Ford, 18 December 1907; article by W.G. Hunt, Calgary, 11 March 1908; article by Rev. F.B. Stacey, 21 July 1909; prairie correspondent, 20 April 1910; 4 May 1910; article by Rev. J.W. Saunby, *Western Methodist Times*, March 1906; Allen Papers, Proceedings of the Commission on Foreign Missions in Western Canada, Winnipeg, 28 August 1909.

12 Saskatchewan conference news, *Christian Guardian*, 6 November 1912. See Voisey, *Vulcan*, and Voisey, *A Preacher's Frontier*, for information about real estate booms and busts in two Alberta towns.

13 Alberta conference news, *Christian Guardian*, 12 September 1906.
14 Allen Papers, Woodsworth, Winnipeg, to Allen, 15 November 1907;
Woodsworth to Rev. C.E. Manning, 23 December 1907.
15 Ibid., Allen to Darwin, 22 October 1906.
16 Ibid., Allen to Darwin, 27 December 1907.
17 Ibid., Darwin to Allen, 20, 29 October and 10, 11 November 1909;
Allen to Darwin, 21, 29 October 1909; Allen to Rev. J.W. Switzer, president of the Saskatchewan conference, 11 November 1909.
18 Ibid., Darwin to Allen, 25 November 1909.
19 Ibid., Darwin to Allen, 29 October 1909.
20 Ibid., Allen to D.J. Thom, Regina, 4 March 1910.
21 Carman Papers, G.W. Brown, Regina, to Carman, 31 December 1909.
In March 1910, after investigation, the general board blamed Darwin for
the faulty communication. As Allen was accustomed to written transactions, he had viewed Darwin's brief verbal communication in his office
as casual conversation. The written information, which Darwin failed to
submit through Allen, was inadequate. On 2 April 1910 Darwin apologised to Allen and agreed to written communications for their future
business transactions. Allen Papers, Allen to Darwin, 11 November 1909
and 2 April 1910; Allen to Rev. J.W. Switzer, 11 November 1909, and
8 March 1910; Allen to Rev. J.T. Harrison, Balcarres, Saskatchewan,
18 March 1910. Despite the general board's findings, the Alberta conference mission superintendent, the Rev. T.C. Buchanan, had made emergency allocations for church and parsonage sites and supplied the
necessary information after the fact. See Sutherland Papers, Buchanan to
H.H. Fudger, Mission Rooms, 14 March 1908; Buchanan to J.N. Shannon, 23 July 1909.
22 Allen Papers, Allen to Rev. C.H. Huestis, Edmonton, 23 October 1906
and 19 November 1906; Allen to Rev. James Woodsworth, 16 November
1906; Allen to T.C. Buchanan, 10 November 1906.
23 Ibid., report of the committee on western mission policy, general board
of missions, October 1909; Allen to Rev. Frank M. Wooten, Moose Jaw,
16 December 1909; Rev. W.K. Allen, Red Deer, Alberta, secretary of the
Alberta conference, to James Allen, 7 June 1910 (copy of the Alberta
conference committee's report, Missionary Autonomy in the West); Minutes, Saskatchewan conference, 1910, report of committee on local
administration in home missionary affairs in the prairie provinces, 79–
81; stenographic report of proceedings of the general board of missions
for 1909, Christian Guardian, 2 February 1910, supplement.
24 *Journal of Proceedings*, general conference, 1906, report no.3 of the general board of missions, 119–20.
25 Allen Papers, Allen to Darwin, 14 December 1907; *Annual Report*,
Missionary Society, 1909–10, 41. The control of monies was vested in a

ten-man prairie region committee that could act in consultation with the prairie mission superintendents.

26 *Journal of Proceedings*, general conference, 1910, report no. 2 of the committee on missions, 394–5, and 104; report of committee on general superintendency, 71, 74, 380–1; Allen Papers, Allen to T.C. Buchanan, Oliver Darwin, and James Woodsworth, 24 October 1910.

27 The Missionary Society's policy of 1912 slowed the expansion of missions in order to secure for the missionaries their full minimum salaries. See chapter 5.

28 Minutes, missionary committee (UCAW).

29 Minutes, Manitoba and Northwest conference, 1892, 64.

30 Minutes, Manitoba conference, 1906, report of the committee on memorials.

31 *Western Methodist Times*, April 1906. See also Minutes, Alberta conference, report of committee on the Christian Guardian, 36–7. During the church year 1904–5, the *Christian Guardian*'s prairie circulation dropped by 241, including 104 fewer subscriptions in the Alberta conference. The statistic of three thousand for the *Christian Guardian* is an estimate. It is based on Milliken's statement that one in ten members in central and western Canada subscribed to it.

32 *Journal of Proceedings*, general conference, 1906, report of book and publishing committee, 172–3. The Maritime conferences always had their own journal, the *Wesleyan*, and were in the committee's Eastern section. The central Canadian conferences, hitherto in the committee's Western section, were placed in a new central section.

33 Journal of Proceedings, general conference, 1910, 324; 1914, 271–2.

34 Alberta conference news, Christian Guardian, 19 June 1907.

35 Ibid., 7 February 1912.

36 Report of the general conference proceedings, ibid., 3 October 1906. Kerby believed that such a paper would have financial problems and hence would be of poor quality. A British Columbia minister doubted that Winnipeg was the best place for a Western journal.

37 Allen Papers, proceedings of the Commission on Foreign Missions in Western Canada, Winnipeg, 28 August 1909.

38 Stenographic report of the 1909 annual meeting of the general board of missions, comment by James Allen, *Christian Guardian*, 2 February 1910, supplement.

39 Manuscript minutes, Alberta conference, 1913 (PAA).

40 See chap. 1 for a statement by Moody. See chap. 8 for other Manitoba opponents of non-Anglo-Saxon mission work.

41 Semple, The Lord's Dominion, 334–9.

42 Semple, "Ontario's Religious Hegemony," 20–5. The increase of lay representation on church courts in 1884, argues Semple, "did not

represent real democratization of the institution; rather it reinforced the domination of leading laymen and bolstered their denominational loyalty." Thus, in this article Semple characterizes the church as an "*urban*, respectable, middle class institution" (my italics).

43 Van Die, "Genuine Revival," 543–4, 554–5, 559n101.

44 Mussio, "The Origins and Nature of the Holiness Movement Church," 82, 96. As Mussio argues, "many farmers and skilled labourers" opposed "middle-class urban" values.

45 Marks, *Revivals and Roller Rinks*, appendix B. Marks sensibly places farmers in the category of "other."

46 Ibid., 10, 13, 157. Although characteristic of early Methodist revivalism, notes Marks, emotionalism was anathema to Methodists by the 1880s. Thus the "middle and working class alike" interpreted the emotional appeal of Army services (with their "shouting, crying, and jumping up and down in the name of salvation") as a "class-based challenge to respectable churchgoing."

47 Ibid., 71–3.

48 Darroch, "Scanty Fortunes," 634, 636–7, 654.

49 Ibid., 655, inferred from his evidence and comment on Gaffield's argument.

50 Wilson, "Tenancy as Family Strategy."

51 Emery and Emery, *A Young Man's Benefit*, chap. 2.

52 Marks, *Revivals and Roller Rinks*, 28, 144. The price for Methodists included pew rents, envelope subscriptions, and the cost of Sunday clothes. The social profiles of Methodists and Odd Fellows varied from one church or lodge to another.

53 Johnson, *Saving and Spending*; Emery and Emery, *A Young Man's Benefit*, 16–17.

54 Mussio, "Holiness Movement Church," 82, 96. Lynne Marks works within Semple's model of middle-class hegemony. Although she notes working-class counter-discourses that challenged church-based respectability, she locates them outside the church, in the Salvation Army and Knights of Labour movements. Within the church, poor working-class women were less likely than middle-class women to join ladies aids, which were fundraising institutions. However, Marks attributes this to financial, time, and social constraints, rather than to alternative values. Marks, *Revivals and Roller Rinks*, 10, 13, 71–3, 157.

55 Methodist and Presbyterian Churches, Social Surveys, St Catherines, 5–16; Huron County, 17; London, 45–6.

56 Marks, *Revivals and Roller Rinks*, chaps. 2–3, 100–1; Van Die, "Genuine Revival," 535–40.

57 Marks, *Revivals and Roller Rinks*, 13–14, 30–7, 68–9.

58 Cavanagh, "'No Place for a Woman.'"

CHAPTER THREE

1 Semple, *The Lord's Dominion*, 16–17, 54, 132.
2 Christ's atonement had "awakened a 'prevenient' grace, identified by some as conscience, which allowed human beings to choose between right and wrong." Ibid.
3 Ibid., 139.
4 Ibid., 19.
5 Mann, *Sect, Cult, and Church in Alberta*, 37, 51–2.
6 Van Die, "Genuine Revival," 529; Westfall, *Two Worlds*, chap. 5.
7 Semple, *The Lord's Dominion*, 211–12; Christie and Gauvreau, *Full-Orbed Christianity*, xii.
8 Semple, "'The Nurture and Admonition of the Lord'"; Semple, *The Lord's Dominion*, 363–9.
9 Marks, *Revivals and Roller Rinks*, 24–5.
10 Rev. Alexander Sutherland, "The Twentieth Century and Missions," *Methodist Magazine and Review,* January 1901, 19.
11 "J.H.," to editor, *Christian Guardian*, 29 May 1905.
12 Ibid., 17 December 1913. See also W. Harrison, "Christianity in the First and Nineteenth Centuries," *Canadian Methodist Quarterly,* October 1891, 500–3.
13 Of American origin, this slogan had been adopted by the Forward Movement for Missions, a program to interest young people in overseas mission work. For use of the slogan by Canadian Methodists, see *Christian Guardian*, 1 September 1900; editorial, 16 October 1907; 18 December 1907; editorial, 5 September 1911.
14 William Williams, "The Christian Missionary, the Pioneer of Civilization," *Canadian Methodist Quarterly* 5 (1893), 29. See also article by Rev. Alexander Sutherland, ibid., 17–23; "The Federation of Empire," *Methodist Magazine and Review,* August 1897, 178–9; Rev. Hugh Johnston, "Anglo-Saxon Brotherhood," ibid., February 1899, 122 (lecture given in Carleton Street Methodist Church, Toronto); Rev. Thomas, "An Anglo-Saxon Alliance," ibid., July 1898, 146–9; article by Professor W.F. Osborne, Wesley College, *Christian Guardian*, 6 May 1903. See also 4 November 1896; 26 May 1897; 2 June 1897; 16 June 1897 (Rev. W.H. Withrow speculates that an Anglo-Saxon alliance might hasten the millennium); review of a book by a French author, Edmund Desmoulin, 5 April 1899; 3 January 1900 (speculation that the American occupation of the Philippines is a step forward in the "White Man's Burden.")
   The millennium was the thousand-year reign of Christ on earth, which was to precede the final judgment. Premillennialists believed that the millennium could be brought about only by Christ's return to earth and that attempts to reform earthly life prior to Christ's return were doomed

to failure. Postmillennialists hoped, with God's help, to bring about the millennium by Christianizing life on earth; they felt that Christ would return at the end of the millennial period of perfection.

15 Brouwer, *New Women for God*; Gagan, *A Sensitive Independence*; Wright, *A World Mission*; Austin, *Saving China*; Ion, The Cross and the Rising Sun.

16 *Annual Report*, Missionary Society, 1911–12, vii. The Methodists arrived at their obligation mathematically. Canada was responsible for forty million of the world's estimated one billion unevangelized people, based on the nation's percentage of the world's Anglo-Saxon population. Methodists had a third of Canada's protestant population and hence a third of the national share.

17 Semple, *The Lord's Dominion*, chap. 12; *Methodist Yearbook, 1915*, 24, 56.

18 *Missionary Outlook*, December 1913, cover page (quotation from the Edinburgh conference of 1910); article by Rev. F.A. Cassidy, *Christian Guardian*, 29 January 1896. The outreach also expressed anxiety. If Canada and other Anglo-Saxon powers failed to evangelize the world, then heathen lands could threaten civilization. Ibid., 6 July 1906; article by Rev. G.J. Bond, a former editor of the Guardian, 1 December 1909; report of an address by Dr James Endicott, a China missionary, to an audience in Regina, 13 August 1913; *Missionary Outlook*, December 1912.

19 Semple, *The Lord's Dominion*, 349–55.

20 McClung, *The Next of Kin* (1917), cited in Hancock, *No Small Legacy*, 64–5.

21 See chap. 8.

22 In 1906, for example, John Holmes's preaching of disbelief in eternal punishment got him purged from the ministry. See Minutes, quarterly board, Binscarth-Foxwarren, Manitoba, 2 August 1906 (UCAW).

23 Brody, *Workers in Industrial America*, 50. For welfare capitalism in Canada, see McCallum, "Corporate Welfarism"; Emery and Emery, *A Young Man's Benefit*, chap. 5.

24 Gauvreau and Christie, "World of the Common Man."

25 Warne, *Literature as Pulpit*, chap. 1.

26 Ibid.

27 For contemporary discussion of problems raised by biblical criticism, see Rev. W.H. Hincks, Toronto conference, to editor, *Christian Guardian*, 25 January 1905.

28 Rev. L. Lashley Hall, Fernie, BC, to editor, Ibid., 16 October 1907; article by the general superintendent, S.D. Chown, 14 August 1912; Minutes, Toronto conference, 1896, pastoral address.

29 Rev. L. Lashley Hall to editor, *Christian Guardian*, 16 October 1907.

30 Gauvreau, "Taming of History," 328–34; Van Die, An Evangelical Mind, chap. 4; Burwash, *History of Victoria College*, chaps. 7, 11, 12. Nelles was

principal of Victoria College (1850–87). Burwash was dean of theology (1873–87) and then president and chancellor (1887–1913).

31 Gauvreau, "The Taming of History," 334–8.

32 Semple, *The Lord's Dominion*, 266.

33 Allen Papers, Rev. John Maclean, Morden, Manitoba, to the Rev. C.E. Manning, 8 February 1911; Carman Papers, Kenner to Carman, 4, 25 March 1909; 10 February, 4 March, 23 April, and 25 October 1910; 30 January 1911.

34 Carman Papers, Kenner to Carman, 4, 25 March 1909; 10 February, 4 March, 23 April, and 25 October 1910; 30 January 1911; Riddell, *Methodism in the Middle West*, 230; *Christian Guardian*, 2 July 1913. Riddell left Wesley College to become principal at the new Alberta College in 1903.

35 Interview with Byles, 21–22 May 1974.

36 Van Die, *An Evangelical Mind*, 91–113; Mussio, "The Holiness Movement Church"; Semple, *The Lord's Dominion*, 267–75. As noted above, the social gospel was in part a countertrend. Although for some it developed from liberal theology, it also accompanied a rejection of theology and a return to experience as the chief authority for religion. See Christie and Gauvreau, *Full-Orbed Christianity*.

37 Marks, *Revivals and Roller Rinks*, chaps. 6–7; Mussio, "The Holiness Movement Church."

38 Marks, *Revivals and Roller Rinks*, 156–7.

39 Mussio, "The Holiness Movement Church."

40 Westfall, *Two Worlds*, chap. 7.

41 Van Die, *An Evangelical Mind*, chaps. 5–6.

42 Article by Rev. George W. Kerby, *Christian Guardian*, 15 July 1903; James Woodsworth to editor, 20 April 1904; Rev. T.J. Johnston, Strathcona, Alberta, to editor, 25 January 1905; Rev. W.P. Gourd, Hartney, Manitoba, to editor, 22 March 1905; Rev. Oliver Coleman, Sperling, Manitoba, to editor, 13 May 1908; article by Nathanael Burwash, 14 February 1912; J.E. Collins, Strathcona, Alberta, to editor, 14 June 1911; Rev. S.D. Chown, Vancouver, to editor, 10 December 1913; *Annual Report*, Missionary Society, 1907–8, 3–4.

43 Manitoba and Northwest conference news, *Christian Guardian*, 17 March 1897; "West." to editor, 2 November 1904; W.G. Bradford, Avonmore, Ontario, to editor, 20 April 1904; Rev. Henry Lewis, Melita, Manitoba, to editor, 20 April 1904; R.A.A. McConnell, Lancaster, Ontario, to editor, 4 January 1905; meeting of Grace Church congregation, Winnipeg, 14 February 1906; "a superfluous preacher," to editor, 28 October 1908; George W. Playfair, Sr, Baldur, Manitoba, to editor, 15 February 1911; "St Mary's," to editor, 7 June 1911; Rev. S.D. Chown, Vancouver, to editor, 10 December 1913; departments of social service and evangelism of

the Methodist and Presbyterian Churches, Rural Survey, Swan River Valley, Manitoba, 1914, 50–1, 58; Rural Survey, Turtle Mountain District, Manitoba, 1914, 61–3; Carman Papers, John George, Port Elgin, Ontario, to Carman, 29 December 1904; Allen Papers, J.H. Ashdown, Winnipeg, to Allen, 20 April 1909.

44 Article by Rev. S.G. Bland, Wesley College, *Christian Guardian*, 26 February 1908; Fred C. Middleton, Winnipeg, to editor, 3 June 1908.

45 Account of the congregational meeting at Grace Church, Winnipeg, ibid., 14 February 1906.

46 Article by Rev. W.P. Gourd, Hartney, Manitoba, ibid., 22 March 1905.

47 Rev. Ernest J. Tate, Alix, Alberta, to editor, ibid., 1 April 1908. See also Manitoba conference news, 15 January 1908; Rural Survey, Swan River Valley, 62; Voisey, *Vulcan*, chap. 8.

48 Alberta conference news, *Christian Guardian*, 31 January 1906; Saskatchewan conference news, 21 March 1906; Carman Papers, Rev. Edward S. Bishop, Okotoks, Alberta, to Carman, 6 January 1906; Rev. David C. Day, Pipestone, Manitoba, to Carman, 17 February 1908; Rev. J.H. White, superintendent of missions for the British Columbia conference, to Carman, 1 February 1906. Carman's correspondence contains eight other instances of delayed church construction plans, all in Ontario.

49 *Christian Guardian*, 17 July 1912.

50 See ibid., 24 August 1910; Minutes, general conference, 1906, report of committee on church union, 81–7; 1910, 329–30; 1914, 282–5. For the content of the basis, see a series of seven articles by Rev. J.S. Ross in *Christian Guardian*, 8 September to 27 October 1909; article by Rev. S.G. Bland, 8 June 1910. In 1925 Methodists united with the Congregational Church and two-thirds of the Presbyterian Church to form the United Church of Canada. For literature on church union, see Silcox, *Church Union in Canada*; Grant, *Canadian Experience of Church Union*; Clifford, *Resistance to Church Union*; Van Die, *An Evangelical Mind*; Semple, *The Lord's Dominion*.

51 Carman Papers, Oliver Darwin to Carman, 24 March 1911; L.L. Meech, Conquest, Saskatchewan, to Carman, 26 July 1912; W.G. Hunt to Carman, 27 June 1912; *Christian Guardian*, 10 February 1909; 3 March 1909; 15 March 1911; 3 April 1912; 6 August 1913, Manitoba conference news; Allen Papers, quadrennial report of James Woodsworth, 1914; J.T. Brown to N.W. Rowell, 10 July 1912; Silcox, *Church Union in Canada*, 215.

52 Manitoba conference news, *Christian Guardian*, 6 August 1913; Allen Papers, quadrennial report of James Woodsworth, 1914; J.T. Brown to N.W. Rowell, 10 July 1912; Carman Papers, W.G. Hunt to Carman, 27 June 1912.

53 Carman Papers, Resolutions of the general conference special committee re union churches and property, 7 April 1911 to 9 January 1913; report of the general conference special committee executive's meeting with Presbyterian representatives, Brantford, 7 October 1912; note of Carman's, dated 27 January 1913; L.L. Meech, Conquest, Saskatchewan, to Carman, 26 June 1912; report of the special committee appointed by the representatives of the union congregations in Regina, 3 April 1913, to confer with Dr Chown of the Methodist Church and Rev. W.A. Mackinnon, representing Dr Grant of the Presbyterian Church, concerning the status and future relations of the union congregations with the Presbyterian, Methodist and Congregational churches, now negotiating union in Canada; *Christian Guardian*, 18 December 1912; Silcox, *Church Union in Canada*, 219–42.

54 Conference news columns, *Christian Guardian*.

55 Editorial comment by Rev. W.B. Creighton, ibid., 8 January 1913; see also article by Rev. C.H. Cross, Saskatchewan conference, 11 January 1911.

56 Moore Papers, Rev. G.G. Webber, Vegreville, Alberta, to Rev. T. Albert Moore, Toronto, 13 September 1912; Byles, "Canadianization of a Yorkshire Lad."

57 *Christian Guardian*, 9 September 1903; see also "The Methodist Pulpit in Toronto," 24 May 1899; article by Rev. C.H. Huestis, 11 September 1907; Miss Millie Magwood, Brantford, to editor, 30 June 1908.

58 Ibid., 23 December 1903; 29 April 1903; Minutes, Manitoba conference, 1911, 54–6.

59 *Christian Guardian*, 29 April 1903.

60 Ibid., 15 May 1912, article by Milliken. For the traditional conversion-centred approach, see articles by Rev. C.H. Huestis, 20 January 1904, and 30 October 1907; article by Rev. R.B. Chadwick, 28 December 1910; editorial on the itineracy, 10 October 1910.

61 Ibid., 8 January 1908.

62 Ibid., 8 May 1907 (Medicine Hat, Alberta); 15 May 1907 (Carman, Manitoba); 21 May 1913 (Davidson, Alberta).

63 Hunt conducted services at Killarney, Manitoba, without "fads or eccentricities." Ibid., 5 February 1905; for other examples of restraint on emotional display see 19 September 1900 (Grenfell, NWT); 22 March 1905 (Blackfalds, Alberta); 17 February 1907 (Medicine Hat, Alberta).

64 Ibid., 25 July 1906; 9 October 1907.

65 Ibid., 18 July 1902.

66 Ibid., 11 April 1906.

67 Ibid., 19 April 1905; 7 March 1906.

68 Ibid., 7, 28 August 1901.

69 Thomas H. Morris, Hamilton, to editor, ibid., 31 July 1907; see also 19 December 1900; Rev. James R. Aikenhead, Gravenhurst, Ontario, to

editor, 3 June 1903; Rev. W.G. Clarke, Little Britain, Ontario, to editor, 1 March 1905; Rev. W. McMullen, Florence, Ontario, to editor.

70 Minutes, Alberta conference, 1910, report of committee on state of the work, 68–71.

71 *Journal of Proceedings*, general conference, 1910, 335. See also Minutes, Alberta conference, 74–5.

72 *Christian Guardian*, 15 February 1895; article by Rev. W.L. Armstrong, 23 July 1907.

73 Bodrug, *Independent Orthodox Church*, 10.

74 Van Paassen, *Days of Our Years*, 57–9.

75 Minutes, Quarterly Official Board, Century Methodist Church, Medicine Hat, 1894–1917 (examined in Century United Church, Medicine Hat).

76 Allen Papers, Rev. Frank Coop, Wilcox, Saskatchewan, to the Rev. James Woodsworth, Winnipeg, 21 November 1907; letter from Howarth, The Pas, *Missionary Bulletin*, 1914, 447.

77 Quote from the Neepawa Register, *Christian Guardian*, 19 January 1910.

78 Carman Papers, C.B. Keenleyside, Saskatchewan conference, to Carman, 1 October 1910.

79 Minutes, Manitoba and Northwest conference, 1896, 66.

80 Report of Manitoba and Northwest conference, *Christian Guardian*, 26 June 1901.

81 Minutes, Manitoba and Northwest conference, 1897, 79; 1902, 74–5; *Christian Guardian*, 19 February 1902; 19 November 1902; *Journal of Proceedings*, general conference, 1902, 194–8.

82 *Christian Guardian*, 18 July 1906.

83 Minutes, Assiniboia conference, 1906, 37; Minutes, Alberta conference, 1906, 45.

84 *Christian Guardian*, 24 August 1904; Minutes, Alberta conference, 1910, 72–4.

85 *The Doctrine and Discipline of the Methodist Church*, 1906, 22–5.

86 *Christian Guardian*, 3 February 1897.

87 Ibid., 9 October 1907.

88 Ibid., 14 December 1904; see also 27 December 1905; 9 October 1907; Rev. A.W. Kenner's account of movie censorship in Winnipeg, 1 March 1911.

89 Voisey, *A Preacher's Frontier*, 23. In 1911 Holdom supported temperance but opposed prohibition at a meeting of the Moral Reform League in Vulcan. Although he ended up supporting Vulcan's local option campaign, he distanced himself from the League's "blind fanaticism."

90 Dr Chris Connolly to Allen, 16 August 1912, Allen Papers; T.C. Buchanan to Allen, 16 September 1912.

CHAPTER FOUR

1 See *Annual Report*, Missionary Society, 1913–14, 511–25.

2 Allen Papers, Allen to Rev. Thomas Neal, Kingston, 26 September 1912; see also Allen to Rev. J.M. Harrison, Macleod, Alberta, 24 October 1910; *Annual Report*, Missionary Society, 1911–12, "A Message from the General Board of Missions."

3 *Annual Report*, Missionary Society, 1911–12, x, xxii; 1912–13, xx. See also Allen Papers, Allen to Rev. J.W. Sparling, principal of Wesley College, 8 November 1907.

4 *Christian Guardian*, 26 October 1910.

5 Gagan, *A Sensitive Independence.*

6 *Methodist Year Book*, 1915, 38.

7 Report of the Church and Parsonage Aid Fund, *Journal of Proceedings*, general conference, 1902, 303–4; 1906, 284–5; 1910, 327; *Christian Guardian*, 17 December 1913. The church added just $5,000 to the capital amount ($32,749) of the Church and Parsonage Aid Fund during the quadrennium 1906–10 and $1,231 during the following three years. See Allen Papers, Allen to Oliver Darwin, 25 April 1908; Allen to T.C. Buchanan, 12 July 1910; Sutherland Papers, Buchanan to J.N. Shannon, Mission Rooms, 4 March 1910.

8 Allen Papers, James N. Shannon, Mission Rooms, to Rev. W.T. Gunn, Toronto, 20 December 1907.

9 Report of the general board of missions, *Journal of Proceedings*, general conference, 1906, 370.

10 *Christian Guardian*, 20 April 1904.

11 Methodists built large, costly buildings in prairie cities. In five cases the costs were $117,000 (Winnipeg, 1904), $80,000 (Moose Jaw, 1905), $63,000 (Calgary, 1905), $80,000 (Regina, 1907), and $67,000 (Calgary, 1912). Ibid., 25 April 1904, 22 February 1905, 30 October 1907, 9 October 1907, 3 January 1912.

12 Calculated from data ibid., 11 October 1911 (appropriations), 25 September 1912 (income).

13 Calculated from *Annual Reports*, Missionary Society, 1898 to 1914. The Manitoba conference data for calculation exclude the Port Arthur and Rainy River districts, which were in Ontario.

14 One should interpret the data with caution. The writer used an American price index (Series E185, in *Historical Statistics of the United States*, 212) because a Canadian one is unavailable for years before 1913. Perforce, the estimates assume that prices in the two countries followed similar trends.

15 *Christian Guardian*, 11 October 1911.

16 *Journal of Proceedings*, general conference, 1906, 387.

17 *Annual Report*, Missionary Society, 1909–10, 57–8; *Journal of Proceedings*, general conference, 1906, report of the Young People's Forward Movement for Missions, 387–96; article by F.C. Stephenson, secretary of the Young People's Forward Movement for Missions, *Christian Guardian*, 2 October 1902.

18 *Annual Report*, Missionary Society, 1909–10, 57–8.

19 *Journal of Proceedings*, general conference, 1906, 387–96.

20 *Methodist Year Book*, 1915, 47–51.

21 *Canada's Missionary Congress*, 246; *Annual Report*, Missionary Society, 1908–9, 7.

22 *Christian Guardian*, 27 March 1907.

23 *Canada's National Missionary Congress*, 241. For reports of meetings elsewhere, see *Christian Guardian*, 13 January 1909 (special LMM issue); 24 November 1909 (Macleod, Lethbridge); 1 December 1909 (Virden, Manitoba); 15 December 1909 (Oak Lake, Saskatchewan).

24 *Canada's National Missionary Congress*, 231–42, 244, 246. See also *Missionary Outlook*, May 1909.

25 Letter from J.R. Paterson, Brantford, to Alexander Sutherland, *Missionary Outlook*, March 1908. For previous apathy towards missions, see address by Mr W.J. Robertson, St Catharines, to the laymen of the Hamilton conference, *Christian Guardian*, 16 October 1901; Rev. T. Manning, Whitby, to editor, 4 March 1896.

26 Calculated from information in *Annual Reports*, Missionary Society, 1903–4, 1913–14.

27 MacKinnon, "New Evidence on Canadian Wage Rates, 1900–1930."

28 Allen Papers, J.H. Ashdown to Allen, 20 April 1909. See also Sutherland Papers, J.A.M. Aikins to Sutherland, 25 May 1909.

29 Calculated from information in *Annual Report*, Missionary Society, 1913–14, lxx–lxxi. For contributors to Winnipeg city missions, see 570–4.

30 Carman Papers, G.W. Brown, Regina, to Carman, 31 December 1909.

31 In contrast, the $1 million Twentieth Century Fund of 1898 was for general purposes. Toronto's Metropolitan Methodist congregation, for example, raised $57,000 to discharge the mortgage on their building. *Metropolitan Church Yearbook*, Toronto, 1897–8; 1899–1900; 1900–1. The Save St James Fund of 1902 was for paying off a $513,000 debt on the Methodist "mother church" in Montreal.

32 Report of the general board of missions, *Journal of Proceedings*, general conference, 1906, 370; *Christian Guardian*, 1 April 1903; Carman Papers, Manitoba and Northwest conference, 1903, 78–9.

33 Allen Papers, Mission Plant Fund, receipts to January 20, 1914.

34 Ibid., Report of the special committee appointed by the general board of missions to consider the question how to provide the additional men and money required for home and foreign missions; Allen to Rev. John

Corbett, Bowmanville, 10 December 1910. See *Annual Report*, Missionary Society, 1910–11, 12–13.

35 Also on the executive were Edward Gurney of Toronto; Chester D. Massey, the Toronto farm-implement manufacturer; W.A. Kemp, an appliance manufacturer and past president of the Toronto board of trade and the Canadian Manufacturers Association; H.H. Fudger of Toronto, the president of the Robert Simpson Company and the treasurer of the Missionary Society; T.H. Preston, the editor and publisher of the *Brantford Expositor*; Cyrus A. Birge, an industrialist, past-president of the Hamilton board of trade, and past-president of the Canadian Manufacturers' Association; J.D. Flavelle of Lindsay, the managing director of the Flavelle Milling Company and brother of Joseph Flavelle; F.E. O'Flynn of Belleville, the general manager of Canadian Securities Limited and member of the Toronto Stock Exchange; and W.H. Goodwin of Montreal, the managing director of Goodwins Limited, a large department store. Ibid., Report of the special committee for home and foreign missions.

36 Ibid., Allen to Rev. J.W. Sparling, Winnipeg, 20 December 1910.

37 Ibid., Allen to J.D. Flavelle, Lindsay, Ontario, 25 January 1911; Allen to J.A.M. Aikins, Winnipeg, 30 January 1911.

38 Ibid., Rev. C.E. Manning, field secretary for the home mission department, to Allen, 23 June 1911.

39 Ibid. C.E. Manning's report to the general board of missions on the mission plant and extension fund, October 1912.

40 Ibid. Allen to T.C. Buchanan, 17 January 1912. Allen assured Buchanan that the Western conferences were to receive $17,500 of the $19,000 reserved for home missions.

41 Ibid., copy of the proposal submitted to the Winnipeg subcommittee by J.H. Ashdown, H.W. Hutchinson, and Rev. T.E. Shore, May 1912. The resolution failed partly because the executive committee of the general board had already spent as much in the western conferences as was expected from them. The Winnipeg subcommittee agreed to these terms provided that subscribers could designate where their contributions were to be spent and provided that the first instalments from Winnipeg would be spent in that city. See Ibid., C.E. Manning's report to the general board of missions on the Mission Plant and Extension Fund, October 1912; resolution passed by a committee of Methodist laymen of Winnipeg and agreed to by a Winnipeg subcommittee.

42 For description of plans for The Pas, see *Christian Guardian*, 29 July 1914. The Pas had a mill, and construction of the Hudson's Bay Railway was taking place. Twenty-nine nationalities lived there.

43 *Annual Report*, Missionary Society, 1913–14, 511–25.

44 Allen Papers. C.E. Manning's report to the general board of missions on the mission plant and extension fund, October 1912. See also *Journal of*

Proceedings, general conference, 1914, report of the general board of missions, 195.

45 Carman Papers, stationing committee, Alberta conference, 1910 (PAA).

46 Carman Papers, stationing committee, Alberta conference, 1905–14 (PAA); Saskatchewan conference 1905–14 (PAS); Manitoba conference 1886–1914 (UCAW).

47 Darwin, *Pioneering with Pioneers*, 51.

48 Carman Papers, missionary committee, Manitoba and Northwest conference, 1885–1903 (UCAW).

49 Carman Papers, quarterly official board, Elkhorn, Manitoba (UCAW), 10 August 1899; 6 August 1900.

50 Darwin, *Pioneering with Pioneers*, 45.

51 Carman Papers, quarterly board, Irma, 1911; Camrose, 27 August 1912; Carmangay-Champion, 29 January 1913 (PAA).

52 Carman Papers, stationing committee, Alberta conference (PAA); Carman Papers, district meeting for Edmonton, 1903 (PAA); Portage la Prairie, 1897; Carman, 1911 (UCAW); Arcola, 1909, Battleford 1910 and 1914 (PAS); Carman Papers, quarterly board, Pincher Creek, Carstairs, Sturgeon, Viking (PAA); Minitonas-Bowsman, Sheho (UCAW); *Methodist Year Book*, 1915, 16–20.

53 Brown, "Over the Red Deer," 10.

54 Silcox, *Church Union in Canada*, 215. For a history of the co-operation movement, see Silcox, *Church Union in Canada*, 214–42; Rev. S.D. Chown, *Story of Church Union*, 50–60; *Christian Guardian*, 22 March 1911; Carman Papers, "Historical Sketch of the Movement for Co-operation in Home Mission Work," n.d.

55 Carman Papers, Woodsworth to Sutherland, December 1902.

56 Sutherland Papers, Buchanan, Edmonton, to Sutherland, 9 December 1902. See also Oliver Darwin, Moose Jaw, to Sutherland, 12 December 1902.

57 Sutherland Papers, the Woodsworth to Sutherland, n.d. (estimate, December 1902). For local-level rivalry, see Allen Papers, Rev. J.W. Flatt, Manor, Saskatchewan, to Rev. Charles Endicott, Arcola, Manitoba, 10 October 1906.

58 Account of the Alberta meeting by Rev. C.H. Huestis, *Christian Guardian*, 25 January 1911. Carman Papers, "Historical Sketch of the Movement for Co-operation in Home Mission Work," n.d.; Silcox, *Church Union in Canada*, 216–22.

59 *Christian Guardian*, 26 March 1913; 2 April 1913; 17 December 1913, on the benefits of co-operation at Wadena, Saskatchewan; Allen Papers, Oliver Darwin to Rev. C.E. Manning, Toronto, 28 July 1913; James Woodsworth's report for the quadrennium 1910–14.

60 Thus size of the Missionary Society's grant to Methodist mission stations
was as large as before the Presbyterians had withdrawn. See Allen
Papers, C.H. Cross, superintendent of missions for Northern
Saskatchewan, to Allen, 28 July 1913; quadrennial report of Oliver
Darwin for the Saskatchewan conference, 1914.

61 *Acts and Proceedings*, general assembly, 1912, appendix, 20.

62 Allen Papers, Allen to Rev. W.W. Andrews, president of Regina College,
26 May 1911; Allen to Rev. J.A. Doyle, president of the Saskatchewan
conference, Prince Albert, 11 April 1913.

63 Ibid., meeting of the representatives of the Methodist churches of Winnipeg at Grace Church, 2 January 1913; Allen to Rev. T.C. Buchanan,
9 January 1913; Rev J.H. Riddell, Edmonton to Rev. W.A. Lowie, Edmonton, 13 January 1912; Riddell to Rev. Thomas Powell, Edmonton, 13 January 1912; Riddell to Buchanan, 13 January 1912; Allen to Rev. W.J.
Haggith, W.G. Hunt, and W.H. Cushing, Calgary, and Rev. George W.
Hazen, London, 14 April 1913; Allen to Rev. A.E. Oke, Gregg, Manitoba, 10 November 1913. Of the $7,500 in grants that Winnipeg saved,
$3,000 was for salaries in Manitoba, $2,500 for salaries in Alberta, and
$2,000 for salaries in Saskatchewan.

64 Ibid., Allen to the Rev. A.W. Kenner, Swan River, 13 February 1914.

65 *Annual Report*, Missionary Society, 1913–14, 569–74. Lady Aikins, however, gave $5.

66 *Journal*, general synod, Anglican Church, 1915, 19–23.

67 *Acts and Proceedings*, general assembly, 1899–1914, appendix, reports of
the home mission committee, western section.

68 *Acts and Proceedings*, general assembly, 1913, appendix, 68–9. Compared
to 1912–13, the Presbyterians had eighteen fewer missions and thirty-
four more augmented charges in 1914–15, the comparable year for the
Methodist and Anglican statistics.

CHAPTER FIVE

1 Allen Papers, Allen to James Woodsworth, 15 February 1907; Allen to T.C.
Buchanan, 29 December 1906; T.C. Buchanan to Allen, 11 January 1907.

2 Allen Papers, Allen to Rev. W.H. Sparling, Kingston, 12 March 1907;
Allen to James Woodsworth, 15 February 1907; Allen to Rev. Charles H.
Woltze, Campbell, Ontario, 25 March 1907; report of James Woodsworth, senior superintendent of missions, submitted 1914; report of the
employment of theological students during the summer vacation, July
1910; *Annual Report*, Missionary Society, 1907–8, 60; 1909–10, 41.

3 *Acts and Proceedings*, general assembly, 1914, calculated from information
in "Statistical and Financial Returns."

4 Ibid., 1912, appendix, 4–5.

5 Riddell, *Methodism in the Middle West*, 148–9.
6 Minutes, Manitoba, Saskatchewan, and Alberta conferences, 1914, 6, 78, 156.
7 *The Discipline*, 1906, Methodist Church, 382–3; *Journal of Proceedings*, general conference, 1902, report of committee on discipline, 96; 1906, report of committee on course of study, 129; J.N. Shannon to Rev. W.T. Gunn, Toronto, 20 December 1907, Allen Papers.
8 Riddell, *Methodism in the Middle West*, 262, 298. Born in Ontario in 1864, Riddell was professor of classics and New Testament exegesis at Wesley College, 1896–1902; the founder and principal of Alberta College, 1903–11; and principal of Wesley College, 1917–38. See Friesen, "Principal J.H. Riddell."
9 *Acts and Proceedings*, general assembly, 1907, appendix, 8–9; 1911, appendix, 3, 14; 1912, appendix, 4–5. In 1908 Rev. J.A. Carmichael, the mission superintendent for the Manitoba and Saskatchewan synods, hired thirty-eight men from Scotland.
10 In 1901 the Canadian church had 8 local preachers for every 1,000 church members. This compared to 83 for Britain's Primitive Methodists; 53 for Britain's Bible Christians; 28 for Britain's New Connexion Methodists; 27 for Britain's Wesleyan Methodists; 22 for the American Primitive Methodist Church; and 5 for each for the American Methodist Episcopal Churches. Calculated from data in Cornish, *Cyclopaedia of Methodism*, vol. 2, 41, 47–48.
11 *Christian Guardian*, July 15, 1896; see also J.A. Irwin, London, to editor, 7 July 1907; "Fairbanks" to editor, 14 June 1905; *Journal of Proceedings*, general conference, 1910, 319; Minutes, Manitoba conference, 1906, 44–6.
12 Report of a meeting of the local preachers of Winnipeg, *Christian Guardian*, 26 November 1913; see also 16 August 1905; "M.E.B." to editor, 21 October 1908; "A Local Preacher" to editor, 5 June 1912; Rev. Charles Bishop to editor, 4 December 1912; I.C. Morris, New Brunswick and Prince Edward Island conference, to editor, 8 January 1913; editorial, 30 July 1913; report of a meeting of local preachers at Grace Methodist church, Winnipeg, 26 November 1913; *Annual Report*, Missionary Society, 1907–8, 63.
13 Minutes, Moose Jaw district, 31 May 1904 (PAS).
14 Minutes, prairie conference stationing committees; Minutes, prairie conference annual meetings.
15 Minutes, Edmonton district, 1903 (PAA); Crystal City district, 1893; Neepawa district, 1897; Brandon district, 1899; Portage La Prairie district, 1905; Binscarth-Foxwarren quarterly board, 1906 (UCAW); Moose Jaw district, 1902; Saskatoon district 1909; Weyburn district, 1910 (PAS). In 1897 E.T. Carter left the Gilbert Plains mission (Neepawa district) to take work in the Baptist Church. In 1899 Melville Shaver, a four-year

probationer in the Brandon district, resigned to enter the ministry of
another church.

16 Article by Rev. W. McMullen, Florence, Ontario, *Christian Guardian*,
   11 January 1905; see also article by Rev. G.R. Turk, 9 September 1903;
   article by Professor Cecil E. Race, Alberta College, 18 August 1909.

17 See *Journal of Proceedings*, general conference, 1906, report of committee
   on course of study, 132–6; *Doctrine and Discipline of the Methodist Church*,
   1906, 93–103.

18 Calculated from information in Cornish, *Cyclopaedia of Methodism.*

19 Darwin, *Pioneering with Pioneers*, 1.

20 "A probationer," to editor, and Rev. R.S. Stevens, Wapella, Saskatchewan,
   to editor, *Christian Guardian*, 13 April 1910; "a Methodist," to editor,
   2 May 1910; Rev. Gustavus A. Colpitts, to editor, 30 March 1910; "One
   who is desirous for the good of the Church of Christ," to editor, 2 February 1910; editorial, 11 November 1908.

21 Rev. G.A. Gifford, to editor, ibid., 23 March 1910; see also C.W. Swallow, to editor, 20 April 1910.

22 Cornish, *Cyclopaedia of Methodism.* For examples, see entries for William
   B. Chegwin, Menotti C. Flatt, Samuel Gaudin, William Pascoe Gourd,
   James Thomas Harrison, and Thomas J. Johnston.

23 The *Discipline* provided for the transfer of "at least four married men"
   from Newfoundland, "if such men so desire. Men who were transferred
   into the Newfoundland conference had the right to return after ten
   years. Not more than one minister from the Newfoundland conference
   could be transferred into any one conference without the consent of its
   president. See the *Discipline*, 60.

24 For example, the WMS missionaries Ethelwyn Chace and Emoline Black
   were lay delegates to the Fort Saskatchewan district meeting in 1915.
   Minutes, Fort Saskatchewan district (PAA).

25 *Christian Guardian*, 3 June 1908. The church allowed women to serve as
   delegates to general conference in 1918 but declined to ordain them
   through to church union in 1925. For Methodist careers for women, see
   Gagan, *A Sensitive Independence* and Semple, *The Lord's Dominion*, 414.

26 Korinek, "No Women Need Apply." See also Thomas, "Servants of the
   Church," 395; Warne, *Literature as Pulpit.*

27 Minutes, Alberta conference stationing committee, 1908 (PAA).

28 Allen Papers, J.N. Shannon to Rev. W.T. Gunn, Toronto, 20 December
   1907, Allen to Rev. W.T. Gunn, 14 January 1908; Rev. B.W.J. Clements,
   Wessington, Alberta, to Allen, 13 February 1907; *Annual Report*, Missionary Society, 1907–8, 67; Rev. James A. Spencely, Rosetown, Saskatchewan,
   to editor, *Christian Guardian*, 19 February 1913; see also statement by the
   chairman of the Balcarres district, Saskatchewan conference, 6 November 1907; statement by James Woodsworth, 27 November 1907.

29 Brown, "Over the Red Deer."
30 Allen Papers, Allen to Rev. J.I. Dawson, Sackville, New Brunswick, 31 December 1907.
31 *Christian Guardian*, 11 September 1912.
32 Allen Papers, Oliver Darwin, superintendent of missions for the Saskatchewan conference, to James Woodsworth, Winnipeg, 30 June 1906; Woodsworth to Allen, 5 January 1907; Woodsworth to Rev. C.E. Manning, field secretary for the Department of Home Missions, Toronto, 22 July 1909; Report of Oliver Darwin for the year ending 10 June 1911; Darwin to Manning, 28 July 1913; quadrennial report of Oliver Darwin, June 1914; T.C. Buchanan to Allen, 18 June 1912; *Annual Report*, Missionary Society, 1907–8, 61, 66; letter from the Rev. T.C. Buchanan, *Missionary Bulletin*, 1912, 1287–8, 1294; *Christian Guardian*, 3 April 1901; 16 April 1902; editorial, 3 February 1904; 27 July 1904; 16 May 1905; 21 March 1906; 6 March 1907; 31 July 1907; plea from James Woodsworth, 8 May 1907; 23 March 1910; 31 July 1912; report of the General Board of Missions annual meeting, 11 October 1911; 11 September 1912; 9 October 1912; *Methodist Year Book*, 1915, 16.
33 Article by Rev. Thomas Holling, *Christian Guardian*, 3 April 1907.
34 Ibid., 21 January 1903; 13 May 1903; 11 May 1904; Rev. James A. Spencely, Rosetown, Saskatchewan, to editor, 19 February 1913.
35 Rev. G.H. Ord, Benito, Saskatchewan, to editor, ibid., 28 August 1912; *Annual Report*, Missionary Society, 1908–9, 7; Sutherland Papers, Rev. E.J. Carson, Neepawa, Manitoba, to Sutherland, 13 June 1906. Gagan, *A Sensitive Independence*, makes this argument for the WMS missionaries.
36 *Journal of Proceedings*, general conference, 1898, report of committee on missions, 138–40; report of the proceedings of the London conference, *Christian Guardian*, 22 June 1898; report of the proceedings of the Hamilton conference, 14 June 1899; Minutes, Toronto conference, 1897, 48.
37 Allen Papers, T.C. Buchanan to Allen, 18 December 1909; *Missionary Outlook*, May 1907; Rev. J.H. White, New Westminster, BC, to editor, *Christian Guardian*, 7 November 1906.
38 Allen Papers, Allen to James Woodsworth, 8 November 1907; Allen to Rev. J.C. Speer, Brampton, president of the Toronto conference, 8 November 1907; Allen to Oliver Darwin, 7 December 1907; Allen to Rev. J.L. Dawson, Sackville, NB, 31 December 1907; articles by James Woodsworth and Rev. C.H. Cross, Cartwright, Manitoba, *Christian Guardian*, 7 May 1902; "J.W.L.F.," to editor, 6 May 1903.
39 Allen Papers, Thomas Kirkup, England, to James Woodsworth, 3 August 1912; James Woodsworth's report of his visit to England, 1907; *Christian Guardian*, 9 January 1907.
40 Darwin, *Pioneering with Pioneers*, 39–40.

41 *Annual Report*, Missionary Society, 1909–10, 41; 1913–14, xiv; *Christian Guardian*, 11 September 1912; 26 October 1910. Woodsworth secured 30 in 1905, 50 in 1906, 63 in 1909, 43 in 1910, and 25 in 1912. At least one of these recruits went to British Columbia, and some withdrew from the ministry shortly after arriving, like many Canadian recruits. See also Allen Papers, Oliver Darwin to James Woodsworth, 30 June 1906, Woodsworth's report of his visit to England, 1907; Woodsworth to Allen, 25 September 1909; Woodsworth, England, to Rev. C.E. Manning, Toronto, n.d., 1909; "The Contingent from British Methodism," *Christian Guardian*, 4 December 1907; "Notes from the New Recruits," 22 January 1908.

42 Allen Papers, Buchanan to Allen, 18 December 1909.

43 Allen Papers, James Woodsworth to Allen, 22 July 1909; Allen to Buchanan, 20 March 1911; Allen to Rev. John Corbett, Bowmanville, 27 March 1908; Allen to Woodsworth, England, 6 August 1912; Rev. F.H. Langford, Regina, to Rev. T.A. Moore, Toronto, 2 June 1914; Allen to Rev. C.H. Cross, Saskatoon, 10 February 1914; *Christian Guardian*, 17 October 1906; Alberta conference news, 9 March 1910; Carman Papers, James Woodsworth to Carman, 15 December 1903, Riddell, *Methodism in the Middle West*, 234. Woodsworth, Buchanan, and Langford were Ontario-born. James Allen was Irish-born but had lived in Ontario from the age of three.

44 "One of the many," to editor, *Christian Guardian*, 1 January 1913; see also "Another of the many," to editor, 26 March 1913; A.J. Warman, Broadview, Saskatchewan, to editor, 26 March 1913; Alfred G. Schofield, Wilberforce, Ontario, to editor, 5 February 1913. For evidence that some English recruits could "fit in," see Harold White, Albert College, Belleville, to editor, 5 February 1913; "Was Green," to editor, 26 February 1913.

45 "Another of the Many," to editor, ibid., 5 February 1913.

46 M.S. Lehigh, Avonmore, Ontario, to editor, ibid., 12 March 1913; see also "Englishmen in Canada – A Friendly Word," by "Exeter Hall," 11 December 1907.

47 Allen Papers, Darwin to Allen, 30 June 1906.

48 Ibid., Buchanan to Allen, 18 December 1909. For other Western appeals to the East, see Allen to Buchanan, 20 March 1911; Rev. Oliver Darwin to Rev. C.E. Manning, 28 January 1913; letter from Rev. T.C. Buchanan, *Missionary Bulletin*, 1912, 1287–8; *Annual Report*, Missionary Society, 1903–4, xii; 1907–8, 61; 1908–9, 7. In Buchanan's view, most of the recruits came from rural areas, where conservative values were entrenched. See letter from Rev. T.C. Buchanan, *Missionary Bulletin*, 1912, 1014.

49 Allen Papers, Allen to Darwin, 6 July 1909; Allen to Rev. J.C. Hartley, secretary of the Saskatchewan conference, 5 August 1909.

50 Ibid., Rev. James Woodsworth to Allen, 22 July 1909; Allen to Rev. C.H. Cross, Saskatoon, Saskatchewan, 14 February 1910; Allen to Rev. John Coburn, Staynor, Ontario, 5 February 1907; Allen to Rev. John Corbett, Bowmanville, Ontario, 27 March 1908; Allen to Rev. J.A. Jewitt, Elmwood, Ontario, 24 April 1908.

51 During the years 1896–1904, the losses in the Manitoba and Northwest conference were equal to 19 percent of the clergy in the conference in 1903. As table 5.2 shows, the comparable statistic for central Canada was 6 percent. Thus the loss was 3.2 times higher (19/6) in the Manitoba and Northwest conference. The comparable statistic for the period 1905–14 was 3.3 (26/8). The data in the table are calculated from information in conference Minutes and the *Journal of Proceedings*, general conference, 1906, 236; 1910, 429.

52 Rev. A. Mosely, Park Hill, Alberta, to editor, *Christian Guardian*, 2 April 1913; see also James Woodsworth, to editor, 13 August 1902.

53 Minutes, quarterly official boards, prairie conferences (PAA, PAS, UCAW).

54 For the high cost of living in the West, see Minutes, Manitoba and Northwest conference, 1904, report of the committee on memorials, 86–7; Allen Papers, Rev. F.I. Woodsworth, Lesser Slave Lake, to C.E. Manning, 15 August 1911.

55 The real amount of the minimum salary for probationers in 1914 was 1.2 times that for 1898. For comparison with wages of ministers in the United States and with incomes in the business world, see Allen Papers, James Woodsworth's report of his visit to England, 1907; "H.H." to editor, *Christian Guardian*, 14 August 1907; 7 December 1904; Robert H. Davis, Kitscoty, Alberta, to editor, 17 November 1909; Rev. R.S. Stevens, Wapella, Saskatchewan, to editor, 13 April 1910. On the general inadequacy of ministerial salaries, see Allen Papers, Rev. W.E.S. James, Ayr, Ontario, to C.E. Manning, 16 January 1913, Oliver Darwin to James Woodsworth, 30 June 1906; Rev. B.W.J. Clements, Wessington, Alberta, to Allen, 13 February 1907; Allen to Rev. W.S. Reid, Souris, Saskatchewan conference, 8 February 1911; Carman Papers, Rev. F. William Westwood, Belle Plain, Saskatchewan, to Carman, 31 October 1913; Sutherland Papers, Rev. James C. Kirk, Merna, Alberta, to Alexander Sutherland; Rev. W.W. Adamson, Dauphin, Manitoba, to James Allen, 21 June 1907; Manitoba and Northwest conference news, *Christian Guardian*, 4 January 1899; Rev. H. Evans Marshall, McTaggert, Saskatchewan, to editor, 15 April 1908; Israel Taylor, London, Ontario, to editor, 9 April 1913; "A Western Itinerant" to editor, 9 April 1913; 5 October 1910.

56 Minutes, Edmonton district meeting, 1906, 32 (PAA); see also Allen Papers, Allen to W. Henry, Esq., Verdun, Montreal, 22 December 1910.

57 Minutes, Edmonton district meeting, 1910, resolution of principal J.H. Riddell and the Rev. T.J. Johnston (PAA); Minutes, missionary committee, Manitoba and Northwest conference, 1885–1903 (UCAW).

58 Allen Papers, Rev. B.W.J. Clements, Wessington, Alberta, to Allen, 13 February 1907.

59 Manuscript minutes, Alberta conference, 1912 (PAA).

60 Allen Papers, Allen to Rev. R.L. Dawson, PEI, 20 April 1914 Allen to Rev. John Moore, board of missions, Nashville, Tennessee, U.S.A., 6 August 1912.

61 Ibid., quadrennial report of T.C. Buchanan, superintendent of missions for the Alberta conference, 15 June 1910; Allen to Rev. C.W. Watch, Huntsville, Ontario, 16 July 1907; Allen to James Woodsworth, 8 November 1907; Allen to Rev. W.T. Gunn, Toronto, 20 December 1907; Allen to Rev. W.J. Smith, Hamilton, 6 February 1913; Allen to Rev. George W. Hazen, London, 14 April 1913; Manitoba conference news, *Christian Guardian*, 2 July 1913.

62 *Christian Guardian*, 22 May 1912. See also Allen Papers, Oliver Darwin to Allen, 30 June 1906.

63 Manuscript minutes, Alberta conference, 1912 (PAA). See also Allen Papers, Allen to Rev. A.B. Aldridge, president of the Alberta conference, Calgary, 19 May 1911; Allen to Rev. W.S. Reid, president of the Saskatchewan conference, Souris, 20 May 1911; Allen to Rev. T.V. Wilson, president of the Manitoba conference, Selkirk, 20 May 1911; circular letter issued in response to an Alberta conference memorial on salary issues; Allen to Rev. G.W. Kerby, Calgary, 29 May 1907; *Christian Guardian*, 23 October 1912; *Annual Report*, Missionary Society, 1907–8, 58.

64 Allen Papers, Allen to Rev. W.W. Andrews, president of Regina College, 26 May 1911; Allen to Rev. J.A. Doyle, president of the Saskatchewan conference, Prince Albert, 11 April 1913.

65 Minutes, Missionary Society, 1914, 566; Minutes, Manitoba, Saskatchewan, and Alberta conferences, 1914, 126. The writer's sources lack information for Alberta. Of the $5,422 issued by the society, $3,750 went to a special Saskatchewan fund of $10,698 to pay salary deficiencies for 1912–13.

66 Minutes, Minitonas-Bowsman quarterly board (UCAW).

67 Minutes, quarterly board, Austin-Sidney, Manitoba, 4 August 1903; Elm Creek, Manitoba, 10 August 1912; Durban, Manitoba, 31 October 1912 (UCAW); Speers (New Ottawa) Saskatchewan, 9 July 1913 (PAS).

68 Minutes, quarterly board, Fort Macleod, 2 September 1914 (PAA).

69 Minutes, quarterly board, Neepawa, 18 May 1896; Carman district meeting, 1898; Birtle district meeting, 1904, 1912; Portage la Prairie district meeting, 1906, 1912 (UCAW); Stettler district, 1908; Olds district, 1912 (PAA).

70 Minutes, Calgary district, 1902; Moose Jaw district, 1905; Yorkton district, 1914.
71 Manuscript minutes, Alberta conference, 1912, communication from the Alberta probationers' association (PAA).
72 *Journal of Proceedings*, general conferences, 1902, 1906, 1910 and 1914, reports of the general conference statistician.
73 *Christian Guardian*, 16 August 1911; Darwin's annual report, 14 July 1911, Allen Papers.
74 "Westerner" to editor, *Christian Guardian*, 30 November 1912; see also "Sirux" to editor, 4 December 1912.
75 Interview with Byles, 21–22 May 1974.
76 *Christian Guardian*, 11 October 1911.
77 Allen Papers, Rev. T.P. Perry, president of the Alberta conference, Lethbridge, to Allen, 23 August 1912; report of Oliver Darwin for the year ending June 1912.
78 Report of the Alberta correspondent, *Christian Guardian*, 28 September 1904. In 1907 Rev. Arthur Barner advocated the reduction in the size of districts, so that district chairmen were responsible for a maximum of six missions. In 1913 Rev. C.H. Cross, now a mission superintendent, argued the need for more ordained men. Allen Papers, the Rev. Arthur Barner, Alix, Alberta, to Allen, 29 January 1907.
79 Assiniboia conference news, *Christian Guardian*, 29 September 1905. See also Allen Papers, the Rev. Arthur Barner, Alix, Alberta, to Allen, 29 January 1907.
80 Darwin, *Pioneering with Pioneers*, 42–3.
81 Riddell, *Methodism in the Middle West*, 155.
82 Report of the superintendent of missions for the Manitoba and Northwest, and British Columbia conferences, *Journal of Proceedings*, general conference, 1898, 128–32; report of the committee on missions, 1902, 119–20.
83 Darwin, *Pioneering with Pioneers*, foreword. Dorey was a native of the Channel Islands whom Woodsworth recruited in 1905. In 1954 he was elected moderator of the United Church of Canada.
84 Allen Papers, Darwin to James Woodsworth, 30 June 1906.
85 Sutherland Papers, Rev. J.W. Dickenson, president of the Assiniboia conference, Virden, Manitoba, to Sutherland, 20 November 1905; Carman Papers, memorial to the general board of missions from the Assiniboia conference, 5 September 1905. In Alberta, Rev. Arthur Barner opined, T.C. Buchanan could have had his hands full without visiting any missions. See Allen Papers, Barner, Alix, Alberta, to Allen, 29 January 1907.
86 Allen Papers, Darwin to Rev. C.E. Manning, 15 May 1912 and 15 April 1910. Darwin's first car was ruined when the flywheel struck against a

stone and cracked the crankcase. The Missionary Society bought him a new car.

87 Ibid., W.H. Cushing, Calgary, to Allen, 29 May 1912; Rev. T.P. Perry, president of the Alberta conference, Lethbridge, to Allen, 23 August 1912; Rev. C.H. Huestis, Macleod, to Allen, 24 August 1912; report of Oliver Darwin, superintendent of missions for the Saskatchewan conference, for the year ending June 1912; Allen to Barner, Red Deer, 12 October 1912 and 5 December 1912; Allen to Cross, Qu'Appelle, Saskatchewan, 22 January 1913.

88 Byles, "The Canadianization of a Yorkshire Lad"; writer's interview with Byles, 21–22 May 1974.

89 The Saskatchewan conference list of stations placed Lashburn under the local supervision of the ordained man at Radisson, who was Thomas Lawson. Lawson was also district chairman, however. Perhaps for that reason, he rearranged the local supervision for his district.

90 His classification was that of lay supply under the "temporary provisions" for probationers of 1902–10.

91 Minutes, Battleford district, 1910 (PAS).

92 The biographical information is from conference obituaries; Methodist pension records; obituaries in the United Church *New Outlook* and *Observer*; the *Christian Guardian*; Morgan, *Canadian Men and Women of the Time*; and Cochrane, *Men of Canada*.

93 In 1902 the Manitoba and Northwest conference hired twenty-two probationers and twelve others "as persons likely to enter the ministry." According to J.H. Riddell, "ninety percent or more [of the thirty-four] came from Canadian homes." Riddell, *Methodism in the Middle West*, 261.

94 Saskatchewan conference news, *Christian Guardian*, 6 November 1907; 27 November 1907; Allen Papers, J.E. Robinson, England, to Allen, 8 November 1912, Allen to Rev. C.H. Cross, 22 January 1913.

95 Rev. J.A. Spencely, Rosetown, Saskatchewan, to editor, *Christian Guardian*, 19 February 1913.

96 Ibid., 19 June 1907.

97 Darwin, *Pioneering with Pioneers*, chap. 8.

98 The writer lacks information about three of the forty-seven district chairmen for these years. Three of the five mission superintendents were from England. Oliver Darwin (southern Saskatchewan) had immigrated from Yorkshire in 1884. Charles Cross (northern Saskatchewan) had come from Nottingham in 1884. Arthur Barner (southern Alberta) had left England in 1890.

99 Nine of the Canadian born men were at Wesley College (J.W. Sparling, Andrew Stewart, Salem Bland, George John Blewett, J.H. Riddell, W.F. Osborn, William T. Allison, J.W. Melvin, and N.R. Wilson). The others were Charles E. Bland and F.S. McCall at Alberta College, Edmonton,

and G.W. Kerby of Mount Royal College, Calgary. The Irish-born Milliken was principal at Regina College.

CHAPTER SIX

1 *Christian Guardian*, 7 October 1908 (Regina); 20 October 1909 (Calgary); 1 January 1908 (Winnipeg).
2 Allen Papers, Rev. John Maclean, Morden, Manitoba, to C.E. Manning, Toronto, 8 February 1911.
3 Ibid., D.H. Kennedy, High Bluff, Manitoba, to C.E. Manning, Toronto, 16 February 1911.
4 *Christian Guardian*, 8 February 1911.
5 Editorial and Clarke Keane to editor, ibid., 2 April 1913; T.R. Clarke to editor and C.W. Swallow to editor, 23 April 1913; George C. Wood, Moulinette, Ontario, to editor, 9 April 1913; Allen Papers, Rev. John Maclean, Morden, Manitoba, to C.E. Manning, 8 February 1911; Rev. Wellington Bridgeman, Winnipeg, president of the Manitoba conference, to Allen, 11 September 1908.
6 *Christian Guardian*, 2 April 1913; W.B. Smith, Hespeler, Ontario, to editor, 23 April 1913; see also "Our Manitoba Letter" and George C. Wood, Moulinette, Ontario, to editor, 9 April 1913; article by Rev. George J. Bond, 23 April 1913.
7 The Manitoba totals exclude two of the conference districts that were in northern Ontario. The total for Manitoba for 1911 includes 3,522 members in Manitoba districts that were transferred from the Saskatchewan conference in 1910. Methodist statistics did not make the correction until 1912.
8 The census did not report age profiles for denominational populations until 1931. In that year the percentage of the United Church population under age fifteen was 31 for the prairie region and 26 for Ontario. In 1914 the elementary division held 48 percent of Methodist Sabbath scholars in the prairie region, compared to 42 percent for Ontario.
9 Congregations declared some members "ceased" because they had lost track of them, not because those persons had necessarily left the church. In 1912 the editor of the *Christian Guardian* attributed the church's "unprecedented" number of ceased members for that year (9,198) to "carelessness and lack of system in our methods of transferring members who remove from one part of the country to another, and chiefly from east to west." See *Christian Guardian*, 31 July 1912. His speculation notwithstanding, the church's highest ceased rates were in western Canada.
10 Minutes, quarterly board, Elkhorn, Manitoba, 12 May 1902; Boissevain, Manitoba, 2 May 1910 (UCAW); Sintaluta, Saskatchewan, 11 May 1912 (PAS); Fort Macleod, February 1914 (PAA).

11 Minutes, Arcola district, Saskatchewan conference, 1910 (PAS); Souris district, 1904 (UCAW).

12 Minutes, quarterly board, Lashburn, 24 April 1909 (PAS).

13 Ibid.; interview with Byles, 21–22 May 1974.

14 *Christian Guardian*, 17 July 1912. Rev. T.A. Moore, secretary of the general conference, reported the numbers of qualified voters under four categories: official board, members eighteen years of age and older, members under eighteen years of age, and adherents. The data used here exclude the adherents. Those who voted outnumbered the qualified voters in the official board category for the London conference; in this case, the writer estimated the number of qualified voters from the numbers who voted. He used the same procedure for the category of members under eighteen for the Alberta conference, whose number of qualified voters was not reported.

15 Taken from information in Minutes, quarterly boards, for ninety-one prairie stations (PAA, PAS, UCAW).

16 Silcox, *Church Union in Canada*, 434. The Presbyterian term for members was "communicants on roll."

17 For a copy of the pamphlet, see box 11, item 327 PAA.

18 *A Preacher's Frontier*, 110.

19 Voisey, *Vulcan*, 13–16.

20 *A Preacher's Frontier*, 53.

21 Ibid., 134.

22 The Methodist statistics are calculated from information in the *Methodist Year Book*, 1915. James Robertson, "the great superintendent," was the sole Presbyterian superintendent for Western Canada during the years 1881–1902. On his death, the church named J.C. Herdman for Alberta and British Columbia and J.A. Carmichael for Manitoba and Saskatchewan. After Herdman's death in 1910 and Carmichael's death in 1912, the general assembly provided for seven prairie superintendents: S.C. Murray for Manitoba, P. Strang for southern Saskatchewan, M.F. Munro for central Saskatchewan, C.G. Young for northern Saskatchewan, W. Simons for northern Alberta, W. Shearer for central Alberta, and J.T. Ferguson for the Presbyteries of High River, Macleod, and Kootenay, BC.

23 Boon, *The Anglican Church*, 289–90.

24 The Manitoba statistics are for the Rupertsland and Keewatin dioceses; the Saskatchewan statistics are for the Saskatchewan and Qu'Apelle dioceses; and the Alberta statistics are for the Calgary, Edmonton, and Athabaska dioceses. Documentary sources: *Church of England Yearbook*, 1919; *Journal of General Synod*, 1918, 361–3 and appendix 3, 62.

25 Barber, "Fellowship of the Maple Leaf," 154; Thomas, "The Church of England"; Boon, *The Anglican Church*, chap. 9. The British missionary

societies active in western Canada included the Colonial and Continental Church Society, the Society for the Propagation of the Gospel, the Church Missionary Society, and the Society for the Propagation of Christian Knowledge.

26 Grant, *The Church in the Canadian Era*, 94–5.

27 Voisey, *A Preacher's Frontier*, 110.

28 *Methodist Year Book*, 1915, 107.

29 The Presbyterian statistics for Sunday schools appear to be complete for student-mission fields, in contrast to the Presbyterian statistics for church membership. The Presbyterian statistics included union schools, whereas the Methodists reported them separately.

30 *Acts and Proceedings*, Presbyterian general assembly, 1914, 27, 30.

31 Interview with Byles, 21–22 May 1974.

32 Calculated from information in Parker, *Who's Who and Why*, 1915–16, vols. 6–7; *Who's Who in Western Canada*, 1911, vol. 1; Morgan, *Canadian Men and Women of the Time*, 1912; McRaye, *Pioneers and Prominent People in Manitoba*, 1925.

33 The estimates credit the Presbyterians with the 17 percent who were Presbyterian in 1931 and with 40 percent of the United Church adherents.

34 *Acts and Proceedings*, general assembly, 1914, appendix, 57.

35 *Christian Guardian*, 17 September 1902.

36 Bicha, "The Plains Farmer"; U.S. Bureau of the Census, *Religious Bodies, 1916*, part I, 109–11.

37 *Acts and Proceedings*, general assembly, 1911, appendix, 14; 1912, appendix, 21–2. The superintendents concerned were Rev. J.A. Carmichael and Rev. W.D. Reid. The 1911 census found just 9,331 Hungarians.

38 Riddell, *Methodism in the Middle West*, 312. Rev. William Wyman, the pastor at the Maple Street branch of the All People's Mission, handled the chaplaincy duties at Winnipeg. In 1913 the Manitoba conference named William Somerville to succeeded him on a full-time basis.

39 *Christian Guardian*, 4 September 1907, article by Rev. James Woodsworth, Winnipeg; Allen Papers, quadrennial report of the committee on immigration, July 1910; *Journal of Proceedings*, general conference, 1914, 223; report of the Committee on Immigration, 1906, 287; *Annual Report*, Missionary Society, 1906–7, cx; 1909–10, 51.

40 *Journal of Proceedings*, general conference, 1914, 226; Walter Giddings, Gleichen, Alberta, to editor, *Christian Guardian*, 15 February 1911; Reynolds, *The British Immigrant*, 219–25; McCormack, "Cloth Cap and Jobs." In contrast, British Anglican immigrants felt at home in the Canadian Anglican church, whose service matched their own.

41 Allen Papers, quadrennial report of the Committee on Immigration, July 1910; article by the Rev. C.E. Manning, *Missionary Outlook*, October 1910.

42 *Journal of Proceedings*, general conference, 1914, 223–4; Allen Papers, Allen to Judge S.A. Chesley, Lunenburg, NS, 2 January 1909; *Annual Report*, Missionary Society, 1913–14, xxiii.

43 Riddell, *Methodism in the Middle West*, 312. See also Allen Papers, Rev. Arthur Barner, Alix, Alberta, to Allen, 29 January 1907; Rev. T.J. Johnson, Clover Bar, Alberta, to Allen, 15 September 1908; article by H.H. Fudger, lay treasurer of the Missionary Society, *Missionary Outlook*, June 1906; article by "T.A.P.," October 1912.

44 Silcox, *Church Union in Canada*, 434–43. Silcox also observed, though not specifically for the prairie region, a reluctance of many adults in communities of Scottish highlanders to "come to the Lord's Table, or become members in full communion, even though they lived circumspect Christian lives."

45 *Acts and Proceedings*, general assembly, 1914, 23–4. The superintendent was Rev. S.C. Murray.

46 *Journal of the General Synod*, Anglican Church, 1915, 33.

47 Voisey, *Vulcan* 166, 182–98.

48 Christie and Gauvreau, *Full-Orbed Christianity*, 13. See also Voisey, *Vulcan*, 190.

49 Marks, *Revivals and Roller Rinks* 25–6.

50 Van Die, "The Marks of a Genuine Revival," 529.

51 Marks, *Revivals and Roller Rinks* 30–7.

52 Brown, "Over the Red Deer," 11; Allen Papers, Rev. B.W.J. Clements, Wessington, Alberta, to Allen, 13 February 1907; Rev. A.R. Aldridge, Vermillion District, Alberta, to Allen, 17 September 1907; Rev. W.P.M. Haffie, Shaunauvon, Alberta, to Allen, 20 August 1914.

53 Christie and Gauvreau, *Full-Orbed Christianity*, xii.

54 Hallet, *Firing the Heather*, 188–9, 194–5. Hallet's evidence is for the 1920s. McClung maintained, however, that she had formed her fundamental beliefs in childhood.

55 Voisey, *Vulcan*, introduction, chap. 8, conclusion. Environment is nature, exclusive of human-made things. Metropolitan is any outside influence on the locality. Frontier, which is conceptually distinct from environment, is the process of building communities where none previously existed.

CHAPTER SEVEN

1 *Christian Guardian*, 29 May, 1901.

2 Allen Papers, Bridgeman to Allen, 11 September 1908.

3 *Christian Guardian*, 8 June 1898; see also 28 June 1899; 9 September 1903; 29 April 1908; 6 June 1909.

4 Ibid., 9 September 1903.

5 Woodsworth, *Strangers within Our Gates*, 273. See also *Christian Guardian*, 3 June 1908; 2 March 1910; *Annual Report*, Missionary Society, 1909–10, 38–40 (a recommendation for the exclusion of paupers and criminals); Minutes, general board of missions, "recommendations of the commission on work among European immigrants, October 7th, 1909," 166–70.

6 Sifton was a lay preacher and "faithful member of his church" who practised daily family worship. See Hall, *Clifford Sifton*, vol. 1, 23–4.

7 Petryshyn, "Sifton's Immigration Policy."

8 In 1906 it provided for the exclusion of any class of persons deemed undesirable. It also required strict medical inspections and minimum landing funds for immigrants. The change in government policy had little influence on the Ukrainian immigrant stream, however. The key influences were conditions in central Europe, free homestead lands on the prairies, and chain migration. See Lehr, "Peopling the Prairies with Ukrainians"; Martynowych, *Ukrainians in Canada*, chap. 3.

9 Martynowych, *Ukrainians in Canada*, 43–6.

10 *Christian Guardian*, 17 May 1897; 12 May 1897; 20 July 1898; 27 July 1898; Friesen, *The Canadian Prairies*, 342.

11 *Missionary Outlook*, June 1906; *Christian Guardian*, 20 July 1898; 3 May 1899.

12 Allen Papers, Proceedings of the Commission on Foreign Missions in Western Canada, 28 August 1909.

13 *Christian Guardian*, 2 February 1910.

14 Allen Papers, report of a "Special Committee Appointed by the General Board of Missions to consider the question how to provide the additional men and money required for home and foreign missions," 8 December 1911.

15 J.K. Smith to Manning, 29 January 1919, Manning Papers.

16 Skwarok, *Ukrainian Settlers*, 122.

17 *Christian Guardian*, 21 November 1900; 15 January 1908.

18 Ibid., 21 April 1909; *Missionary Outlook*, March 1911. The lack of a compulsory attendance law also opened the door to separate schools without double taxation in districts whose population had not organized a public school.

19 *Christian Guardian*, 19 March 1913.

20 Ibid., 29 January 1913.

21 Woodsworth Papers, clipping from the *Manitoba Free Press*, 2 August 1912; *Christian Guardian*, 29 January 1913.

22 Anderson, *Education of the New Canadian*, 102.

23 Martynowych, *Ukrainians in Canada*, 343.

24 Manning Papers, Pike to Manning, 19 May 1919.

25 Lupul, "Ukrainian Language Education." The provision for foreign language instruction dated from 1903.

26 Martynowych, *Ukrainians in Canada*, chap. 13; Skwarok, *Ukrainian Settlers*, chaps. 5, 7.

27 Martynowych, *Ukrainians in Canada*, chap. 7.

28 *Christian Guardian*, 22 January 1902; 28 January 1909.

29 Martynowych, *Ukrainians in Canada*, 238–9.

30 Weber makes this argument for nineteenth-century France in his *Peasants into Frenchmen*. The argument also applies to Ukrainians in their homelands of Galicia and Bukovynia. See Martynowych, *Ukrainians in Canada*, chap. 1.

31 Ibid., chap. 7.

32 Ibid., chap. 10; Skwarok, *Ukrainian Settlers*; Lupul, "Ukrainian Language Education."

33 Bodrug, *Independent Greek Orthodox Church*, 56–7; see also chap. 8.

34 Canadian Ukrainians founded a third ethnic denomination, the Ukrainian Orthodox Church, in 1918. In was, in many ways, a reincarnation of the defunct Independent Greek Church. See Martynowych, *Ukrainians in Canada*. In 1911 the Baptist Ruthenian-Canadian conference had seven churches and six missionaries. For the Baptists, see Fitch, *Baptists of Canada*, 276–7; McLaurin, *Pioneering in Western Canada*, 386–96. For the Baptists in the Ukraine, see Marunchak, *Ukrainian Canadians*, 99.

After the 1890s Anglicans did not engage in non-Anglo-Saxon mission work, in no small part because their church lacked the resources to act on the problem. High-church Anglicans regarded Greek Orthodox immigrants as catholic co-religionists and declined to minister to them unless the immigrants lacked clergy of their own. See Powell, "Church of England and the Immigrants," "Church of England and the 'Foreigner'"; Barber, "Nationalism, Nativism, and the Social Gospel.

35 Ukrainian nationalism has a complex, dynamic history that dates from 1815; it differed somewhat between Austria and Russia. Pan-Russianist and pan-Ruthenianism (later pan-Ukrainianism) were the dominant constructions of nationalism in Galicia, and a third construction, peasant socialism, later jockeyed for influence. Clerics were the early nationalists. The pan-Ruthenian movement had anticlerical tendencies but relied on priests for local influence. In Russia, where Ukrainians were a wholly peasant society and the Russian Orthodox church was antinationalist, the peasant socialist movement was strongly anticlerical, sometimes atheist, and sometimes pro-Protestant (pro-Stundist, Russian Baptist). Thus, Ukrainian nationalism was no monolith but rather had multiple constructions, in the Old World as in Canada. See Himka, *Ukrainians in Canada*, 135–68.

36 Lehr, "Peopling the Prairies with Ukrainians." The writer inferred the ratio of Galicians to Bukovynians from the ratio of Greek Catholics to Greek Orthodox supporters in the 1911 census.

37 Himka, *Ukrainians in Canada*, 158.

38 Martynowyich, *Ukrainians in Canada*, chap. 1.

39 Ibid., 185–7.

40 Himka makes this argument for Galicia in *Religion and Nationality*, 154.

41 Tremblay, *Le Père Delaere*; Marunchak, *Ukrainian Canadians*, 99–114.

42 The monks once were worldly, with a fondness for cards, drink, dirty jokes, and ditties, and they suffered from an acute shortage of vocations. In 1882 the order began twenty years of Jesuit-managed reforms, imposed by the Vatican. See Himka, *Religion and Nationality*, 79–84.

43 In 1914 popular pressure forced the Belgian Redemptorists to leave their established monastery at Yorkton and start afresh in poor unchurched settlements in the Gimli-Komarno area of Manitoba. Tremblay, *Le Père Delaere*; Marunchak, *Ukrainian Canadians*, 234–47.

44 Martynowych, *Ukrainians in Canada*, chap. 8.

45 Bodrug, *Independent Greek Orthodox Church*; Martynowych, *Ukrainians in Canada*.

CHAPTER EIGHT

1 Martynowych, *Ukrainians in Canada*, 266.

2 *Christian Guardian*, 19 August 1908.

3 The writer's sources do not show when Mcguire left the mission. In 1914 she returned for its twenty-fifth anniversary celebration as Mrs J.J. Hughes. *Christian Guardian*, 26 July 1899; 5 August 1914.

4 The last place rented was adjacent to a hotel bar. Methodist legend reports that one bar patron wandered into a prayer meeting by mistake, stayed, and was converted!

5 *Christian Guardian*, 23 November 1898.

6 Ibid., 13 April, 20 April 1898.

7 Ibid., 26 July 1899.

8 Woodsworth Papers, vol. 29, clipping from Methodist Sunday school publication, the *Banner*, 1911; vol. 28, superintendent's report, All People's, 1907.

9 The association responded by discussing the enlargement and extension of the mission. In November 1904, it asked six churches to raise $825 for the mission's kindergarten work. See Minutes, Methodist Ministerial Association of Winnipeg, vols. 1–3, UCAW.

10 *Missionary Bulletin*, 1907, 27–30.

11 Sutherland Papers, Rev. J.V. Kovar to Sutherland, 21 February 1906.

12 Woodsworth Papers, vol. 28, superintendent's report, All People's, 1907.

13 Sutherland Papers, Dojacek to Sutherland, 31 March 1905.

14 *Christian Guardian*, 3 January 1906.

15 Sutherland Papers, Wigle to Sutherland, 31 March 1905.

16 Woodsworth, *Strangers within Our Gates,* chap. 23; Mills, *Fool for Christ,* 16, 36.

17 Ibid., 36.

18 Woodsworth, *My Neighbor,* 168.

19 Woodsworth, *Strangers within Our Gates,* chap. 23.

20 Ibid., 306. Woodsworth was misinformed about the Redemptorist mission at Yorkton, whose constituency was Ukrainian, not Polish.

21 Ibid., 305.

22 *Christian Guardian,* 18 September 1907.

23 Woodsworth, "Some Aspects of the Immigration Problem," *The Young Women of Canada,* December 1909, 147–8, in Woodsworth Papers, vol. 28.

24 Woodsworth, *My Neighbor,* 167.

25 *Missionary Bulletin,* 1908, 153.

26 *Missionary Outlook,* June 1912.

27 Woodsworth, "Immigration Problem," 147.

28 *Missionary Outlook,* June 1912.

29 Woodsworth, *Strangers within Our Gates,* 222.

30 Toronto *Globe,* 14 March 1910. Henceforth, the newspapers cited, other than the *Christian Guardian,* are from scrapbooks in the Woodsworth Papers.

31 Winnipeg *Evening Telegram,* 8 December 1908.

32 Article by "J.A.," *Manitoba Free Press,* 1 May 1909.

33 Ibid., 11 November 1909.

34 Ibid., 20 May 1909 (article in the Woodsworth Papers by someone other than Woodsworth).

35 Woodsworth, *My Neighbor,* 168–9.

36 Ibid., 172.

37 *Epworth Era* (Toronto), July 1911.

38 Martynowych, *Ukrainians in Canada,* 230–2, 236.

39 McNaught, *A Prophet in Politics,* 26.

40 Fort William *Herald,* 16 June 1910.

41 *Christian Guardian,* 23 September 1914.

42 Christie and Gauvreau, *A Full-Orbed Christianity,* 11.

43 Woodsworth, *Strangers within Our Gates,* 341. Woodsworth left the ministry in 1918, but over his Church's support for the war effort, not out of a crisis of faith.

44 Mills, *Fool for Christ,* 21. This perspective, finds Mills, presaged his "later, discrepant mixture of *de facto* atheism, deism, and pantheism." For more on Woodsworth's religious journey, see Cook, *The Regenerators,* chap. 11.

45 Christie, *A Full-Orbed Christianity,* xii–xiii, 3–12, 50–1.

46 As Christie and Gauvreau write, "*Woodsworth* ... combined industrial education with evangelistic meetings ... At the Maple Street Mission

Woodsworth and his workers held two Gospel services on Sunday, three prayer meetings ... and a series of special revival meetings, where forty-five adults and seven children were converted." Ibid., 50–1 (my italics).

47 With his evangelical goals, Chambers held lodging house meetings and lantern services. Woodsworth Papers, "Practical Christianity," 10–11; "Organized Helpfulness," 21–2.

48 *Missionary Bulletin*, 1911, 512.

49 Winnipeg *Tribune*, 5 September 1912.

50 Woodsworth, *Strangers within Our Gates*, 320.

51 Sutherland Papers, Rev. J.H. Morgan to Sutherland, 23 February 1906; 23 July 1906, Dojacek's monthly report for March 1905; *Missionary Outlook*, July 1906.

52 Sutherland Papers, Kovar to Sutherland, 21 February 1906.

53 Marunchak, *Ukrainian Canadians*, 310; Martynowych, *Ukrainians in Canada*, 230, 332–3.

54 Woodsworth Papers, "Practical Christianity," 3; Woodsworth, *My Neighbor*, 322–32. The Bethlehem Slavic mission also was on Stella Avenue.

55 *Annual Report*, Missionary Society, 1907–8, 63–6.

56 *Christian Guardian*, 18 December 1907, 1 April 1908.

57 Ibid., 18 December 1907, 25 March 1908; Woodsworth, *Strangers within Our Gates*, 306–9.

58 *Christian Guardian*, 30 June 1909.

59 Sissons Papers, Woodsworth to C.B. Sissons, 10 April 1908, quoted in Mills, *Fool for Christ*, 37.

60 Allen Papers, Allen to James Woodsworth, 28 November 1907; *Christian Guardian*, 30 June 1909; Woodsworth Papers, "Organized Helpfulness," *Annual Report*, All People's Mission, 1911–12, 21–2; Sissons Papers, J.S. Woodsworth to C.B. Sissons, 10 April 1908, quoted in Mills, *Fool for Christ*, 37.

61 Woodsworth, *Strangers within Our Gates*, 328.

62 *Christian Guardian*, 27 September 1911.

63 *Missionary Bulletin*, 1911, 512.

64 *Manitoba Free Press*, 24 February 1912.

65 Winnipeg *North Ender*, 29 September 1910.

66 *Manitoba Free Press*, 27 May 1911.

67 Winnipeg *North Ender*, 29 September 1910, 23 March 1912.

68 Ibid., 29 September 1910.

69 *Manitoba Free Press*, 27 May 1911.

70 Ibid., 27 May 1911. See also Woodsworth, *My Neighbor*, 322–32.

71 Article by "Kilmeny", *Manitoba Free Press*, 24 February 1912; Winnipeg *North Ender*, 26 September 1912.

72 Article by Woodsworth, *Christian Guardian*, 2 September 1914.

73 Ibid., 22 October 1913.

74 McNaught, *Prophet in Politics*, 59.

75 *Christian Guardian*, 23 September 1914.

76 Allen Papers, Rev. William Somerville, Cypress River, Manitoba, to Rev. James Allen, 28 November 1911.

77 Manning Papers, Bridgman to Manning, 8 April 1915. See also Bridgman *Breaking Prairie Sod*, 168–9. For Moody, see chap. 1.

78 On one occasion the mission's nonsectarian character produced a sectarian outcome. In 1925 John Korchik was the eldest of four children born to Galician parents in Winnipeg. His mother, a devout Ukrainian Catholic, wanted him to become a priest. When his Catholic schooling failed to satisfy Korchik, his brother introduced him to Rev. J.M. Shaver and the All People's Mission. Korchik admired Shaver's truth-seeking, nonsectarian approach and emphasis on Christian character, and in 1928, with his mother's blessing, he entered Wesley College medical school to become a United Church medical missionary. John Korchik, "Confidential Report on the Leading Ukrainian Districts of Western Canada," Board of Home Missions, United Church, 1929.

79 The Brandon mission was short-lived. In 1909 Brandon Second was founded to serve some 250 families to the north of the CPR tracks in the city. Sixty of the families were Anglo-Canadian, and 30 were German Lutheran. The balance included 17 Jewish, 87 Roman Catholic (German, Galician, and Polish) and 20 Galician Greek Orthodox households. Sunday school classes at Brandon Second soon attracted 150 children weekly. Rev. Pohlman, a Lutheran pastor from Lemburg, Saskatchewan, used the building once monthly for a nominal fee. In 1911, however, Rev. Robert Milliken, principal of Regina College, advised James Allen that further expenditure was unwise. The local leadership was lacking, and the "foreign" population was stable due to the "quiet steadiness" of the city. See Allen Papers, Report on European Foreigners, n.d. (est. 1909); Rev. Charles R. Sing, Brandon, to Oliver Darwin, 10 March 1909; Rev. Robert Milliken, Brandon, to Rev. James Allen, 11 September 1911.

CHAPTER NINE

1 The census of 1901 reports 3,193 Austrians, 2,518 Russians, and 4 Rumanians for the Alberta district. The census of 1911 reports 14,369 Austrians and 2,224 Russians, Poles, and Rumanians for the Victoria district. The enumeration of 1921 reports 19,468 Ukrainians, 9,646 Austrians, and 3,939 Poles and Russians for the Alberta census districts 10, 13, and 14.

2 Manning Papers, Smith to Manning, 5 October 1919.

3 Allen Papers, Rev. W.A. Lewis, Edmonton, to Allen, 5 May 1911, *Christian Guardian*, 8 October 1913.

4 Manning Papers, Taranty Hannochko, Bellis, letter submitted to the *Missionary Bulletin*, 10 January 1922; Kostash, *All of Baba's Children*, 61.

5 Pike, "The Flame," 1.

6 *Missionary Bulletin*, 1904, 202; Martynowych, *Ukrainians in Canada*, chap. 4. Kostash, *All of Baba's Children*, gives a feisty rebuttal to romantic interpretations of the settler's experience.

7 Martynowych, *Ukrainians in Canada*, 85–6.

8 Manning Papers, Lawford to Manning, 29 July 1919.

9 *Christian Guardian*, 8 December 1909. For another expression, of Lawford's anti–Roman Catholicism, see *Missionary Bulletin*, 1911, 336. For background, see Miller, "Anti-Catholicism in Canada," 25–48.

10 *Missionary Bulletin*, 1908, 451.

11 Ibid., 1904, 202. The shortage of priests was a long-term problem. In 1929 Greek Catholics had only four priests for their thirty-five churches in Alberta; only two churches had weekly services. See Korchik, "Confidential Report."

12 *Missionary Bulletin*, 1908, 223, 451.

13 Ibid., 1908, 223; 1910, 52–3.

14 Minutes, WMS, Alberta branch, 1913 (PAA).

15 Ibid., 1915, 387–92.

16 Ibid.

17 *Christian Guardian*, 25 September 1907.

18 Manning Papers, Buchanan to Manning, 10 September 1919.

19 Interview, Edmonton, 16 August 1972.

20 *Missionary Bulletin*, 1904, 202; 1910, 192, 335; Allen Papers, Lawford to Allen, 15 May 1911.

21 *Missionary Bulletin*, 1909, 501.

22 *Edmonton Journal*, 10 August 1952; Lawford, "A Short History"; *Missionary Bulletin*, 1904, 199–200. In 1879 Lawford's father had accepted the position of farm instructor to Indians in the Riding Mountains, near the future site of the village of Rossburn, Manitoba.

23 Interview, Edmonton, 16 August 1972.

24 Ironside, "Development of Victoria Settlement"; Mills, *Fool for Christ*, 9.

25 *Missionary Bulletin*, 1904, 201.

26 Ibid., 1904, 202–4; Pike, "The Flame," 4. "Sometimes, while conducting services through an interpreter," Pike recalled, "the doctor became a bit impatient [when] the interpreter rambled on with explanations instead of straight interpreting. One Sunday morning the doctor interjected with his own imperfect Ukrainian. He was talking about the man who was let down at the feet of Jesus in a home in Galilee. Now the word for *bed* and the words for *spoon* are very similar in Ukrainian. He convulsed the congregation by saying *they let him down on a spoon.*"

27 Pike, "The Flame," 15.

28 Chace, "Wahstao Memories," PAA.

29 Manning Papers, T.C. Buchanan, Edmonton, to Manning, 10 April 1919.

30 Ibid., Wildfong to Manning, 20 July 1922. In 1922 the Methodist missionary, J.D. Wildfong, wrote that the Ukrainians "lack the nursing instinct. In sickness they resort to patent remedies such as Beef Iron & Wine as pain killers & medicine of that nature. In cuts & wounds they resort to pure carbolic acid & bind the part with green cabbage leaves." When epidemic smallpox broke out in 1925, the local priests viewed it as a divine visitation and warned the people away from the Methodist doctor lest this tempt providence. Manning Papers, Rev. W.R. Donagh to Rev. Lloyd Smith, Toronto, 27 April 1926; May Monthly Report, Vita General Hospital, 1925.

31 *Missionary Bulletin*, 1904, 203. The doctors nearest Lawford, both Methodists, were Dr Harry R. Smith and his wife (formerly Dr Martha Doyle) at Star.

32 Lawford, "A Short History." For Lawford's car, see Kolokreeka Diary, PAA.

33 *Missionary Bulletin*, 1905, 606.

34 Lawford, "A Short History."

35 The cost was $4,000. Pike, "The Flame," 25; Allen Papers, Allen to Lawford, 21 March 1907; *Missionary Bulletin*, 1907, 169.

36 Manning Papers, Dr C.F. Connolly to Manning, 4 April 1912.

37 *Missionary Bulletin*, 1907, 623–4. Lawford was the hospital's superintendent. In Edmonton, Dr Harry R. Smith and Rev. T.C. Buchanan acted as a two-man advisory board for Methodist hospitals in the Alberta conference. Smith had just given up a medical practice in the village of Star. Buchanan was the newly appointed superintendent of missions for the Alberta conference. In 1915 the missionary society created a fourteen-person board of directors to manage hospitals in Alberta. See Allen Papers, H.R. Smith to Allen, 3 April 1907; "First Meeting of the Board of Directors for the Administration of Hospitals in Alberta," 9 November 1915. See Hoffman, "Women of God," for protestant children in Catholic schools.

38 *Missionary Bulletin*, 1910, 56.

39 Allen Papers, Smith to Allen, 8 May 1912.

40 *Missionary Bulletin*, 1910, 56.

41 Allen Papers, Lawford to Allen, 20 August 1912; Buchanan to Allen, 16 September 1912. The correspondence dealing with Connolly's dismissal lasted from November 1911 to January 1913. Lawford had several reasons for firing Connolly, one of them a well-founded suspicion that Connolly was after his job while he, Lawford, was bed-ridden for four months with a hip injury. Although worried about the controversy that followed Lawford's action, T.C. Buchanan agreed that "a man at the

head of an institution in connection with the Methodist Church should neither smoke nor play cards either publicly or privately."

42 Lawford admitted this in 1912, when a hip injury left him bed-ridden for four months. During the years 1913–15 he paid the $300 deficit of the hospital out of his own salary. Allen Papers, Lawford to Allen, 10 June 1912; "First meeting of the Board of Directors for the Administration of Hospitals in Alberta," 9 November 1915.

43 Ibid., Lawford to Allen, 4 March 1908.

44 Ibid., Lawford to Allen, 4 March 1908; *Missionary Bulletin*, 1908, 223. Basilian monk-priests from Galicia were active in the Star colony. See chap. 7.

45 *Missionary Bulletin*, 1908, 449.

46 Ibid., 1908, 450–1; 1910, 501; 1912, 1399.

47 *Missionary Outlook*, August 1909; Pike, "The Flame," 17.

48 *A Century of Progress*, Minutes, WMS, Alberta branch, 1913 (PAA).

49 Pakan Austrian Circuit Register, PAA.

50 *Missionary Bulletin*, 1910, 192.

51 *Missionary Outlook*, February 1911; Pike, "The Flame," 18.

52 Sutherland Papers, Lawford to Sutherland, 20 December 1909.

53 *Missionary Bulletin*, 1910, 49.

54 *Christian Guardian*, 5 October 1910.

55 Personal communication from D.M. Ponich, 4 January 1972; Pike, "The Flame," 18. Metro was always welcome in his parents' home, and his father gave him a deathbed blessing.

56 Ethelwyn Chace's address to the Sixth Annual Convention of Methodist Ruthenian Workers in Alberta, Wahstao, 31 July–3 August 1917, Manning Papers.

57 Wahstao Diary, 1911–27.

58 Chace, "Wahstao Memories," PAA.

59 Pike, "The Flame," 5. See McGregor, *Vilni Zemli*, back cover page, for a superbly detailed map of "the colony" in 1910.

60 *Christian Guardian*, 17 August 1904; 28 September 1904; *Missionary Outlook*, February 1907; January 1908; Pike, "The Flame," 5–13; Chace and Edmonds, "Wahstao Memories," PAA. "The school room occupied most of the ground floor, behind were living room and pantry. Upstairs were two bedrooms and two very tiny ones. A lean-to kitchen and another small bedroom completed the structure. It was heated by two big box-stoves, but it grew cold on winter nights."

61 Chace, "Wahstao Memories," PAA. Chace joined the Wahstao staff in 1907. She wrote her memoir in the form of retrospective letters to Edith Weekes.

62 Edmunds required rest and surgery in Edmonton in March and August of 1905. Munro, reported Chace, was a "city girl" from Peterborough

and older and less robust than Edmonds, a farm girl. Before serving at Wahstao, she had been invalided home from Japan.

63 Pike, "The Flame"; Gagan, *A Sensitive Independence*, 181.

64 Chace, "Wahstao Memories."

65 *Christian Guardian*, 25 September 1907.

66 Reminiscence of Ethel Hickman, WMS collection, PAA.

67 *Christian Guardian*, 25 September 1907; Pike, "The Flame."

68 *Missionary Outlook*, March 1909.

69 Chace, "Wahstao Memories."

70 Pike, "The Flame," 4.

71 Chace, "Wahstao Memories"; Pike, "The Flame," 15; Gagan, *A Sensitive Independence*, 182–3. To Gagan the poultry incident evidenced the ladies' "agonizing difficulty speaking Ukrainian" and the "marginally rewarding results of their work." That is not the interpretation presented here.

72 Minutes, WMS, Alberta branch, 1914 (PAA).

73 Gagan, *A Sensitive Independence*, 184–5.

74 Manning Papers, Buchanan to Manning, 10 April 1919.

75 Conversion, let alone Methodist Church membership, carried risk for the convert. In 1913 Rev. J.K. Smith told of a young female convert who "was whipped by her father because she refused to go to confession, and has since been compelled to flee her home." See *Missionary Outlook*, November 1913, 245.

76 Wahstao Dairy, 1911–27, PAA.

77 Allen Papers, J.K. Smith to Rev. Arthur Barner, 15 February 1915.

78 *Christian Guardian*, 16 September 1914.

79 Allen Papers, Rush to F.C. Stephenson, 31 October 1914; *Missionary Outlook*, 1916, 361–4. The village and district paid $12,000 of the $15,000 cost. The General Board paid the balance, operated the hospital, and owned the property.

80 *Missionary Bulletin*, 1917, 293–6. For social-services and educational-cultural societies organized in Edmonton by Ukrainians, see Martynowych, *Ukrainians in Canada*, 271–2.

81 *Missionary Outlook*, October 1911.

82 Ibid., February 1914.

83 Interview with Pike, 8 September 1972. His upbringing also gave him a prejudice against the Church of England.

84 Allen Papers, Rev. W.A. Lewis, Edmonton, to James Allen, 5 May 1911; Pike, "The Flame," 20; interview with Rev. W.H. Pike, Ottawa, 17 April 1968.

85 *Missionary Bulletin*, 1912, 1018–9.

86 *Christian Guardian*, 19 January 1910; Allen Papers, Methodist Ruthenian Workers to the General Board of Missions, 18 December 1917; Manning

Papers, Minutes of the sixth annual meeting of Ruthenian workers, 31 July 1917; Minutes of general board committee on the proposed amalgamation of the *Canadian* with *Ranok*, 6 January 1917. The circulation for 1917 was 850, including 119 in Saskatchewan and Manitoba. Methodist Ruthenian workers had increased the circulation in an effort to save the *Canadian* from amalgamation with *Ranok*.

87 Allen Papers, "Report of Investigation of Conditions of Foreign Settlements" by Rev. Edmund Chambers, 1914. This was the judgment of Chambers, who had studied language in Poland during the years 1909–11, then served at All People's Mission in Winnipeg (1911–14).

88 W.H. Pike, "A Canadianizer's Ideal of Canadian Citizenship," *Missionary Outlook*, 16, 2 (1920); interview with Pike, 8 September 1972.

89 Manning Papers, Responses to questionnaire on churches and missions using a foreign language, 1922.

90 Interview with E. May Laycock, 16 August 1972.

91 Pike, "The Flame," 16; *Missionary Bulletin*, 1913, 453–6; 1914, 307.

92 Allen Papers, Rev. Arthur Barner, Calgary, to Rev. C.E. Manning, Toronto, 16 July 1914, "Report on the Work among Non-English Speaking Peoples in the Southern Superintendency of the Alberta conference."

93 *Missionary Bulletin*, 1915, 211–14; 1915, 387–92.

94 Ibid., 1915, 211–14, 387–92; 1920, 733–6; 1922, 433–6.

95 Personal communication from D.M. Ponich, 4 January 1972.

96 Allen Papers, Buchanan to Allen, 29 January 1915.

97 Ibid., Methodist Ruthenian Workers to the General Board of Missions, 18 December 1917. Ponich was among the signatories, and the petition strongly endorsed Michael Bellegay, the Ukrainian editor of the Methodist paper.

98 Manning Papers, Chace to Rev. J.H. Riddell, Winnipeg, 18 March 1918.

99 W.T. Cherrington, Moon Lake, to Mrs Florence Schoffield, St Stephens, 12 March 1967, PAA. Three big steam engines pulled the buildings in a nine-day operation that required the contractor and fifteen men. Cherrington was one of the crew.

100 Pakan Austrian Mission Circuit Register, PAA.

101 Manning Papers, Lawford to Manning, 29 July 1919.

102 Interview with Laycock, 16 August 1972; interview with Pike, 8 September 1972.

103 Manning Papers, Maddex to T.C. Buchanan, 15 July 1914; Smith to Manning, 11 January 1918; W.H. Garred, Pakan, to Manning, 16 October 1920; Lawford to Manning, 25 January 1921.

104 Ibid., Minutes of general board committee on the proposed amalgamation of the *Canadian* with *Ranok*, 6 January 1917; Minutes of a joint meeting of representatives of the Methodist and Presbyterian Churches

on the proposed amalgamation, Winnipeg, 10 May 1917. Silcox reports that the amalgamation took effect in 1920. See Silcox, *Church Union in Canada*, 232.

105 Manning Papers, Pike's "Report of the Methodist-Presbyterian Mission to New Canadians in Edmonton and Vicinity for 1921."

106 Ibid., Annual report, Lamont Public Hospital, 1923.

107 Ibid., Thomas D. Jones to Manning, 2 October 1919.

108 Lawford, "A Short Survey," 8.

109 *Missionary Outlook*, 1916, 689–92.

Bibliography

ABBREVIATIONS

GMA Glenbow Museum and Archives, Calgary
NA   National Archives, Ottawa
PAA Provincial Archives of Alberta, Edmonton
PAS Provincial Archives of Saskatchewan, Saskatoon
UCA United Church Archives, Toronto
UCAW United Church Archives, Winnipeg

MANUSCRIPT COLLECTIONS

Allen Papers, 1906–18, UCA. Rev. James Allen was general secretary, Department of Home Missions, Missionary Society of the Methodist Church.
Carman Papers, UCA. Rev. Albert Carman was general superintendent, 1884–1915.
Dobson Papers, 1912–51, microfilm, UCA. Rev. Hugh Dobson taught in Wesley College, 1911–12, and was the western field secretary for the Department of Evangelism and Social Service, 1913–24.
Fitzpatrick Papers, 1902–5, NA. Hon. Charles Fitzpatrick was minister of justice.
Manning Papers, 1906–25, UCA. Rev. Charles E. Manning was field secretary for the home mission department, then Allen's successor as general secretary in 1918.
Moore Papers, UCA. Rev. Thomas Albert Moore held several important positions, including secretary of the general conference, joint secretary of the

Dominion Alliance, secretary of the Canadian Lord's Day Alliance and membership on the executive of the Moral and Social Reform Council of Canada.

Oliver Papers, PAS. Rev. E.H. Oliver was principal of St Andrews College, Presbyterian Church, Saskatoon.

Sifton Papers, 1897–1903, microfilm, NA. Hon. Clifford Sifton was minister of the interior (1896–1905) and a Methodist.

Sutherland Papers, 1905–6, UCA. Rev. Alexander Sutherland was general secretary of the Missionary Society until 1906, then general secretary for its foreign mission department.

Ukrainian Mission Collection, PAA. Diaries, circuit registers, and reminiscences for Pakan, Wahstao, Kolokreeka, and other points in the Smoky Lake district.

Winnipeg All People's Collection, UCAW.

Woodsworth Papers, NA, group 27, series 3, vol. 28–9, scrapbooks of press clippings relating to the work of Rev. J.S. Woodsworth during his superintendency of All People's Mission, Winnipeg, 1907–13. Vols. 1–4, containing correspondence relating to his early life and to his attempt to resign from the ministry.

INTERVIEWS

Byles, Stephen R. London, 21–22 May 1974. Byles was a Methodist probationer in the Saskatchewan conference, 1908–16.

Laycock, E. May. Edmonton, 16 August 1972. Laycock was a WMS Ukrainian missionary during the 1920s.

Pike, William Henry. Ottawa, 17 April 1968, 8 September 1972. Pike served on Ukrainian missions in Alberta.

Ponich, Demetrius Metro. Correspondence, 4 January 1972. Ponich was a Ukrainian convert missionary in Alberta.

OFFICIAL RECORDS

Acts and Proceedings. General Assembly, Presbyterian Church in Canada, 1896–1914.

Annual Reports. Missionary Society of the Methodist Church, 1896–1914.

Annual Reports. Woman's Missionary Society, Methodist Church, 1896–1914.

Canada's Missionary Congress: Addresses Delivered at the Canadian National Missionary Congress, Held in Toronto, March 31 to April 4, 1909, with Reports of Committees. Toronto, Canadian Council of the Laymen's Missionary Movement, 1909.

Doctrine and Discipline of the Methodist Church, The. 1906. Departments of Social Service and Evangelism of the Methodist and Presbyterian Churches. Social Surveys, Regina, 1913; London, 1913; St Catharines, 1913; Fort William,

1913; Swan River Valley, Manitoba, 1914; Turtle Mountain District, Manitoba, 1914; Huron County, 1914; Toronto, 1915.

Journal of Proceedings. General Conference, Methodist Church, 1894, 1898, 1902, 1906, 1910, and 1914.

Journal of Proceedings. General Synod, Anglican Church of Canada 1893, 1896, 1902, 1905, 1908, 1911, and 1914.

Metropolitan Methodist Church Yearbook. Toronto, 1897–98 to 1911–12.

Minutes. Conference Stationing Committees for Alberta (PAA), Saskatchewan (PAS), and Manitoba (UCAW).

Minutes. District meetings. Alberta (PAA): Calgary, Edmonton, Fort Saskatchewan, High River, Red Deer, Stettler, Olds, Wetaskiwin. Saskatchewan (PAS): Arcola, Battleford, Goose Lake, Moosemin, Regina, Saskatoon, Weyburn, Yorkton. Manitoba (UCAW): Birtle, Brandon, Carman, Crystal City, Deloraine, Dauphin, Neepawa, Portage la Prairie, Souris, Winnipeg South.

Minutes. Executive Committee, General Board of Missions, Methodist Church 1908–19.

Minutes. General Board of Missions, Methodist Church, 1901–7.

Minutes. Methodist and Presbyterian Co-operation Committee, MacLeod District, 1911–21, PAA.

Minutes. Quarterly Official Boards. Alberta (PAA): Camrose, Bashaw, Bankhead All Peoples, Beaver Hills, Bowden, Crossfield, Carstairs, Carmangay-Champion, Calgary (Central Methodist), Claresholm, Clive-Alix, Fort Macleod, High River, Irma, Lloydminster, Medicine Hat, Nanton, Okotoks, Olds, Oyen, Penhold, Sturgeon, Taber, Tofield, Vermillion, Viking, Wainwright. Saskatchewan (PAS): Abernethy, Alsask, Arcola, Ardath, Bigger, Blaine Lake, Birch Hills, Boharm, Bredenbury, Elstow, Flaxcombe, Glenhurst, Grand Coulee, Grenfell, Lashburn, Laura, Lemberg, Macklin, Macoun, Maple Creek, Moosemin, North Portal, Prince Albert, Qu'Appelle, Rocanville, Sheho, Sintaluta, Speers (New Ottawa), Talmage, Weyburn, Woleysey. Manitoba (UCAW): Austin-Sydney, Binscarth-Russell, Boissevain, Carberry, Cartwright (Holmfield), Crystal City, Durban (Benito-Kenville), Eastland, Elkhorn, Elm Creek, Foxwarren, Glenboro (trustee board), Hamiota, Hartney, Hayfield-Carroll, High Bluff, High Bluff Prospect, Kelwood-McCreary, Lyleton (Elva)/Pierson, MacGregor, Manitou, Melita, Miami, Minitonas-Bowsman, Minnedosa, Murillo, Neepawa, Oak Lake, Oakville, Portage la Prairie, Rapid City, Rivers, Roland.

Minutes. WMS, Alberta branch, 1909–18. PAA.

Minutes (Manuscript). Alberta Conference (PAA); Saskatchewan Conference (PAS); Manitoba and Northwest Conference and Manitoba Conference (UCAW).

Minutes (printed). Toronto, Hamilton, London, Bay of Quinte, and Montreal conferences, 1896–1914; Manitoba and Northwest conference, 1890–1903;

Manitoba, Assiniboia (later Saskatchewan), and Alberta conferences 1904–14.

The Social Service Congress, Report of Addresses and Proceedings. Ottawa and Toronto 1914.

U.S. Department of Commerce. *Bureau of the Census, Religious Bodies,* 1916. Part 1. Washington 1919, 109–11.

NEWSPAPERS AND PERIOD JOURNALS

Assiniboia Church Advocate. Moose Jaw, monthly, vol. 1, nos. 1–9, October 1904 to June 1905, UCA.

Canadian Methodist Quarterly. Toronto, 1889–95, UCA.

Christian Guardian. Toronto, weekly, 1895–1914, UCA.

Methodist Magazine. Toronto, 1890–95, UCA.

Methodist Magazine and Review. Toronto, 1896–1906, UCA.

Missionary Bulletin. Toronto, quarterly, 1903–14, UCA. Publication of the Young People's Forward Movement for Missions, with "Letters from Missionaries and Missionary Superintendents to their Fellow Workers at Home."

Missionary Outlook. Toronto, monthly, 1896–1914, UCA. Published jointly by the Missionary Society and the WMS.

Western Methodist Bulletin. Winnipeg, monthly, vol. 1, nos. 6–11, December 1904 to May 1905, UCA.

Western Methodist Times. Winnipeg, monthly, vol. 2, nos. 7–12, January 1906 to July 1906, UCA.

UNPUBLISHED MANUSCRIPTS

Bay, Theodore. "The Historical Sketch of the Background and the Beginning of the Protestant Movement in Canada among the Ukrainian People in Canada." 1964. PAA.

Brooks, William H. "Methodism in the Middle West in the Nineteenth Century." PHD diss., University of Manitoba, 1972.

Byles, Stephen R. "The Canadianization of a Yorkshire Lad." Photocopy, in writer's possession, 1973.

Korchik, John. "Confidential Report on the Leading Ukrainian Districts of Western Canada." Board of Home Missions, United Church, 1929, UCA.

Lawford, Charles, H. "A Short History of Pioneer Life in the Western Provinces from 1849 and Mission Work of the United Church in the Pakan District." GMA, n.d., file 1084.

Pike, W.H. "The Flame: A Story of the Church's Ukrainian Work in Alberta." UCA, 1966.

Royce, Marion V. "The Contribution of the Methodist Church to Social Welfare in Canada." MA thesis, University of Toronto, 1940.

Wenstob, Murray. "The Work of the Methodist Church among the Settlers of Alberta up to 1914, with Special Reference to the Formation of New Congregations and Work among the Ukrainian People." BD thesis, St Stephens College, University of Alberta, 1959, GMA, microfilm.

Wilson, Catharine Anne. "Tenancy as a Family Strategy for Survival: Starting Up and Winding Down in Mid-Nineteenth Century Ontario." Paper presented to the Canadian Conference on Economic History, Niagara on the Lake, May, 1997.

Zuk, Michael. "The Ukrainian Protestant Missions in Canada." STM thesis, Faculty of Divinity, McGill University, ca. 1956.

BIOGRAPHICAL SOURCES

Bibliographical File, GMA, Calgary.

Charlesworth, Hector, ed. *A Cyclopaedia of Canadian Biography.* Toronto 1919.

Cochrane, Rev. William. *Men of Canada.* Vols. 1–5. Brantford, ON, 1891–1896.

Christian Guardian, 1896–1924, UCA.

Greene, B.M., ed. *Who's Who and Why, 1921.* Toronto 1921.

Hamilton, Ross. *Prominent Men of Canada, 1931–32.* Montreal, 1932.

McRaye, Walter, ed. *Pioneers and Prominent People in Manitoba.* Winnipeg 1925.

Magurn, A.J., ed. *The Canadian Parliamentary Guide,* 1898, 1901, 1905, 1909.

Minutes, Annual Conferences, obituaries, 1896–1925.

Morgan, Henry, ed. *Canadian Men and Women of the Time, 1912.* Toronto, 1912.

New Outlook, United Church of Canada, 1925–38, UCA.

Parker, Dr C.W., ed. *Who's Who in Western Canada,* Vol. 1, 1911. Vancouver, 1911.

– *Who's Who and Why, 1915–16.* Vols. 6–7. Toronto, 1916.

Pension Records, Methodist Church, UCA.

United Church Observer, 1939–68.

Wallace, W. Stewart, *The Dictionary of Canadian Biography.* Toronto, 1919.

– *The Canadian Who's Who.* Toronto, 1910.

PUBLISHED LITERATURE

Acheson, T.W. "Methodism and the Problem of Methodist Identity in Nineteenth-Century New Brunswick." In *The Contribution of Methodism to Atlantic Canada,* ed. Charles H.H. Scobie and John Webster Grant. Montreal and Kingston: McGill-Queen's University Press, 1992, 107–26.

Airhart, Phyllis D. Review of *Secularizing the Faith,* by David B. Marshall. *Canadian Historical Review* 74, 4 (1993): 607–9.

– *Serving the Present Age: Revivalism, Progressivism, and the Methodist Tradition in Canada.* Montreal and Kingston: McGill-Queen's University Press, 1992.

Akenson, Donald Harman. *Small Differences: Irish Catholics and Irish Protestants,*
1815–1922. Montreal and Kingston: McGill-Queen's University Press, 1988.
– *Surpassing Wonder: The Invention of the Bible and the Talmuds, 1815–1922.*
Montreal and Kingston: McGill-Queen's University Press, 1998.
Allen, Richard. "Salem Bland and the Spirituality of the Social Gospel:
Winnipeg and the West, 1903–1913." In *Prairie Spirit: Perspectives on the Her-*
itage of the United Church of Canada in the West, ed. Dennis L. Butcher, et al.
Winnipeg, MB: University of Manitoba Press, 1985, 217–32.
– "The Social Gospel and the Reform Tradition in Canada." *Canadian Histor-*
ical Review 49 (1968): 381–99.
– *The Social Passion: Religion and Social Reform in Canada, 1914–28.* Toronto:
University of Toronto Press, 1971.
Anderson, J.T.M. *The Education of the New Canadian.* Toronto: J.M. Dent, 1918.
Archer, John H. "The Anglican Church and the Indian in the Northwest."
Journal of the Canadian Church Historical Society 28, 1 (1986): 19–30.
Arnold, Abraham. "New Jerusalem on the Prairies: Welcoming the Jews." In
Visions of the New Jerusalem: Religious Settlement on the Prairies, ed. Benjamin
G. Smillie. Edmonton, AB: NeWest Press, 1983, 91–107.
Austin, Alvyn J. *Saving China: Canadian Missionaries in the Middle Kingdom,*
1888–1959. Toronto: University of Toronto Press, 1986.
Ayers, Edward L. *Southern Crossing: A History of the American South, 1877–1906.*
New York: Oxford University Press, 1995.
Badertscher, John. "As Others Saw Us." In *Prairie Spirit: Perspectives on the Her-*
itage of the United Church of Canada in the West, ed. Dennis L. Butcher, et al.
Winnipeg, MB: University of Manitoba Press, 1985, 44–64.
Bagley, Ray. "Lacombe in the Nineties." *Alberta History* 10, 3 (1962): 18–27.
Barber, Marilyn. "The Fellowship of the Maple Leaf Teachers." In *The Anglican*
Church and the World of Western Canada, 1820–1965, ed. Barry G. Ferguson.
Regina, SK: Canadian Plains Research Centre 1991, 154–66.
– "Nationalism, Nativism, and the Social Gospel: The Protestant Church
Response to Foreign Immigrants in Western Canada, 1897–1914." In *The*
Social Gospel in Canada, ed. Richard Allen. Ottawa: National Museum of
Canada, 1975, 186–226.
Barclay, Wade Crawford. *The M.E. Church, 1845–1939.* New York: Methodist
Church Board of Missions, 1957.
Baswick, Daryl. "Social Evangelism, the Canadian Churches, and the Forward
Movement, 1919–1920." *Ontario History* 89, 4 (1997): 303–20.
Barnhart, Gordon. "The Prairie Pastor: E.H. Oliver." *Saskatchewan History* 37,
3 (1984): 81–94.
Becker, A. "The Lake Geneva Mission, Wakaw, Saskatchewan." *Saskatchewan*
History 29, 2 (1976): 51–64.
Berkowitz, Edward, and Kim McQuaid. *Creating the Welfare State: The Political*
Economy of Twentieth Century Reform. New York: Praeger 1988.

Bicha, Karel Denis. *The American Farmer and the Canadian West, 1896–1914*.
Lawrence KS: Coronado Press 1968.

– "The Plains Farmer and the Prairie Province Frontier, 1897–1914." *Proceedings of the American Philosophical Society* 109, 6 (December 1965): 398–440.

Binnema, Theodore. "'A Feudal Chain of Vassalage': Limited Identities in the Prairie West, 1870–1896." *Prairie Forum* 20, 1 (1995): 1–18.

Bliss, Jacqueline. "Seamless Lives: Pioneer Women of Saskatoon, 1883–1903." *Saskatchewan History* 43, 3 (1991): 84–101.

Bliss, J.M. *A Canadian Millionaire: The Life and Times of Sir Joseph Flavelle, Bar., 1858–1939*. Toronto: MacMillan of Canada, 1978.

– "The Methodist Church and World War I." *Canadian Historical Review* 49 (1968): 213–33.

Bodrug, Ivan. *Independent Greek Orthodox Church: Memoirs Pertaining to the History of a Ukrainian Canadian Church in the Years 1903 to 1913*. Toronto: Ukrainian Canadian Research Foundation, 1982.

Boon, T.C.B. *The Anglican Church from the Bay to the Rockies: A History of the Ecclesiastical Province of Rupert's Land and Its Dioceses From 1820 to 1950*. Toronto: Ryerson Press 1962.

Bowen, Desmond. *The Idea of the Victorian Church*. Montreal: McGill University Press, 1968.

Braverman, Harry. *Labor and Monopoly Capital: The Degradation of Work in the Twentieth Century*. New York: Monthly Review Press 1974.

Bridgeman, Rev. Wellington. *Breaking Prairie Sod*. Toronto: Musson, 1920.

Brody, David. *Workers in Industrial America: Essays on the Twentieth Century Struggle*. New York: Oxford University Press, 1980.

Brooks, William H. "The Primitive Methodists in the North-West." *Saskatchewan History* 29, 1 (1976): 26–37.

– "The Uniqueness of Western Canadian Methodism, 1840–1925." *Journal of the Canadian Church Historical Society* 26, 1–2 (1977): 57–74.

Brouwer, Ruth Compton. "The 'Between-Age' Christianity of Agnes Machar." *Canadian Historical Review* 65, 3 (1984): 347–70.

– *New Women for God: Canadian Presbyterian Women and the India Missions, 1876–1914*. Toronto: University of Toronto Press, 1990.

– "Opening Doors through Social Service: Aspects of Women's Work in the Canadian Presbyterian Mission." In *Women's Work for Women: Missionaries and Social Change in Asia*, ed. Leslie A. Fleming. Boulder, CO: Westview Press, 1989.

– "Transcending the 'Unacknowledged Quarantine': Putting Religion into English-Canadian Women's History." *Journal of Canadian Studies/Revue d'études canadiennes* 27, 3 (1992): 47–61.

Brown, Violet. "Over the Red Deer: Life of a Homestead Missionary." *Alberta History* 33, 3 (1985): 9–18.

Bucke, Emory Stevens, ed. *The History of American Methodism*. Vol. 2. Nashville, IN: Abingdon Press, 1964.

Burkinshaw, Robert K. *Pilgrims in Lotus Land: Conservative Protestantism in British Columbia, 1917–1981.* Montreal and Kingston: McGill-Queen's University Press, 1995.

Burnet, Jean. *Next-Year Country: A Study of Rural Social Organization in Alberta.* Toronto: University of Toronto Press, 1951.

Burr, Christina. "The Business Development of the Methodist Book and Publishing Company, 1870–1914." *Ontario History* 85, 3 (1993): 251–72.

Burwash, Nathanael, *A History of Victoria College.* Toronto: Victoria College Press, 1927.

Butcher, Dennis L., et al., eds. *Prairie Spirit: Perspectives on the Heritage of the United Church of Canada in the West.* University of Manitoba Press, 1985.

Caldwell, J. Warren. "The Unification of Methodism in Canada, 1865–1914." *The Bulletin,* United Church Archives, 1967.

Campbell, Douglas F. "Class, Status, and Crisis: Upper-Class Protestants and the Founding of the United Church of Canada." *Journal of Canadian Studies/ Revue d'études canadiennes* 29, 3 (1994): 63–84.

Carnes, Mark C. *Secret Ritual and Manhood in Victorian America.* New Haven, CT: Yale University Press, 1989.

Carter, David J. "The Rev. Samuel Trivett." *Alberta Historical Review* 21, 2–3 (1973): 13–19, 18–27.

Cavanagh, Catharine. "'No Place For a Woman': Engendering Western Canadian Settlement." *Western Historical Quarterly* 28, 4 (1997): 493–520.

Century of Progress: An Historical Study of the Waskatenau, Smoky Lake, Warspite, Bellis, Vilna, and Spedden School Communities, 1867–1967. Edmonton, AB, 1967.

Chalmers, John W. "The Church at Spring Lake." *Alberta History* 31, 3 (1983): 33–6.

– "John W. Niddrie." *Alberta History* 19, 1 (1971): 26–9.

– "Missions and Schools in the Athabaska." *Alberta History* 31, 1 (1983): 24–9.

Chown, Rev. Samuel Dwight. *The Story of Church Union in Canada.* Toronto: Ryerson Press, 1930.

Christie, Nancy, and Michael Gauvreau. *A Full-Orbed Christianity: The Protestant Churches and Social Welfare in Canada, 1900–1940.* Montreal and Kingston: McGill-Queen's University Press, 1996.

Clifford, N. Keith. "Church Union and Western Canada." In *Prairie Spirit: Perspectives on the Heritage of the United Church of Canada in the West,* ed. Dennis L. Butcher, et al. Winnipeg, MB: University of Manitoba Press, 1985, 283–95.

– *The Resistance to Church Union in Canada, 1904–1939.* Vancouver, BC: University of British Columbia Press, 1985.

Clark, S.D. *Church and Sect in Canada.* Toronto: University of Toronto Press, 1948.

Cook, G. Ramsay. "Ambiguous Heritage: Wesley College and the Social Gospel Re-considered." *Manitoba History* 19 (1990): 2–11.

– "Church, Schools and Politics in Manitoba." *Canadian Historical Review* 39 (1958): 1–23.

– *The Regenerators: Social Criticism in Late Victorian English Canada*. Toronto: University of Toronto Press, 1985.

Cook, Sharon Anne. "'Do Not … Do Anything That You Cannot Unblushingly Tell Your Mother': Gender and Social Purity in Canada." *Histoire sociale/ Social History* 30, 60 (1997): 215–38.

– *"Through Sunshine and Shadow": The Woman's Christian Temperance Union, Evangelicalism, and Reform in Ontario, 1874–1930*. Montreal and Kingston: McGill-Queen's University Press, 1995.

Cornish, Rev. George H. *Cyclopaedia of Methodism in Canada*. Vols. 1–2. Toronto: Methodist Book and Publishing House, 1881, 1903.

Crouse, Eric. "The 'Great Revival': Evangelical Revivalism, Methodism, and Bourgeois Order in Early Calgary." *Alberta History* 47, 1 (1999): 18–23.

Crysdale, Stewart. *The Industrial Struggle and Protestant Ethics in Canada*. Toronto: Ryerson Press, 1961.

Danysk, Cecilia. *Hired Hands: Labour and the Development of Prairie Agriculture, 1880–1930*. Toronto: McClelland and Stewart, 1995.

Darlington, James W. "The Ukrainian Impress on the Canadian West." In *Canada's Ukrainians: Negotiating an Identity*, ed. Lubomyr Luciuk and Stella Hryniuk. Toronto: University of Toronto Press, 1991, 53–80.

Darroch, Gordon. "Scanty Fortunes and Rural Middle-Class Formation in Nineteenth-Century Central Ontario." *Canadian Historical Review* 79, 4 (1998): 621–59.

Darwin, Oliver. *Pioneering with Pioneers*. Toronto: United Church, 1949.

Dawson, Carl Addington. *Group Settlement: Ethnic Communities in Western Canada*. Toronto: Macmillan, 1934.

Dempsey, Hugh A. "The Last Letters of George McDougall." *Alberta History* 15, 2 (1967): 20–30.

Donaghy, James A. "Recollections and Reminiscences as a Student Missionary." *Saskatchewan History* 7, 2 (1954): 60–8.

Emery, George. *Facts of Life: The Social Construction of Vital Statistics, Ontario, 1869–1952*. Montreal and Kingston: McGill-Queen's University Press 1993.

– "The Lord's Day Act of 1906 and the Sabbath Observance Question." In *Documentary Problems in Canadian History*. Vol. 2, ed. J.M. Bumsted. Georgetown, ON: Irwin-Dorsey 1969, 23–52.

– "Methodist Missions among the Ukrainians." *Alberta History* 19, 2 (1971): 8–19.

– "Ontario Denied: The Methodist Church on the Prairies, 1896–1914." In *Aspects of Nineteenth Century Ontario*, ed. F.H. Armstrong, H. Stevenson, and D. Wilson. Toronto: University of Toronto Press, 1974, 312–26.

Emery, George, and J.C. Herbert Emery. *A Young Man's Benefit: The Independent Order of Odd Fellows and Sickness Insurance in the United States and Canada, 1860–1929*. Montreal and Kingston: McGill-Queen's University Press, 1999.

England, Robert. *The Central European Immigrant in Canada*. Toronto: Macmillan, 1929.

Essar, D. "A Letter from an Early Saskatchewan Settler." *Saskatchewan History* 29, 2 (1976): 65–72.

Fast, Vera K. "Eva Hassell and the Caravan Mission." In *The Anglican Church and the World of Western Canada, 1820–1965*, ed. Barry G. Ferguson. Regina, SK: Canadian Plains Research Centre, 1991, 167–75.

Ferrier, Thompson. "Indian Education in the North-West." Pamphlet, Methodist Church, Toronto, 1906.

Fitch, Rev. E.R. *The Baptists of Canada.* Toronto: Standard Publishing, 1911.

French, Goldwin. "The Evangelical Creed in Canada." In *The Shield of Achilles*, ed. W.L. Morton. Toronto: McClelland and Stewart, 1967.

– *Parsons and Politics.* Toronto: Ryerson Press, 1962.

Friesen, Gerald. *The Canadian Prairies: A History.* Toronto: University of Toronto Press, 1984.

– "Principal J.H. Riddell: The Sane and Safe Leader of Wesley College." In *Prairie Spirit: Perspectives on the Heritage of the United Church of Canada in the West*, ed. Dennis L. Butcher, et al. Winnipeg, MB: University of Manitoba Press, 1985, 250–64.

Friesen, John W. "John McDougall: The Spirit of the Pioneer." *Alberta Historical Review* 22, 2 (1974): 9–17.

Gagan, David. "'For Patients of Moderate Means': The Transformation of Ontario's Public General Hospitals, 1880–1950." *Canadian Historical Review* 70, 2 (1989): 151–79.

Gagan, Rosemary R. *A Sensitive Independence: Canadian Methodist Women Missionaries in Canada and the Orient, 1881–1925.* Montreal and Kingston: McGill-Queen's University Press, 1992.

Gauvreau, Michael. *The Evangelical Century: College and Creed in English Canada from the Great Revival to the Great Depression.* Montreal and Kingston: McGill-Queen's University Press, 1991.

– "The Taming of History: Reflections on the Canadian Methodist Encounter with Biblical Criticism, 1830–1900." *Canadian Historical Review* 65, 3 (1984): 315–46.

– "War, Culture and the Problem of Religious Certainty: Methodist and Presbyterian Church Colleges, 1914–1930." *Journal of the Canadian Church Historical Society* 29, 1 (1987): 12–31.

Gauvreau, Michael, and Nancy Christie. "'The World of the Common Man Is Filled with Religious Fervour': The Labouring People of Winnipeg and the Persistence of Revivalism, 1914–25." In *Aspects of the Canadian Evangelical Experience*, ed. G.A. Rawlyk. Montreal and Kingston: McGill-Queen's University Press, 1997, 337–50.

Goldin, Claudia. *Understanding the Gender Gap: An Economic History of American Women.* New York: Oxford University Press, 1990.

Grant, J. Webster. *The Canadian Experience of Church Union.* London: Butterworth, 1967.

– *The Church in the Canadian Era.* Toronto: McGraw-Hill Ryerson, 1972.

– *Moon of Wintertime: Missionaries and the Indians of Canada since 1534.* Toronto: University of Toronto Press, 1984.

– *A Profusion of Spires: Religion in Nineteenth-Century Ontario.* Ontario Historical Studies Series. Toronto: University of Toronto Press, 1988.

Grant, William Lawson, and Frederick Hamilton. *Principal Grant.* Toronto: Morang, 1904

Gray, Susan. "Methodist Indian Day Schools and Indian Communities in Northern Manitoba, 1890–1925." *Manitoba History* 30 (1995): 2–16.

Greenlee, James G., and Charles M. Johnston. *Good Citizens: British Missionaries and Imperial States, 1870 to 1918.* Montreal and Kingston: McGill-Queen's University Press, 1999.

Hall, D.J. *Clifford Sifton: The Young Napoleon, 1861–1900.* Vol. 1. Vancouver, BC: University of British Columbia Press, 1981.

Hallett, Mary, and Marilyn Davis. *Firing the Heather: The Life and Times of Nellie McClung.* Saskatoon, SK: Fifth House Publishers, 1993.

Hancock, Carol L. "Nellie L. McClung: A Part of a Pattern." In *Prairie Spirit: Perspectives on the Heritage of the United Church of Canada in the West,* ed. Dennis L. Butcher, et al. Winnipeg, MB: University of Manitoba Press, 1985, 203–15.

– *No Small Legacy: Canada's Nellie McClung, Blazing a Trail for Faith and Justice.* Winfield, BC: Wood Lake Books, 1986.

Headen, Christopher. "Women and Organized Religion in Mid and Late Nineteenth Century Canada." *Journal of the Canadian Church Historical Society* 20, 1–2 (1978): 3–18.

Hiemstra, Mary. *Gully Farm.* Toronto: McClelland and Stewart 1955.

Himka, John-Paul. *Religion and Nationality in the Western Ukraine: The Greek Catholic Church and the Ruthenian National Movement in Galicia, 1867–1900.* Montreal and Kingston: McGill-Queen's University Press, 1999.

Hoffman, Barbara. "Women of God: The Faithful Companions of Jesus." *Alberta History* 43, 4 (1995): 2–12.

Holmes, Mrs Robert. "Experiences of a Missionary's Wife." *Alberta History* 12, 2 (1964): 18–25.

Holmgren, Eric J. "William Newton and the Anglican Church." *Alberta Historical Review* 23, 2 (1975): 17–25.

Hryniuk, Stella. "'Sifton's Pets': Who Were They?" In *Canada's Ukrainians: Negotiating an Identity,* ed. Lubomyr Luciuk and Stella Hryniuk. Toronto: University of Toronto Press, 1991, 3–16.

Hutchinson, Gerald. "British Methodists and the Hudson's Bay Company, 1840–54." In *Prairie Spirit: Perspectives on the Heritage of the United Church of Canada in the West,* ed. Dennis L. Butcher, et al. Winnipeg, MB: University of Manitoba Press, 1985, 28–43.

Inglis, Kenneth Stanley. *Churches and the Working Classes in Victorian England.* London: Routledge and Kegan Paul, 1963.

– "Patterns of Religious Worship in England and Wales." *Journal of Ecclesiastical History* 2 (1960): 74–6.

Ion, A. Hamish. *The Cross and the Rising Sun: The Canadian Protestant Missionary Movement in the Japanese Empire, 1872–1931.* Wilfrid Laurier University Press, 1990.

Ironside, R.G., and E. Tomasky. "Development of Victoria Settlement." *Alberta History* 19, 2 (1971): 20–9.

Joanette, Nelson K. "Am I My Brother's Keeper: Nineteenth and Early Twentieth Century Pension Development for Methodist Preachers." *Journal of the Canadian Church Historical Society* 36, 2 (1994): 135–47.

Johnson, Paul. *Saving and Spending: The Working-Class Economy in Britain 1870–1935.* Oxford: Clarendon Press, 1985.

Johnson, Stanley C. *A History of Emigration from the United Kingdom to North America, 1763–1912.* London: G. Routledge, 1913.

Jones, David C. *Empire of Dust: Settling and Abandoning the Prairie Dry Belt.* Edmonton, AB: University of Alberta Press, 1987.

Kerr, Don, and Stan Hanson. *Saskatoon: The First Half-Century.* Edmonton, AB: NeWest Press, 1982.

Kinnear, Mary. *A Female Economy: Women's Work in a Prairie Province, 1870–1970.* Montreal and Kingston: McGill-Queen's University Press, 1998.

– "Margaret McWilliams and Her Social Gospel: The Formation of an Interwar Feminist." *Manitoba History* 22 (1991): 30–4.

Korinek, Valerie J. "No Women Need Apply: The Ordination of Women in the United Church, 1918–65." *Canadian Historical Review* 74, 4 (1993): 473–509.

Kostash, Myrna. *All of Baba's Children.* Edmonton, AB: Hurtig Publishers, 1977.

Krawchuk, Andrii. "Between a Rock and a Hard Place: Francophone Missionaries among Ukrainian Catholics." In *Canada's Ukrainians: Negotiating an Identity,* ed. Lubomyr Luciuk and Stella Hyrniuk. Toronto: University of Toronto Press, 1991, 206–17.

Latourette, Kenneth Scott. *A History of Christian Missions in China.* New York: Russell and Russell 1929.

Laudan, Larry. *Progress and Its Problems: Towards a Theory of Scientific Growth.* Berkeley, CA: University of California Press, 1977.

Lehr, John C., "Peopling the Prairies with Ukrainians." In *Canada's Ukrainians: Negotiating an Identity,* ed. Lubomyr Luciuk, and Stella Hryniuk. Toronto: University of Toronto Press, 1991, 30–53.

Lewis, Maurice H. "The Anglican Church and Its Mission Schools Dispute." *Alberta History* 14, 4 (1966): 7–13.

Long, John S. "The Rev. George Barnley, Wesleyan Methodism, and the Fur Trade Company Families of James Bay." *Ontario History* 77, 1 (1985): 43–64.

Lowe, Graham S. *Women in the Administrative Revolution.* Toronto: University of Toronto Press, 1987.

Lupul, Manoly R. "Ukrainian Language Education in Canada's Public Schools." In *A Heritage in Transition: Essays in the History of Ukrainians in*

Canada, ed. Manoly R. Lupul. Toronto: McClelland and Stewart, 1982, 215–43.

Lutz, Jessie G., ed., *Christian Missions in China*. Boston, MA: Heath, 1965.

Lysenko, Vera. *Men in Sheepskin Coats: A Study in Assimilation*. Toronto: Ryerson Press, 1947.

Macdonald, Catherine. "James Robertson and Presbyterian Church Extension in Manitoba and the North West, 1866–1902." In *Prairie Spirit: Perspectives on the Heritage of the United Church of Canada in the West*, ed. Dennis L. Butcher, et al. Winnipeg, MB: University of Manitoba Press, 1985, 85–99.

MacDonald, Christine. "Pioneer Church Life in Saskatchewan." *Saskatchewan History* 13, 1 (1960): 1–16.

MacInnis, Grace. *J.S. Woodsworth: A Man to Remember*. Toronto: Macmillan, 1953.

MacIntosh, William Archibald. *Prairie Settlement: The Geographical Setting*. Toronto: Macmillan, 1934.

MacKinnon, Mary. "New Evidence on Canadian Wage Rates, 1900–1930." *Canadian Journal of Economics* 19,1 (1996): 114–31.

Maclean, John. *Vanguards of Canada*. Toronto: Methodist Missionary Society, 1918.

Macleod, David. "A Live Vaccine: The YMCA and Male Adolescence in the United States and Canada, 1870–1920." *Histoire sociale/Social History* 11, 21 (1978): 5–25.

Maffly-Kipp, Laurie F. *Religion and Society in Frontier California*. New Haven, CT: Yale University Press, 1994.

Magney, William H. "The Methodist Church and the National Gospel, 1884–1914." *The Bulletin*. United Church Archives, 1968.

Mann, William E. *Sect, Cult and Church in Alberta*. Toronto: University of Toronto Press, 1955.

Marks, Lynne. *Revivals and Roller Rinks: Religion, Leisure, and Identity in Late-Nineteenth-Century Small-Town Ontario*. Toronto: University of Toronto Press, 1996.

Marnoch, James D. "John Black." In *Prairie Spirit: Perspectives on the Heritage of the United Church of Canada in the West*, ed. Dennis L. Butcher, et al. Winnipeg, MB: University of Manitoba Press, 1985, 65–84.

Marr, Lucille. "Sunday School Teaching: A Women's Enterprise. A Case Study from the Canadian Methodist, Presbyterian and United Church Traditions, 1919–1939." *Histoire sociale/Social History* 26, 52 (1993): 329–44.

Marshall, David B. Review of *Serving the Present Age*, by Phyllis D. Airhart. *Canadian Historical Review* 74, 4 (1993): 609–11.

– *Secularizing the Faith, Canadian Protestant Clergy and the Crisis of Belief, 1850–1940*. Toronto: University of Toronto Press, 1992.

Martynowych, Orest T. "The Ukrainian Bloc Settlement in East Central Alberta." In *Continuity and Change: The Cultural Life of Alberta's First Ukrainians*, ed. Manoly R. Lupul. Edmonton, AB: Canadian Institute of Ukrainian Studies, 1988, 30–59.

– *Ukrainians in Canada: The Formative Period, 1891–1924.* Edmonton, AB: University of Alberta, Canadian Institute of Ukrainian Studies Press, 1991.

Marunchak, Michael H. *The Ukrainian Canadians: A History.* Winnipeg, MB: Ukrainian Free Academy of Sciences, 1970.

McCallum, Margaret E. "Corporate Welfarism in Canada, 1919–39." *Canadian Historical Review* 71, 1 (1990): 49–79.

McCormack, Ross. "Cloth Caps and Jobs: The Ethnicity of English Immigrants in Canada, 1900–1914." In *Ethnicity, Power and Politics in Canada,* ed. Jorgen Dahlie and Tisssa Fernando. Toronto, 1981, 38–55.

– "Networks among British Immigrants and Acommodation to Canadian Society: Winnipeg, 1900–1914." *Histoire sociale/Social History* 17, 34 (1984): 357–74.

McDougall, John. *George Millward McDougall.* Toronto: William Briggs, 1888.

– "Through the Foothills." *Alberta Historical Review* 23, 2 (1975): 1–3.

McGowan, Don C. *Grassland Settlers: The Swift Current Region during the Era of the Ranching Frontier.* Regina, SK: Canadian Plains Research Centre, 1975.

McGowan, Mark G. "'A Portion for the Vanquished': Roman Catholics and the Ukrainian Catholic Church." In *Canada's Ukrainians: Negotiating an Identity,* ed. Lubomyr Luciuk and Stella Hryniuk. Toronto: University of Toronto Press, 1991, 218–37.

– "Toronto's English-Speaking Catholics, Immigration, and the Making of a Canadian Catholic Identity, 1900–30." In *Creed and Culture: The Place of English-Speaking Catholics in Canadian Society, 1750–1930,* ed. Terrance Murphy and Gerald Stortz. Montreal and Kingston: McGill-Queen's University Press, 1993, 204–45.

McGregor, J.G. *Vilni Zemli, Free Lands: The Ukrainian Settlement of Alberta.* Toronto: McClelland and Stewart, 1969.

McGuinness, Father Robert. "Missionary Journey of Father De Smet." *Alberta History* 15, 2 (1967): 12–19.

McInnis, R. Marvin. "Women, Work and Childbearing: Ontario in the Second Half of the Nineteenth Century." *Histoire sociale/Social History* 24, 48 (November 1991): 237–62.

McKenzie, Charles L. "Growing Up in Alberta, Part 1." *Alberta History* 37, 3 (1989): 14–23.

McLaurin, C.C. *Pioneering in Western Canada: A Story of the Baptists.* Calgary, AB. Published by the author, 1939.

McLoughlin, William G., Jr. *Modern Revivalism.* New York: Ronald Press, 1959.

McNaught, Kenneth. *A Prophet in Politics: A Biography of J.S. Woodsworth.* Toronto: University of Toronto Press, 1959.

McPherson, Margaret E. "Head, Heart, and Purse: The Presbyterian Women's Missionary Society in Canada, 1876–1925." In *Prairie Spirit: Perspectives on the Heritage of the United Church of Canada in the West*, ed. Dennis L. Butcher, et al. Winnipeg, MB: University of Manitoba Press, 1985, 147–70.

Merkley, Paul. "The Vision of the Good Society in the Social Gospel: What, Where and When in the Kingdom of God?" *Historical Papers/Communications historiques* (1987): 138–56.

Miller, J.R. "Anti-Catholicism in Canada: From the British Conquest to the Great War." In *Creed and Culture: The Place of English-Speaking Catholics in Canadian Society, 1750–1930*, ed. Terrance Murphy and Gerald Stortz. Montreal and Kingston: McGill-Queen's University Press, 1993, 25–48.

– *Shingwauk's Vision: A History of Native Residential Schools*. Toronto: University of Toronto Press, 1996.

Millman, T.R. "The Domestic and Foreign Missionary Society of the Church of England in Canada, 1883–1902." *Journal of the Canadian Church Historical Society* 19, 3–4 (1977): 166–76.

Mills, Allen. *Fool for Christ: The Political Thought of J.S. Woodsworth*. Toronto: University of Toronto Press, 1991.

Mitchell, Elizabeth B. *In Western Canada before the War, Impressions of Early Twentieth Century Prairie Communities*. London: J. Murray, 1915; Saskatoon: Western Producer Prairie Books, 1981.

Mitchell, T.S. "Forging a New Protestant Ontario on the Agricultural Frontier: Public Schools in Brandon and the Origins of the Manitoba School Question, 1881–1890." *Prairie Forum* 11, 1 (1986): 33–50.

Moir, John S. *Enduring Witness: A History of the Presbyterian Church in Canada*. Hamilton, ON: Presbyterian Church in Canada, 1974.

Moyles, R.G. *The Blood and Fire in Canada: A History of the Salvation Army in the Dominion 1882–1976*. Toronto: Peter Martin Associates, 1977.

Mussio, Louise A. "The Origins and Nature of the Holiness Movement Church: A Study in Religious Populism." *Journal of the Canadian Historical Association* 7 (1996): 81–104.

Navalkowsky, Anna. "Shandro Church." *Alberta History* 30, 4 (1982): 25–30.

– "Shandro School." *Alberta History* 18, 4 (1970): 8–14.

Nebel, Mabel Ruttle. "Rev. Thomas Johnson and the Insinger Experiment." *Saskatchewan History* 11, 1 (1958): 1–17.

Olender, Vivian. "The Canadian Methodist Church and the Gospel of Assimilation." *Journal of Ukrainian Studies* 7, 2 (1982): 61–74.

– "Symbolic Manipulation in the Proselytizing of Ukrainians: an Attempt to Create a Protestant Uniate Church." In *The Ukrainian Religious Experience: Tradition and the Canadian Cultural Context*, ed. David. J. Goa. Edmonton, AB: University of Alberta, Institute of Canadian Studies, 1989.

Oliver, Edmund H. "The Religious History of Saskatchewan to 1935." Unpublished manuscript, vols. 1–9, PAS, Saskatoon.

– *The Winning of the Frontier*. Toronto: United Church Publishing House, 1930.

Osborne, Brian. "'Non-Preferred' People: Inter-War Ukrainian Immigration to Canada." In *Canada's Ukrainians: Negotiating an Identity,* ed. Lubomyr Luciuk and Stella Hyrniuk. Toronto: University of Toronto Press, 1991, 81–102.

Owen, Michael. "'Building the Kingdom of God on the Prairies': E.H. Oliver and Saskatchewan Education, 1913–1930." *Saskatchewan History* 60, 1 (1987): 22–34.

– "'Keeping Canada God's Country': Presbyterian School-Homes for Ruthenian Children." In *Prairie Spirit: Perspectives on the Heritage of the United Church of Canada in the West,* ed. Dennis L. Butcher, et al. Winnipeg, MB: University of Manitoba Press, 1985, 184–201.

Passmore, F., "Methodist Memories of Saskatchewan." *Saskatchewan History* 8, 1 (1955): 1–16.

Peake, Frank A. "Anglican Theological Education in Saskatchewan." *Saskatchewan History* 35, 1–2 (1982): 25–34; 57–78.

– "Church Missionary Society Personnel and Policy in Rupertsland." *Journal of the Canadian Church Historical Society* 30, 2 (1988): 59–74.

Petryshyn, Jaroslav. "Sifton's Immigration Policy." In *Canada's Ukrainians: Negotiating an Identity,* ed. Lubomyr Luciuk and Stella Hyrniuk. Toronto: University of Toronto Press, 1991, 17–29.

Planting of the Faith, A. Presbyterian Church Women's Missionary Society, 1921.

Platt, Harriett Louise. *A Story of the Years: A History of the Woman's Missionary Society of the Methodist Church.* Vol. 1. Toronto: Methodist Woman's Missionary Society, 1908.

Popowich, Claudia Helen. *To Serve Is to Love: The Canadian Story of the Sisters Servants of Mary Immaculate.* Toronto: Sisters Servants of Mary Immaculate, 1971.

Potyondi, Barry. "Loss and Substitution: The Ecology of Production in Southwestern Saskatchewan, 1860–1930." *Journal of the Canadian Historical Association* (1994): 213–36.

Powell, Trevor. "The Church of England and the 'Foreigner' in the Dioceses of Qu'Appelle and Saskatchewan." *Journal of the Canadian Church Historical Society* 28, 1 (1986): 31–43.

– "The Church of England and the Immigrants in the Diocese of Qu'Appelle." In *The Anglican Church and the World of Western Canada, 1820–1965,* ed. Barry G. Ferguson. Regina, SK: Canadian Plains Research Centre, 1991, 143–54.

Prang, Margaret. *N.W. Rowell: Ontario Nationalist.* Toronto: University of Toronto Press, 1975.

– "'The Girl That God Would Have Me Be': The Canadian Girls in Training, 1915–39." *Canadian Historical Review* 66, 2 (1985): 154–84.

Prokop, Manfred. "Canadianization of Immigrant Children: The Role of the Rural Elementary School in Alberta, 1900–1930." *Alberta History* 37, 2 (1989): 1–10.

Rawlyk, George. *Champions of Truth: Fundamentalism, Modernism, and the Baptists.* Montreal and Kingston: McGill-Queen's University Press, 1990.

– ed. *Aspects of the Canadian Evangelical Experience.* Montreal and Kingston: McGill-Queen's University Press, 1997.

Reynolds, Lloyd G. *The British Immigrant: His Social and Economic Adjustment in Canada.* Toronto: Oxford University Press, 1935.

Riddell, J.H. *Methodism in the Middle West.* Toronto: Ryerson Press, 1946.

Ridout, Katharine. "A Woman of Mission: The Religious and Cultural Odessey of Agnes Wintermute Coates." *Canadian Historical Review* 71, 2 (1990): 208–44.

Rolph, William Kirby. *Henry Wise Wood of Alberta.* Toronto: University of Toronto Press, 1950.

Saunders, J. Clark. "Congregationalism in Manitoba, 1879–1937." In *Prairie Spirit: Perspectives on the Heritage of the United Church of Canada in the West,* ed. Dennis L. Butcher, et al. Winnipeg, MB: University of Manitoba Press, 1985, 122–46.

Scott, W.L. "The Catholic Ukrainian-Canadians." *Dublin Review,* April 1938, reprint.

– "The Ukrainians: Our Most Pressing Problem." Catholic Trust Society of Canada. Pamphlet. Toronto, n.d.

Selles, Johanna M. *Methodists and Women's Education in Canada, 1836–1925.* Montreal and Kingston: McGill-Queen's University Press, 1996.

Semple, Neil. *The Lord's Dominion: The History of Canadian Methodism.* Montreal and Kingston: McGill-Queen's University Press, 1996.

– "'The Nurture and Admonition of the Lord': Nineteenth-Century Canadian Methodism's Response to 'Childhood.'" *Histoire sociale/Social History* 14, 27 (1981): 157–75.

– "Ontario's Religious Hegemony: The Creation of the National Methodist Church." *Ontario History* 77, 1 (1985): 19–42.

Sheehan, Nancy M. "The WCTU on the Prairies, 1886–1930: An Alberta-Saskatchewan Comparison." *Prairie Forum* (spring 1981): 17–35.

Sibbald, Andrew. "West with the McDougalls." *Alberta History* 19, 1 (1971): 1–4.

Silcox, Claris Edwin. *Church Union in Canada.* New York: Institute of Social and Religious Research, 1933.

Sissons, Charles B. *Bi-lingual Schools in Canada.* Toronto: J.M. Dent and Sons, 1917.

– *Church and State in Canadian Education.* Toronto: Ryerson Press, 1959.

– *A History of Victoria University.* Toronto: University of Toronto Press, 1952.

Skwarok, J. *The Ukrainian Settlers of Canada and Their Schools, 1891–1921*. Edmonton, AB: Basilian Press, 1958.

Smillie, Benjamin. *Beyond the Social Gospel: Church Protest on the Prairies*. Saskatoon, SK: Fifth House Publishers, 1991.

– "The Woodsworths: James and J.S., Father and Son." In *Prairie Spirit: Perspectives on the Heritage of the United Church of Canada in the West*, ed. Dennis L. Butcher, et al. Winnipeg, MB: University of Manitoba Press, 1985, 100–21.

– ed. *Visions of the New Jerusalem: Religious Settlement on the Prairies*. Edmonton, AB: NeWest Press, 1983, 91–107.

Smillie, Benjamin, with N.J. Threinen. "Protestant Prairie Visionaries of the New Jerusalem: The United and Lutheran Churches in Western Canada." In *Visions of the New Jerusalem: Religious Settlement on the Prairies*, ed. Benjamin G. Smillie. Edmonton, AB: NeWest Press 1983, 69–90.

Smith, Raymond R. "A Heritage of Healing: Church Hospital and Medical Work in Manitoba, 1900–1977." In *Prairie Spirit: Perspectives on the Heritage of the United Church of Canada in the West*, ed. Dennis L. Butcher, et al. Winnipeg, MB: University of Manitoba Press, 1985, 265–82.

Smith, W.G. *A Study in Canadian Immigration*. Toronto, 1920.

– *Building the Nation: A Study of Some Problems Concerning the Church's Relation to the Immigrants*. Toronto, 1922.

Spence, Ruth E. *Prohibition in Canada*. Toronto: Ontario Branch of the Dominion Alliance, 1934.

Starr, Paul. *The Social Transformation of American Medicine: The Rise of a Sovereign Profession and the Making of a Vast Industry*. New York: Basic Books, 1982.

Stegner, Wallace. *Wolf Willow: a History, a Story, and a Memory of the Last Plains Frontier*. Lincoln, NE: University of Nebraska Press, 1955.

Stephenson, Mrs Frederick C. *One Hundred Years of Canadian Methodist Missions, 1824–1924*. Vol. 1. Toronto: Missionary Society of the Methodist Church, 1925.

Strange, Carolyn, and Tina Loo. *Making Good: Law and Moral Regulation in Canada, 1867–1939*. Toronto: University of Toronto Press, 1997.

Sutherland, Alexander. *The Methodist Church and Missions in Canada and Newfoundland*. Toronto, 1906.

Sweet, William Warren. *Methodism in American History*. New York: Abingdon Press, 1961.

Tavuchis, Nicolas. *Pastors and Immigrants*. The Hague: M. Nijhoff, 1963.

Thomas, John D. "Servants of the Church: Canadian Methodist Deaconess Work, 1890–1926." *Canadian Historical Review* 65, 3 (1984): 371–95.

Thompson, John Herd. *Canada, 1922–1939: Decades of Discord*. Toronto: McClelland and Stewart, 1985.

Thomas, L.G. "The Church of England and the Canadian West." In *The Anglican Church and the World of Western Canada, 1820–1965*, ed. Barry G. Ferguson. Regina, SK: Canadian Plains Research Centre, 1991, 16–28.

Thrift, Gayle. "Women of Prayer Are Women of Power: Women's Missionary Societies in Alberta, 1918–1939." *Alberta History* 47, 2 (1999): 10–17.

Tims, Rev. John W. "Anglican Beginnings in Southern Alberta." *Alberta History* 15, 2 (1967): 1–11.

Tremblay, Emlien. *Le Père Delaere et L'Eglise Ukrainienne du Canada.* N.p., 1960.

Troeltsch, Ernest. *The Social Teachings of the Christian Churches.* New York: Harper, 1960.

Trosky, Odarka. *The Ukrainian Greek Orthodox Church in Canada.* Winnipeg, 1968.

Van Die, Marguerite. *An Evangelical Mind: Nathanael Burwash and the Methodist Tradition in Canada, 1839–1918.* Montreal and Kingston: McGill-Queen's University Press, 1989.

– "'A March of Victory and Triumph of Praise of *The Beauty of Holiness*': Laity and the Evangelical Impulse in Canadian Methodism, 1800–1884." In *Aspects of the Canadian Evangelical Experience,* ed. G.A. Rawlyk. Montreal and Kingston: McGill-Queen's University Press, 1997, 73–89.

– "'The Marks of a Genuine Revival': Religion, Social Change, Gender, and Community in Mid-Victorian Brantford, Ontario." *Canadian Historical Review* 79, 3 (1998): 524–63.

Van Paassen, Pierre. *Days of Our Years.* Camden, NJ: Haddon Craftsmen, 1939.

Van Tigham, Frank, OMI. "Father Leonard Van Tigham, OMI." *Alberta History* 12, 1 (1964): 17–21.

Varg, Paul A. *Missionaries, Chinese and Diplomats.* Princeton, NJ: Princeton University Press, 1958.

Voisey, Paul. "Rural Local History and the Prairie West." *Prairie Forum* 10, 2 (1985): 327–38.

– *Vulcan: The Making of a Prairie Community.* Toronto: University of Toronto Press, 1988.

– ed. *A Preacher's Frontier: The Castor, Alberta Letters of Rev. Martin W. Holdom, 1909–1912.* Calgary, AB: Historical Society of Alberta, 1996.

Warne, Randi R. *Literature as Pulpit: The Christian Social Activism of Nellie L. McClung.* Waterloo, ON: Wilfrid Laurier University Press, 1993.

Waterman, A.M.C. "The Lord's Day Act in a Secular Society: A Historical Comment on the Canadian Lord's Day Act of 1906." *Canadian Journal of Theology* 11 (1965): 108–23.

Weber, Eugen. *Peasants into Frenchmen: The Modernization of Rural France, 1870–1914.* Stanford, CA: Stanford University Press, 1976.

Weir, G.M. *The Separate School Question in Canada.* Toronto: Ryerson Press, 1934.

Wetherell, Donald G., and Irene R.A. Kmet. *Town Life, Main Street and the Evolution of Small Town Alberta, 1880–1947.* Edmonton, AB: University of Alberta Press, 1995.

Weisberger, Bernard A. *They Gathered at the River.* Boston, MA: Little, Brown, 1958.

Westfall, William. *Two Worlds: the Protestant Culture of Nineteenth Century Ontario.* Montreal and Kingston: McGill-Queen's University Press, 1989.

White, Anne. "Emily Spencer Kerby, Pioneer Clubwoman, Educator, and Activist." *Alberta History* 46, 3 (1998): 2–9.

Whitely, Marilyn Färdig. "'Doing Just About What They Please': Ladies' Aids in Ontario Methodism." *Ontario History* 82, 4 (1990): 289–304.

Widdis, Randy. "American Resident Migration to Western Canada at the Turn of the Twentieth Century." *Prairie Forum* 22, 2 (1997): 237–62.

– *With Scarcely a Ripple: Anglo-Canadian Migration into the United States and Western Canada, 1880–1920.* Montreal and Kingston: McGill-Queen's University Press 1998.

Woodsworth, James. *Thirty Years in the Northwest.* Toronto: McClelland, Goodchild, and Stewart 1917.

Woodsworth, J.S. *Strangers within Our Gates.* Toronto: Methodist Missionary Society 1909.

– *My Neighbor.* Toronto: Methodist Missionary Society, 1911.

Worster, Donald. *Under Western Skies: Nature and History in the American West.* New York: Oxford University Press, 1992.

Woywitka, Anne B. "Homesteader's Woman." *Alberta Historical Review* 24, 2 (1976): 20–4.

Wright, Robert. *A World Mission: Canadian Protestantism and the Quest for a New International Order, 1918–1939.* Montreal and Kingston: McGill-Queen's University Press, 1991.

Yuzyk, Paul. *The Ukrainians in Manitoba.* Toronto: University of Toronto Press, 1953.

Young, Charles H. *The Ukrainians: A Study in Assimilation.* Toronto: T. Nelson & Sons, 1931.

Young, Rev. George. *Manitoba Memories.* Toronto: W. Briggs, 1897.

Index

population turnover in prairie region, 113
post-millenialism, 40, 202–3n14
prairies: as a Methodist challenge, 7–19; economic development, 5–7
Presbyterian Church: expansion program, 75–6, 113, 122; mission superintendents, 72–4, 222n22; statistics for church members, 112; Sunday schools, 116–7; supply of clergy, 80, 85; and immigrant coreligionists, 118–23; and the Independent Greek Church,137–8

Regina, 1912 cyclone, 16
revival meetings, 48–50
Riddell, J.H., 7, 213n8
Roman Catholic danger, 12, 161, 166–7
Rose, Arthur, 149, 152–3, 155
Ross, C.W. Watson, 176, 182–3
Rowell, Newton Wesley, 3, 7, 18, 194n9
rural problem, 8–9
Rush, Dr Will T., 177, 182

Sabbath observance, 53
Salvation Army, 43–4

Sanford, Alice, 162, 169
secularization theorists, xv–xviii
Semple, Neil, xv, 30–1, 200–1n42
Sifton, Clifford, 15, 127
Smith, J.K., 129, 158, 176, 178–9
Smoky Lake, Star colony, 160–1, 181
social gospel, 39–42
Star colony, 129, 134, 157–84
Sunday schools and youth organizations, 50–1, 58, 115–8
Sutherland, Alexander, 22, 27, 39, 57
Sutton, Percy G., 179

temperance and prohibition, 52–3
tradition, dynamic definition of, xix, 193n7

Ukrainians: Baptists, 168–9; Bukovynian Greek Orthodox tradition, 134–5; Galician Greek Catholic tradition, 134–5; immigrants, 6, 132–6, 142; immigration, 225n8; language and Methodist missionaries, 172–4, 179, 231n26; Methodist newspaper (see Bellegay, Michael); nationalism, 133–4, 226n35; Roman

Catholic mission, 136–7; women, 159–60, 163, 170–8
urban problem, 13–14

Van Die, Marguerite, xv–xviii, 30
Voisey, Paul, xvi, xx, 6, 113–14, 123–4

Wahstao mission. See Women's Missionary Society missions
Warne, Randi, xvi, 42
Weekes, Edith, 171–4
Wesley College, Winnipeg, 10, 86, 100
Winnipeg, prairie metropolis and gateway city, 140
Winnipeg, Grace Church, 5
Women's Missionary Society: organization, 58; missions, 169–76
Woodsworth, James, 16, 57, 72–3, 86–7, 95
Woodsworth, James Shaver, 11, 26, 41–3, 127, 130–1, 140–55

Young, George, 5

Zacharuk, Stenna, 170, 173